International Criminal Justice Series

Volume 15

Series Information

The *International Criminal Justice Series* aims to create a platform for publications in the whole field of international criminal justice. It, therefore, deals with issues relating, among others, to:

- the work of international criminal courts and tribunals;
- transitional justice approaches in different countries;
- international anti-corruption and anti-money laundering initiatives;
- the history of international criminal law.

The series concentrates on themes pertinent to developing countries. It is peer-reviewed and seeks to publish high-quality works emanating from excellent scholars, in particular from African countries.

Editorial Office

Prof. Dr. Gerhard Werle
Humboldt-Universität zu Berlin
Faculty of Law
Unter den Linden 6,
10099 Berlin, Germany
gerhard.werle@rewi.hu-berlin.de
moritz.vormbaum@rewi.hu-berlin.de

More information about this series at http://www.springer.com/series/13470

Stella Margariti

Defining International Terrorism

Between State Sovereignty and Cosmopolitanism

ASSER PRESS

Springer

Stella Margariti
Naxos
Greece

ISSN 2352-6718 ISSN 2352-6726 (electronic)
International Criminal Justice Series
ISBN 978-94-6265-203-3 ISBN 978-94-6265-204-0 (eBook)
DOI 10.1007/978-94-6265-204-0

Library of Congress Control Number: 2017943237

Published by T.M.C. ASSER PRESS, The Hague, The Netherlands www.asserpress.nl
Produced and distributed for T.M.C. ASSER PRESS by Springer-Verlag Berlin Heidelberg

Printed on acid-free paper

This T.M.C. ASSER PRESS imprint is published by Springer Nature
The registered company is Springer-Verlag GmbH Germany
The registered company address is: Heidelberger Platz 3, 14197 Berlin, Germany

Acknowledgements

This book is based on research conducted for the purpose of a Ph.D. thesis. Therefore I would like to express my most sincere gratitude to all my supervisors during these years, Ms. Elizabeth Kirk, Dr. Jacques Hartmann, Prof. Fiona Raitt and Dr. Padraig McAuliffe, under whose enthusiastic supervision the research was completed. Their support throughout this study was unlimited, and without their help this book would have been impossible to complete.

I would also like to express my gratitude to Asser/Springer for showing confidence in my work and for their help throughout the process of publishing.

I thank colleagues and friends from the University of Dundee in the UK for reading and commenting on several chapters of this book.

I would like to acknowledge with gratitude the love of my family and friends in Greece who gave me endless moral support over the past years. Last but not least, I would like to express my honest gratitude to Manos Primikyrios, for his endless encouragement and patience and for his constant love and support when they were most required.

Contents

Abbreviations

AU	African Union
AC	Appeals Chamber
art(s)	Article(s)
ASP	Assembly of States Parties
col	Column
DRC	Democratic Republic of Congo
edn	Edition
EAW	European Arrest Warrant
EU	European Union
ICC	International Criminal Court
ICJ	International Court of Justice
ICTR	International Tribunal for Rwanda
IHL	International Humanitarian Law
ILC	International Law Commission
IMTs	International Military Tribunals
ITFY	International Tribunal for the Former Yugoslavia
NMT	Nuremberg Military Tribunal
OIC	Organisation of Islamic Countries
p	Page
para(s)	Paragraph(s)
s	Section
STL	Special Tribunal for Lebanon
SWGCA	Special Working Group on the Crime of Aggression
UN	United Nations
UNGA	UN General Assembly
UNSC	UN Security Council
vol	Volume
WWII	World War II
Yrbk	Yearbook

Chapter 1
Introduction

Abstract Drafting definitions for international crimes can be a long and laborious process, not the least because of the need to reflect into the definitions of crimes both sovereignty-related concerns on the part of the States involved and cosmopolitan considerations on the part of international criminal law bodies. The effort of the International Criminal Court to draft an international definition for the crime of aggression manifests this antithesis, an antithesis which should not be exclusively attributed to the nature of the crime of aggression. The struggle between these two poles of State sovereignty and cosmopolitanism is a continuation of the struggle between politics and law in an international criminal law context. This struggle could be also approached from another viewpoint: it can be seen as the very reason why international terrorism has not been defined so far for the purposes of international criminal justice. While there are imperative reasons to allow international criminal justice to play its role in the fight against terrorism, States have been so far strongly opposed to this idea. The reasons for this wary attitude of States should be mainly sought to the potential implications on their sovereign interests and priorities, should international criminal justice assume its role in the fight against terrorism.

Keywords Sovereignty · Cosmopolitanism · Crime of Aggression · International Terrorism · Rome Statute · International Criminal Law

---

Stella Margariti, Naxos, Greece, stllmrgrt@gmail.com, tel: +306932456511.

This book is up to date to 1 July 2015. Therefore, the analysis on issues of international terrorism does not include any reference to the ISIS tragic terrorist actions that have taken place in the last two years. It is in the author's view that these actions might require a separate type of analysis due to their differentiated and unprecedentedly large-scale character. However, it is only a welcome challenge for the author to apply the positions held in this book to the ISIS phenomenon, as part of a future research.

S. Margariti, *Defining International Terrorism*, International Criminal Justice Series 15, DOI 10.1007/978-94-6265-204-0_1

Contents

1.1 Definitions of International Crimes, State Sovereignty and Cosmopolitanism

International criminal law is composed of several elements, the interrelation of which is what ultimately determines its effectiveness: international criminal law bodies (such as international criminal tribunals and more recently the International Criminal Court (ICC)),[1] the commitment of their States Parties to the application of the law as well as the degree of cooperation of non-Parties and finally, the very content and scope of the field of law these bodies are meant to apply. The most recent embodiment of this content and scope of international criminal law is the Rome Statute for an ICC (Rome Statute),[2] entailing definitions of the international crimes of genocide, crimes against humanity, war crimes and the crime of aggression.[3] In this respect, effectiveness consists of, among other things,[4] the

---

[1] UNGA 1998a, b.

[2] Rome Statute of the International Criminal Court, opened for signature 17 July 1998, 2187 UNTS 90 (entered into force 1 July 2002) UN Doc. A/CONF.183/9 (Rome Statute).

[3] Rome Statute, above n. 2, Articles 5–8. The crime of aggression was added as a placeholder in the Rome Statute and it was agreed to decide upon a definition and the conditions for the exercise of the ICC's jurisdiction at a later stage. These issues concerning the crime of aggression were finalised in Resolution RC/Res.6, Annex I, Amendments to the Rome Statute of the International Criminal Court on the Crime of Aggression (11 June 2010) (Kampala Resolution).

[4] See e.g. Damaska 2008, p. 329; Freeland 2008.

drafting and application of definitions which can enhance the principles enshrined in the Preamble of the Rome Statute: international accountability, fight against impunity, respect for the Purposes and Principles of the United Nations (UN) Charter,[5] prohibition of the use of force and respect for the territorial integrity and political independence of all States. The purpose of this study is to argue in favour of a definition for international terrorism in the context of international criminal law, under the prism of two parameters: (i) the modalities of the drafting of the definition of the crime of aggression in Resolution 6 to the Rome Statute of the International Criminal Court on the Crime of Aggression (Kampala Resolution) and (ii) the achievement of due balance between the two mostly antithetical poles of State sovereignty on the one hand, and international criminal justice or cosmopolitan purposes on the other.[6] These two poles represent two, often conflicting, dynamics that have influenced the development of international criminal law in general and the formulation of definitions for international crimes in particular: a State sovereignty-oriented approach gives primacy to the protection of State interests over the need to promote international criminal justice purposes, whereas a cosmopolitan approach[7] prioritises international criminal justice over State sovereign interests and prerogatives. It is the author's view that, for an international terrorism definition to achieve its maximum effectiveness and ensure accountability without disregarding State sovereign prerogatives, both dynamics should be reflected in such a manner so as to push forward the development of international law and the protection it affords without ignoring sovereignty-related considerations.

Turning to extant international criminal law definitions, the definitions for genocide, crimes against humanity and war crimes had already been provided in

[5] Charter of the United Nations, opened for signature 26 June 1945, 1 UNTS XVI (entered into force 24 October 1945) (UN Charter).

[6] For the purposes of this book, 'international criminal justice' or 'cosmopolitan' purposes can be summarised as the protection of all human beings, respect for human rights, fight against impunity and the prevention of grave crimes that 'threaten the peace, security and well-being of the world' (See Rome Statute, above n. 2, Preamble, para 3). The Preamble also reaffirms the Purposes and Principles as enshrined in the UN Charter, meaning that there is substantial convergence between the purposes of these two international institutions.

[7] Generally speaking, the cosmopolitan theory or cosmopolitanism holds that 'universal standards applicable to humankind should take priority in international affairs'. Current developments that can be considered as cosmopolitan steps are the emergence of an international human rights regime and international law, which should aim at the prevalence of universal rights and justice 'over other competing values reflecting particular cultural, religious, social, historical, ethnic or economic perspectives' of States (in Wilson 2009, pp. 2 and 6).

international law[8] long before the drafting of the Rome Statute. However, the recent definition of the crime of aggression was the product of long and laborious negotiations, from the time of the Nuremberg trials[9] and the definition of crimes against peace[10] until the Kampala Resolution in June 2010. From this long drafting process, there are lessons to be learnt on how a definition of an international crime with strong implications for State sovereignty should be approached. Due to the challenges presented by State sovereignty and eventually, by the need for balance between Security Council powers under Chapter VII of the UN Charter and the ICC's potential jurisdiction over aggression, the definition of aggression took more than 50 years since the precedent of the Nuremberg Trials in order to be drafted and firmly established in an international criminal law context. The long negotiations that took place and the analysis of the opposing dynamics that finally shaped the definition can serve as a guidance of how another international crime which evinces similar challenges for State sovereignty can be ultimately defined: international terrorism.

For the purposes of this book, 'international terrorism' will refer to any type of conduct as already specified by the anti-terrorist or 'suppression' conventions[11] but

---

[8] The definition of genocide is provided in the Convention on the Prevention and Punishment of the Crime of Genocide, opened for signature 9 December 1948, 78 UNTS 227 (entered into force 12 January 1951), Article 2. War crimes and crimes against humanity were defined in the Charter of the International Military Tribunal, opened for signature 8 August 1945, 82 UNTS 279 (entered into force 8 August 1945) (Nuremberg Charter) and the Charter of the International Military Tribunal for the Far East, opened for signature 19 January 1946 (entered into force 19 January 1946) (Tokyo Charter) in Articles 6 and 5 respectively. All these three international crimes were also defined in the Statutes of the International Military Tribunal for the Former Yugoslavia (UNSC 1993, Articles 3–5) and of the International Military Tribunal for Rwanda (UNSC 1994, Articles 2–4). However crimes against humanity lacked a widely accepted international law definition until the adoption of the Rome Statute (Schabas 2016). War crimes, referred to also as 'grave breaches of the Geneva Conventions of 12 August 1949', were also specified in the four Geneva Conventions of 12 August 1949, opened for signature 12 August 1949 (entered into force 21 October 1950) and in Articles 11 and 85 of the Protocol Additional to the Geneva Conventions of 12 August 1949, and relating to the Protection of Victims of International Armed Conflicts, opened for signature 8 June 1977, 1125 UNTS 3 (entered into force 7 December 1978) (Additional Protocol I). Nonetheless, the Rome Statute does not always adopt these definitions verbatim. See Cassese 1999, pp. 149–150.

[9] For an analysis of the historical account on the definition of aggression see Chap. 3.

[10] Nuremberg Charter, above n. 8, Article 6; Tokyo Charter, above n. 8, Article 5. Before the definition of 'crimes against peace', the renunciation of war as a means of national policy was already established by Article 1 of the Kellogg-Briand Pact (Treaty between the United States and other Powers) providing for the renunciation of war as an instrument of national policy, opened for signature 27 August 1928, 94 LNTS 57 (entered into force 24 July 1929).

[11] For the purpose of this book, as anti-terrorist or 'suppression' conventions are considered the conventions that oblige States to criminalise particular conducts related to terrorism, e.g. Convention for the Suppression of Unlawful Seizure of Aircraft, 860 UNTS 105 (entered into force 14 October 1971); Convention for the Suppression of Unlawful Acts against the Safety of Civil Aviation, 974 UNTS 177 (entered into force 26 January 1973); Convention on the Prevention and Punishment of Crimes Against Internationally Protected Persons, 1035 UNTS 167 (entered into force 20 February 1977); International Convention Against the Taking of Hostages,

not strictly limited to them, which is committed by either State or non-State actors, bears international dimensions in terms of perpetrators, victims and means used, and takes place only in time of peace.[12] In this respect, the focus of this study will lie on the question of how to define international terrorism in an international criminal law context, departing from the approach followed so far by the anti-terrorist conventions, which oblige States to criminalise particular criminal conducts related to terrorism and which, most of the time, avoid the mere use of the term. The approach followed by these conventions results in the obligation for States to criminalise (but not in the criminalisation *per se* of) a list of criminal acts that relate to terrorism (but do not constitute terrorism *per se*).[13] Thus, criminal conducts related to terrorism are considered as transnational offences whose criminalisation and prosecution are matters of domestic concern only. Instead, this book will attempt to address the question of defining international terrorism by treating it as a crime which is much more than the sum of all the prohibited acts provided by the anti-terrorist conventions. Precisely because defining terrorism for international criminal justice purposes will have implications on State sovereignty, this study will approach the issue of definition by addressing first and foremost the need to achieve due balance between the State sovereignty and cosmopolitan concerns that come into play. The 'State sovereignty versus cosmopolitanism' debate that will form the theoretical framework of this book is part of a much wider

---

(Footnote 11 continued)

1316 UNTS 205 (entered into force 3 June 1983) (International Convention Against the Taking of Hostages); Convention on the Physical Protection of Nuclear Material, 1456 UNTS 246 (entered into force 8 February 1987); Protocol for the Suppression of Unlawful Acts of Violence at Airports Serving International Civil Aviation, Supplementary to the Convention for the Suppression of Unlawful Acts Against the Safety of Civil Aviation, 1589 UNTS 474 (entered into force 6 August 1989); Convention for the Suppression of Unlawful Acts against the Safety of Maritime Navigation, 1678 UNTS 201 (entered into force 1 March 1992); Protocol for the Suppression of Unlawful Acts against the Safety of Fixed Platforms located on the Continental Shelf, 1678 UNTS 304 (entered into force 1 March 1992); International Convention for the Suppression of the Financing of Terrorism, opened for signature 9 December 1999, 2178 UNTS 197, (entered into force 10 April 2002) (International Convention for the Suppression of the Financing of Terrorism); International Convention for the Suppression of Terrorist Bombings, 2149 UNTS 256 (entered into force 23 March 2001) (International Convention for the Suppression of Terrorist Bombings); International Convention for the Suppression of Acts of Nuclear Terrorism, opened for signature 13 April 2005, (entered into force 7 July 2007) UN Doc. A/RES/59/290.88 (International Convention for the Suppression of Acts of Nuclear Terrorism).

[12] Terrorism as a war crime is already regulated by the Geneva Conventions and their Additional Protocols: Geneva Convention (IV) Relative to the Protection of Civilian Persons in Time of War of August 1949, 75 UNTS 287 (entered into force 21 October 1950), Article 33; Additional Protocol I, above n. 8, Article 51(2); Protocol Additional to the Geneva Conventions of 12 August 1949, and relating to the Protection of Victims of Non-International Armed Conflicts, opened for signature 8 June 1977, 1125 UNTS 609 (entered into force 7 December 1978), Article 4(2).

[13] Boister 2009, p. 348. More generally see Boister 2003.

debate between politics and law and perhaps the most representative continuations of politics and law respectively in the context of international criminal justice.

The relevance of this debate to the formulation of international crimes definitions has already been evinced in the drafting of the definition of the crime of aggression in Kampala. Unlike the other international crimes definitions of the Rome Statute, which were either treaty-based or defined in the statutes of international criminal tribunals, the definition of aggression was the product of many years of deliberations that had started before the establishment of the ICC. After its establishment, the work of the Special Working Group on the Crime of Aggression (SWGCA) demonstrated that the Kampala Resolution was the outcome of a long effort to accommodate both State-centred and international criminal justice concerns in a single definition. Therefore, this book will argue that the examination of how State sovereignty and cosmopolitan concerns interacted in the definition of aggression will serve as an example of how they should interact in the quest for a definition of international terrorism in order to ensure that such a definition will promote international law in the field with due consideration of any occurring sovereignty-related implications on States.

Thus, this introductory chapter will first offer a brief explanation of the reasons why terrorism should be defined for international criminal law purposes (Sect. 1.2) and secondly why, despite these reasons, terrorism was not ultimately included into the Rome Statute (Sect. 1.3). Section 1.4 will provide an overview of the two theories that advocate either the predominance of State sovereignty concerns over international law (the State-centric theory) or the priority that is due to cosmopolitan concerns related to international criminal justice over State sovereign interests (the cosmopolitan theory). It will be also shown how these theories are relevant in the context of the ICC project: on the one hand the establishment of the ICC is based on quasi-universal jurisdiction[14]—generally a cosmopolitan ideal—while on the other hand, its complementary jurisdiction is a manifestation of the protection afforded to the sovereign interests of its States Parties regarding the adjudication of international crimes. Finally, Sect. 1.5 will present the architecture of the book, providing a brief description of the chapters that are going to follow.

[14] According to the ICJ, *Arrest Warrant of 11 April 2000 (Democratic Republic of the Congo v Belgium)*, Joint Separate Opinion of Judges Higgins, Kooijmans and Buergenthal, 14 February 2002 ICJ Rep 2002, paras 41–42, 'universal jurisdiction', as a term used in the context of an international treaty, is a misnomer for 'an obligatory territorial jurisdiction over persons…for extraterritorial events'. For an opposing view see O'Keefe 2004, p. 735, who claims that universal jurisdiction can be grounded in treaty law. Article 12(2) of the Rome Statute, above n. 2, provides that the ICC may exercise its jurisdiction when the territorial State or the State of nationality of the accused (or both) are Parties to the Statute or have accepted its jurisdiction ad hoc. However, this jurisdictional link with the territorial or nationality State does not apply in case of a Security Council referral of a situation to the ICC Prosecutor under Chapter VII of the UN Charter, above n. 5 (Rome Statute, above n. 2, Articles 12–13).

1.2 Why Do We Need a Definition for Terrorism?

The questions of why there is a need for an international definition for terrorism and why terrorism should be also prosecuted at an international level (and not only domestically) are the two sides of the same coin. Presumably, the issue of promoting accountability for terrorism can be addressed by what Boister calls 'transnational criminal law',[15] namely the framework provided by the anti-terrorist conventions which oblige States to criminalise particular terrorist conducts for the purpose of national prosecutions. However, it will be demonstrated herein that there is a separate need for an international definition for terrorism to be used in an international criminal law context.

Firstly, the attribution of individual criminal responsibility for terrorist acts will, in some respects, support and protect State sovereignty. Terrorism has been viewed as a crime against the State, 'its security and stability, sovereignty and integrity, institutions and structures, or economy and development'.[16] Having an international mechanism in place to ensure that no terrorist offenders go unpunished strengthens the respect for State sovereignty at an international level, especially that of those States which are not sufficiently powerful to prosecute the offenders themselves. Although international anti-terrorist treaties oblige States to prosecute or extradite alleged terrorist offenders,[17] it cannot be taken for granted that decisions to extradite or prosecute are always taken with due consideration of criminal justice purposes. Some decisions are bound to be shaped by the political dynamics involved in a particular case. Thus, for example, a State might refuse to extradite an alleged offender to the requesting State due to political or diplomatic reasons or for fear of having its foreign relations disturbed or of appearing weak if it gives into an extradition request.[18] In the current state of affairs, it is likely that a terrorist offender can escape prosecution if he or she flees to a State that would deny his or her extradition or prosecution on grounds irrelevant to international criminal justice but relevant to political considerations such as opposing ideology, adverse relations or distrust towards the requesting State.[19] In such cases, the existence of an international mechanism with jurisdiction to prosecute terrorist cases when States

---

[15] Boister 2003.

[16] Saul 2008, p. 3.

[17] For example see: International Convention Against the Taking of Hostages, above n. 11, Article 10; International Convention for the Suppression of the Financing of Terrorism, above n. 11, Article 9(2); International Convention for the Suppression of Terrorist Bombings, above n. 11, Article 9; International Convention for the Suppression of Acts of Nuclear Terrorism, above n. 11, Article 11(1).

[18] In the Lockerbie case, Libya insisted that the suspects be prosecuted by the Libyan authorities. However, the Security Council required the extradition of the suspects, due to evidence that implicated Libya in the commission of the crime (UNSC 1992).

[19] Sailer 1999, p. 338. See also Bassiouni 1996, p. 581; Krohne 1997, p. 159.

are 'unwilling or unable genuinely'[20] to do so, could, arguably, eliminate States' discretion in prosecuting alleged terrorists and bring to the fore terrorist cases that deserve international attention. It could also encourage States to harmonise[21] their domestic law definitions for terrorism with the international one and, at least to some extent, minimise the role of politics in the administration of international criminal justice for terrorist cases.[22]

Secondly, the need to agree upon an international definition for terrorism is also imperative for reasons of clarity. Though the formulation of a definition for terrorism does not, and cannot, fully guarantee that the term will not be open to political abuse, States will be more restricted in their discretion to label political opponents as terrorists in order to exclude any possibility of political dialogue with them and 'as a justification to crush any dissent'.[23] For reasons of 'self-defence', '[national] security', 'law and order', terrorism can be used as a weapon in the hands of those who participate in the 'fight against terrorism'.[24] Without any outer legal criteria of reference, at least as to what 'international terrorism' consists of, States have full discretion to determine what terrorism is and what it is not, something which results in the prevalence of the allegation that terrorism is a tactic mostly used against a State and not by a State against any opposing groups or individuals.[25]

Furthermore, incidents such as the Lockerbie case,[26] the 1998 embassy bombings in Nairobi, Kenya and Dar es Salaam, Tanzania, the 2001 9/11 attack in the United States, the 2002 and 2005 Bali bombings, the 2005 7/7 London bombings, etc. have shown that terrorism can be of such gravity so as to qualify as a threat to international peace and security.[27] This qualification is explicitly declared in several

---

[20] Genuine unwillingness and inability for prosecution are two of the conditions of admissibility of a case before the ICC under the complementarity regime and according to Article 17 of the Rome Statute. For an analysis regarding States' unwillingness or inability to try terrorist cases see Creegan 2010–2011, pp. 257–61.

[21] Cassese argues that the ICC 'was conceived as an instrument for harmonizing national and international criminal justice', in Cassese 2003.

[22] Though one cannot rule out entirely the role of politics in some of the current cases under the ICC's jurisdiction (eg the Darfur situation and the apparent US support to the ICC based on political motives, see Ssenyonjo 2009, p. 397), it is the author's view that the political influences on the ICC's mandate, if any, constitute a general functional weakness that relates to all Article 5 crimes and will not be exclusively manifest in terrorist cases.

[23] Zeidan 2004, p. 495.

[24] Ibid.

[25] Ibid.

[26] ICJ, *Case Concerning Questions of Interpretation and Application of the 1971 Montreal Convention Arising From the Aerial Incident at Lockerbie* (*Libyan Arab Jamahiriya v United Kingdom*), Provisional Measures, Order of 14 April 1992, ICJ Rep 1992, p. 114.

[27] The Security Council has used the term 'threat to the peace' broadly, in situations varying from mass violations of international humanitarian or human rights law to economic and ecological disasters. See generally Cryer 1996, p. 161.

Security Council Resolutions[28] and clearly contradicts the argument made during the Rome negotiations that terrorism is not of sufficient gravity in order to be included into the jurisdiction of the ICC. If a terrorist incident can reach the threshold of being a threat to international peace and security, it is difficult to see why incidents of such a gravity cannot reach the threshold articulated in the Rome Statute of being one of the 'most serious crimes of concern to the international community as a whole'.[29]

Last, but not least, the adjudication of terrorist cases by the ICC will contribute to the improvement of the current extradition system, which is in place for countering terrorism in many anti-terrorist treaties. The weaknesses of this system are analysed elsewhere in this book.[30] In summary, in the current state of affairs, decisions for extradition are driven mostly by political and foreign relations considerations rather than international criminal justice purposes, meaning that the punishment of perpetrators can be foreclosed despite the existence of a system of State cooperation and extradition treaties. In such cases, the ICC can offer an alternative forum for prosecution in the absence of an extradition treaty or in cases of concurrent State jurisdictions over a particular terrorist incident and thus help minimise the role of politics in extradition decision-making.[31] However, the role of politics is not as yet minimised with respect to whether or how terrorism should be defined for international criminal law purposes and this is what the following section attempts to analyse.

1.3 Terrorism and the ICC: Why Terrorism Was Not Included into the Rome Statute

1.3.1 Efforts to Include Terrorism into the Rome Statute

In the Final Act of the Rome Conference in 1998, it was recognised that 'terrorist acts, by whomever and wherever perpetrated and whatever their forms, methods or motives, are serious crimes of concern to the international community' and that it is regrettable that 'no generally acceptable definition of the crimes of terrorism and drug crimes could be agreed upon for the inclusion within the jurisdiction of the Court'.[32] The jurisdiction of the newly established ICC included the so-called core

[28] See indicatively UNSC 1999, 2001a, b.

[29] Rome Statute, above n. 2, Article 5(1).

[30] See Chap. 5.

[31] In the Lockerbie case, an internationalised Scottish court sitting in the Netherlands functioned as an alternative forum for prosecution when the 'extradite or prosecute' principle did not solve the conflict between Libya and the UK/US. See also Plachta 2001, p. 125.

[32] UNGA 1998a, b.

or international crimes or international crimes *stricto sensu*[33] (or Article 5 crimes as will be referred to in this book), namely genocide, crimes against humanity, war crimes and the crime of aggression as a placeholder, for which it was decided that the definition and conditions of the exercise of jurisdiction will be agreed upon at a later stage.[34] It was further provided that the jurisdiction of the ICC can be expanded in the future by a review mechanism.[35] In an international politics context, the Security Council has issued a number of Resolutions denouncing terrorist acts as 'threats to international peace and security'. Specifically, after the event of 9/11, the UN established two expert bodies, the 'Policy Working Group on the United Nations and Terrorism', in October 2001[36] and the 'High-Level Panel on Threats, Challenges, and Change' in 2003, which made it clear that the fight against terrorism needs a comprehensive strategy that should include but not be limited to, coercive measures.[37] In particular, the High-Level Panel recommended that the fight against terrorism be conducted 'within a legal framework that is respectful of civil liberties and human rights, including in the area of law enforcement'[38] and also that the UNGA should conclude the negotiations over a universally agreed upon definition of terrorism and make terrorism an international crime.[39] Finally, the Policy Working Group recommended that the most serious terrorist crimes should be prosecuted by the ICC.[40]

More recently, and before the 2010 Review Conference, the Netherlands submitted a proposal to include terrorism into the ICC's jurisdiction, stating that

---

[33] For the purposes of this book, as international crimes are considered the crimes punishable under the Rome Statute, whose distinctive feature is, as Fletcher suggests, that they are 'wrong in themselves—not wrong by force of the international treaty that defines them' (Fletcher 2005, pp. 22–23). For a distinction between 'international' or 'core' crimes or 'international crimes *stricto sensu*' and 'transnational', 'treaty', 'treaty-based' crimes or 'crimes of international concern' see indicatively Bassiouni 1999, p. 4 (where he makes a distinction between 'crimes of international concern' or 'common crimes against internationally protected interests' and 'international crimes' or 'core crimes'); Kress 2008 (distinction between transnational and supranational international criminal law *stricto sensu*); Cryer and Wilmshurst 2010, pp. 4–5 (transnational and international crimes); Gaeta 2009, p. 69 (international crimes proper and treaty-based crimes). Cassese extends the list of international crimes to include, apart from the Article 5 crimes, torture and international terrorism (Ambos and Timmermann 2014, p. 24). Boister also makes a detailed analysis between international crimes *stricto sensu* and transnational crimes in Boister 2003.

[34] Rome Statute, above n. 2, Articles 5(1) and (2).

[35] UNGA 1998a, b, para 6.

[36] Report of the Policy Working Group on the United Nations and Terrorism 2002.

[37] Secretary-General 2004, para 148.

[38] Ibid.

[39] Ibid., paras 163–64.

[40] Report of the Policy Working Group on the United Nations and Terrorism 2002, para 26.

terrorism is a threat to international peace and security and that international prosecution of terrorist offenders is imperative when States with jurisdiction are unwilling or unable to carry out domestic proceedings.[41] It further proposed that a similar approach to that followed for the crime of aggression could be adopted for the crime of terrorism as well, namely that terrorism be included in the list of Article 5 crimes with a postponement of the ICC's jurisdiction, while at the same time, an informal working group should be established with the task of examining to what extent the Rome Statute needs to be adapted for that purpose.

While most delegations acknowledged the importance of the issue, concerns were expressed about the lack of a legal definition for the crime of terrorism. Some delegations suggested that this proposal should be considered at a later time taking into account the result of the discussions on a UN draft convention on terrorism.[42] It was also suggested that the approach of adding terrorism as a placeholder in the Rome Statute, as happened with the crime of aggression, might not be desirable. It would be more time-consuming for States to consider first whether or not to include terrorism into the Rome Statute and then to start negotiations about its definition. Besides, it was argued that it would be more practical to consider one set of amendments at once, concerning both the incorporation of terrorism into Article 5 together with its definition and conditions for the exercise of the ICC's jurisdiction.[43]

In light of the discussions in the context of a UN draft comprehensive convention on terrorism, delegations suggested that it was not proper for the Assembly of States Parties (ASP) to start discussions related to terrorism. Instead, it seemed more fruitful that the Review Conference 'be invested in issues that have greater probability in proving acceptable'.[44] The existence of several multilateral conventions addressing the issue of terrorism,[45] though most of them do not use the term *per se*, indicated that the need to establish a legal definition was not yet deemed urgent[46] and the issue was put on hold to be considered at a more opportune time. Finally, during the 12th session of the ASP, the Netherlands withdrew its proposal to amend Article 5 and extend the ICC's jurisdiction to the crime of terrorism. None of the other delegations raised this issue.[47]

---

[41] Assembly of States Parties to the Rome Statute of the International Criminal Court 2009, para 41.

[42] Ibid., paras 42–45.

[43] Ibid., para 46.

[44] Ibid., paras 20–21.

[45] Text to above n. 11.

[46] Assembly of States Parties to the Rome Statute of the International Criminal Court 2009, para 22.

[47] Assembly of States Parties to the Rome Statute of the International Criminal Court 2013, para 4.

1.3.2 Why Terrorism Was Not Included into the Rome Statute

Looking back at the early negotiations phase, some States (Algeria, India, Sri Lanka and Turkey) proposed to include terrorism into the Rome Statute as a crime against humanity.[48] Their proposal was met with opposition by some delegations, the US included, mainly for the following reasons: (i) the lack of a universally accepted definition,[49] (ii) the fact that not all acts of terrorism can meet the 'sufficient gravity' threshold posed by Article 5(1) of the Rome Statute, (iii) the general conviction that prosecution and punishment in terrorist cases is more efficient when carried out by national authorities rather than international tribunals and (iv) the risk of politicising the ICC.[50] Although the abovementioned argumentation has some merit, most of the reasons presented cannot go entirely unopposed. Regarding the issue of finding a definition, a question one could ask is not whether the non-inclusion of terrorism to the Rome Statute was due to the lack of an international definition but whether the lack of an international definition for terrorism was the consequence of its non-inclusion into the ICC's jurisdiction. Arguably, one could suggest that, as occurred with aggression whose definition was not finalised during the drafting process of the Rome Statute or with crimes against humanity which, strictly speaking, did not have an international treaty definition, the Rome negotiations could be seen as an opportunity to put terrorism under the ICC's jurisdiction without a definition, with a postponement of jurisdiction over the crime until a future drafting of it. Besides, the lack of a universally agreed upon definition for the crime of aggression[51] did not obstruct its inclusion into the Rome Statute, even though the prospects of reaching an agreement were, at that time, quite uncertain. In the case of aggression, it seemed that the need to establish individual liability for its commission was deemed of such an importance that the ASP was willing to start lengthy, and possibly unfruitful, negotiations on its definition. In the case of terrorism however, the fact that negotiations would be lengthy and possibly unfruitful constituted *per se* a reason why terrorism should not be included into the Rome

[48] Proposal submitted by Algeria, India, Sri Lanka and Turkey on Article 5 1998.

[49] See also UNGA 1998a, b. Resolution E states that it is regrettable that 'no generally acceptable definition of the crimes of terrorism and drug crimes could be agreed upon for the inclusion within the jurisdiction of the Court…'.

[50] Cassese 2001, p. 994. For an analysis of the reasons as difficulties in expanding the ICC's jurisdiction over treaty crimes see also Boister 2009, pp. 345–54; De Londras 2010, p. 175 (arguing that the main reasons were the definitional difficulties and the fact that terrorism at that time was not considered as one of the most serious crimes of concern to the international community).

[51] However, it was already considered as an international crime of customary law status. See UK Court of Appeal (Criminal Division), *R v Jones* (Appellant), Opinions of the Lords of Appeal for Judgment, 29 March 2006, UKHL 16, para 12.

Statute—an argument which might have some merit if coupled with the rest of the arguments for its non-inclusion but not when standing alone. Moreover, and as it will be shown in Chap. 5 referring to several international and regional treaties and national legislation relating to or defining terrorism, there is a certain common ground to be found among these definitions (and obviously points of contention) which could have been used as a starting point for the formulation of an international criminal law definition of terrorism.

Furthermore and regarding the argument that terrorism should not be included into the ICC's jurisdiction because not all terrorist acts are of sufficient gravity, the answer is to be found in Article 1 of the Rome Statute itself: Article 1 imposes the threshold for crimes to fall within the ICC's jurisdiction,[52] and as already happens with crimes against humanity and aggression,[53] further thresholds can be introduced into the definitions themselves in order to ensure that only terrorist acts of particular gravity can fall into the ICC's jurisdiction. Specific incidents of terrorism can amount to a threat to international peace and security and as such, they can, at least conceptually, reach the threshold of sufficient gravity required by Article 5(1) of the Rome Statute.

Thirdly, concerning the argument that all terrorist cases—including those that fall into the ambit of international anti-terrorist treaties—are being more effectively dealt with by national authorities, one key point is worth making: as will be discussed in Chap. 5, this argument takes for granted that the regime established by the anti-terrorist conventions on the suppression of terrorism and the *aut dedere aut judicare* ('extradite or prosecute') principle that these conventions often embody, always works for the benefit of international criminal justice; this argument presupposes that States act in good faith and are driven by a sentiment of commitment to the anti-terrorist conventions or to any extradition treaties they are parties to, something which is not always the case (if ever at all). Also, the anti-terrorist conventions that allow States wide discretion in dealing with terrorist offences in their national realm, take for granted the existence of fully developed domestic penal law systems (where in reality, they might be poorly developed)[54] and appear

[52] Rome Statute, above n. 2, Article 1: '[The ICC]… shall have the power to exercise its jurisdiction over persons for the most serious crimes of international concern…'.

[53] According to Article 7 of the Rome Statute on crimes against humanity, there are three thresholds to be applied: there has to be (i) an attack which is (ii) widespread and (iii) systematic. According to the definition of aggression in Article 8*bis* of the Kampala Resolution an act of aggression should '…by its character, gravity and scale, constitute[s] a manifest violation of the Charter of the United Nations'. These inner thresholds play the role of a jurisdictional filter for the ICC.

[54] Boister 2003, p. 958. Boister sees this reliance of transnational criminal law (as he calls the regime established by international treaties relating to the suppression of transnational crimes) on national criminal law systems as an inherent doctrinal weakness of the anti-terrorist conventions. His view is also shared by Bassiouni 1974, p. 405, who, even before the drafting of many of the international anti-terrorist conventions, was of the view that the main weakness of the suppression of treaty crimes is its State-based system.

to have an implicit faith in how domestic criminal law systems operate.[55] It will be argued in Chap. 5 that this State-centric system of dealing with transnational crimes does not always work in the best interest of international criminal justice. States' decisions to conform to anti-terrorist treaties or to the 'extradite or prosecute' principle are sometimes made on grounds irrelevant to international criminal justice purposes but relevant to political, diplomatic or foreign relations considerations. This state of affairs does not favour an effective operation of the State-based system of transnational cooperation in dealing with terrorist cases but, instead, allows too much room for political considerations to influence States' decisions for prosecution or extradition of terrorist offenders.[56]

The last reason for the non-inclusion of terrorism seems to be the only one that is sustainable. Politicisation of the ICC means that implications for State sovereignty are at stake when an international court is authorised to investigate and prosecute acts of terrorism. These sovereignty-related implications perhaps best explain why the inclusion of terrorism into the ICC's jurisdiction has been obstructed so far.

An illustrative example of this wary attitude of States towards the inclusion of terrorism into the jurisdiction of the ICC can be found in the ministerial reply to a question posed to the UK Secretary of State for the Home Department in 1998, concerning whether the ICC should have jurisdiction over terrorist crimes. A minister replied that:

> There are several reasons for the view that the Court [ICC] should not be able to deal with terrorism. Paramount among them is the need to protect confidential sources, which would be compromised if an international body were to investigate and prosecute terrorist incidents. In practical terms it would be very difficult for the Court to act in terrorist cases, countries naturally having a predilection not to volunteer sensitive national security information.
>
> In any event, the jurisdiction of the International Criminal Court in this area is unnecessary given the range of terrorist conventions in place, including the recently concluded United Nations Terrorist Bombing Convention. These require their parties to co-operate against terrorism and, in some cases, to take extraterritorial jurisdiction over terrorist crimes. Indeed, the involvement of the Court could even undermine or set back progress in combating terrorism, on which there is increasingly effective international co-operation.[57]

It is apparent from the above that the UK was against the prosecution of terrorism by an international body not for reasons relating either to the lack of a universal definition for terrorism or to the lack of the necessary gravity threshold. Instead, the ministerial argument against the inclusion of terrorism in the Rome Statute focuses, on the one hand, on the sensitivity of national security issues that

[55] It can be said that the establishment of the ICC as a complementary judicial authority with jurisdiction over international crimes is based on similar arguments of flawed or absent domestic criminal proceedings.

[56] Arguably, the ICC might be also influenced by political considerations when deciding the admissibility of cases and has been accused of functioning as a neo-colonial court, e.g. in the Darfur situation (see Ssenyonjo 2009). For an opposite view see Mégret 2013.

[57] House of Commons, Written Answers to Questions, 23 June 1998, vol 314, col 441W.

have to be protected in case of having an international body adjudicating over terrorist cases and, on the other hand, on the conviction that the current regime of the anti-terrorist conventions and State cooperation works properly. Regarding the second part of the argument, it has been already mentioned and will also be discussed in Chap. 5 that the State-based system of combatting international terrorism through the anti-terrorist conventions does not always work for the benefit of international criminal justice, since it relies too much on State sovereignty considerations. However, the first part of the argument, namely the protection of national security interests, is closely related to the political dimension of relinquishing jurisdiction for international terrorism to the ICC and evinces the distrust of States towards an international institution[58] (or its States Parties) whose aim, one could argue, extends to the protection of State interests through the anti-impunity mechanisms it establishes.

Lastly and closely connected to this feeling of distrust towards an international court with jurisdiction over terrorism, there is also the question of whether the latter can be seen as an appropriate forum of prosecution.[59] For a State to delegate its adjudicative jurisdiction to an international institution to try terrorist cases means that there will be implications for its sovereignty regardless of whether the concerned State is the victim State or the State whose nationals are being accused. In the latter case, the objections on the part of the State whose nationals are being accused are obvious: that State could question the neutrality of an international court, as has happened with Libya and the 'internationalised' Scottish court established to prosecute the offenders in the Lockerbie case[60] or question the fact that the conduct did indeed constitute terrorism. Similarly, though less obviously, it is still possible that the victim State would have objections in conferring its adjudicative jurisdiction to an international court for terrorist cases. A victim State may hold that its sovereignty is being interfered with if it finds that the international court does not share the same view on the law in the field or that it has different priorities on the matter or that it is not similarly situated in issues of terrorism[61] (or might even consider the ICC sentencing as being too lenient). Thus, even on judicial grounds, States might view that their sovereign interests are being interfered with, if international terrorism is to be included into the ICC's jurisdiction.

So far it has been examined (i) why terrorism needs a universally agreed definition for international criminal law purposes, (ii) why efforts to include terrorism

[58] Morris 2004–2005, p. 409.

[59] See generally Tiefenbrun 2002–2003, p. 386.

[60] Morris 2004–2005, p. 408.

[61] Ibid., For example, in *Prosecutor v Lubanga Dyilo*, the first case that was made admissible through self-referral by the DRC, the Pre-Trial Chamber, although it recognised that the Congolese judicial system 'had undergone certain changes' and was 'able' to prosecute the case under Article 17, declared the case admissible because the accused was not being prosecuted by the national authorities for the same offences as were to be charged by the ICC Prosecutor (ICC, *Prosecutor v Thomas Lubanga Dyilo*, Under Seal Decision of the Prosecutor's Application for a Warrant of Arrest, Article 58, 10 February 2006, Case No. ICC-01/04-01/06-8 (*Lubanga* 2006), paras 35–37).

into the ICC's jurisdiction have been unsuccessful so far and finally (iii) how implications on State sovereignty have obstructed the inclusion of terrorism into the ICC's jurisdiction. However, before going deeper into the architecture of this book, it is essential to present a brief overview of the two theories that reflect views that, on the one hand, prioritise the respect for State sovereignty over international criminal justice purposes and on the other, promote cosmopolitan purposes notwithstanding concerns related to State sovereign interests. As the focus on these theories will endure through this study, the analysis of their relationship with international law will contribute to our understanding of the role they have played in the shaping of international law, and in this respect, of their role in influencing the drafting of definitions for international crimes.

1.4 State Sovereignty Theories and International Law

1.4.1 State-Centric Theory and Cosmopolitanism in International Law

The complicated relationship between State sovereignty and international law stems from the fact that the two concepts incorporate conflicting interests. International law developments are often hampered by sovereignty-related State interests,[62] but it is also equally true that no international law would exist without sovereign States.[63] The traditional definition of sovereignty comprises such concepts as claim and control over a State's territory, State freedom of action towards its citizenry (internal sovereignty) and towards other States (external sovereignty),[64] and political independence.[65] A State, under the Westphalian system, sees international law more as a means of interaction and coexistence between sovereign States rather than a means of cooperation to achieve a common end.[66] However, this horizontal

[62] Cryer 2005, p. 981. Antonio Cassese also views that State sovereignty and international rule of law are incompatible and sees international criminal law as a limit to State sovereignty. On the other hand, when States retain some crucial aspects of their sovereignty and fail to cooperate with international criminal tribunals in international criminal prosecutions, then it is international criminal law's impact that is limited by international politics. See Cassese 1998, pp. 11–17; Broomhall 2003, p. 57.

[63] Bennoune 2002, p. 244. See also Klabbers 1998, p. 345.

[64] Henley 2011, p. 1025. See also PCIJ, *Austro-German Customs Union Case*, Advisory opinion, 5 September 1931, Rep Series A/B No 41.

[65] Bennoune 2002, p. 245 who also argues that sovereignty can mean the 'will of people', namely popular sovereignty. See also Henkin 1999–2000, p. 2.

[66] Wolfgang Friedmann in Cryer 2005, p. 983.

regime of international law in relation to State sovereignty has changed over the years to a more vertical system. Under an 'international order rationale',[67] international law has gradually strengthened—in the aftermath of World War II (WWII) and through the establishment of the UN—as a result of State aspirations to promote international peace and security through the regulation of individual State conduct. The role that international law has played in regulating State conduct in the international arena has given rise to two theories, one defending the primacy of sovereignty over international law and the other viewing sovereignty as a State right, sometimes limited and sometimes protected, but definitely afforded by international law.

According to the traditional State-centric theory, sovereignty is seen as a 'pre-legal, (…) monolithic entity of clearly determinate content'[68] which has arisen 'apart from and prior to its existence as part of international law'.[69] The primacy of sovereignty over international law stems from the fact that international law becomes a part of national law after a State's express or tacit recognition of it.[70] According to Kelsen, who under his monistic theory[71] equates the primacy of sovereignty with the primacy of national law over the international, a State is sovereign only when its national legal order is a supreme order.[72] In this sense, international law can become part of this order only when it has as reason of its validity the 'will' of that State.[73]

The cosmopolitan theory views sovereignty as 'a product of the recognition conferred by the international system itself and not a pre-existing trait inherent in States.'[74] Sovereignty becomes a more flexible concept, 'constitutive of the international legal order' and comprising the rights and duties of States.[75] Under this theory, international law appears as a supreme order, which contains all national legal orders, the latter gaining their validity from their recognition by international

[67] It is the author's view that the 'international order rationale'—which prioritises the international order over the national one—is a manifestation of cosmopolitanism and cosmopolitan theory, in the context of international criminal law. Thus, for the purpose of this book, the term 'cosmopolitanism' or 'cosmopolitan theory' will reflect the supremacy of international law over the national legal orders and, more generally, over State sovereignty interests and considerations.

[68] Cryer 2005, p. 981.

[69] Broomhall 2003, p. 59.

[70] Kelsen 1959–1960, p. 630.

[71] Ibid., p. 629. Under Kelsen's monistic theory, 'international law and national law form a unity'. This unity can be achieved with the primacy of the one over the other. In contrast, the dualistic or pluralistic theory of Kelsen, argues that international law and national law are 'independent of each other in their validity' and therefore can be valid simultaneously. He dismissed the second theory due to logical contradictions.

[72] Ibid., p. 631 '[Sovereignty] is a *presupposition*, viz., the presupposed assumption of a system of norms as a supreme normative order whose validity is not to be derived from a superior order.'

[73] Ibid.

[74] Broomhall 2003, p. 59.

[75] Cryer 2005, p. 982.

law.[76] In this sense, State sovereignty corresponds to State independence from other States but not from international law.[77]

Past and current trends in the development of international law and in State practice at times reflect both theories. For example, the practice of colonisation was a flagrant manifestation of the State-centric theory, in that States were trying to promote and establish their sovereign interests in other lands, while at the same time, internally, States would become increasingly democratic (a political system whose principles converge with cosmopolitan ideals).[78] Moreover, a more recent and indicative example of State practice that favours State sovereignty considerations at the expense of cosmopolitan ideals is the adoption of counter-terrorism legislation (especially after the events of 9/11) with a human rights-oppressive character (for example, the government of Chile used its Anti-Terrorist Law to suppress an indigenous dissident group)[79] or the adoption of restrictive immigration and asylum legislation by States and the European Union, as a response to Security Council anti-terrorist resolutions.[80] On the other hand, the establishment of an international human rights regime through the creation of international human rights treaties, the establishment of international or regional human rights institutions such as the European Court of Human Rights or the UN Human Rights Committee, and finally the creation of the ICC can be seen as steps towards implementing cosmopolitan ideals, since their aim is to offer protection, first and foremost, to individuals rather than States.

Be that as it may, these two mostly antithetical approaches should not be seen as totally incompatible. The assumption of international legal obligations may put constraints on some aspects relating to the sovereignty of the consenting States but that does not obviously result in the total erosion of their sovereignty.[81] States, acting in free will, may subject themselves to international law when they recognize its nature as binding but they are still regarded as sovereign with respect to one another.[82] However, complications are still present and depend, as Clapham suggests, on what one chooses to understand as sovereignty.[83] As Cryer rightly puts it, the absolutist view of the State-centric theory that sovereignty ought to have primacy over international law 'derive[s] an "ought" from an "is", or more accurately

[76] Kelsen 1959–1960, p. 632.

[77] Ibid.

[78] Henley 2011, p. 1025.

[79] Nagle 2010, p. 97.

[80] Norberg 2010, p. 12.

[81] Broomhall 2003, p. 59.

[82] Kelsen 1959–1960, p. 633. Sovereign equality, according to Kelsen, is a principle that 'cannot be maintained on the basis of primacy of national law.' Kelsen presents a very interesting scheme where national law in the narrower sense is equal to the national legal order and national law in the wider sense is composed of the national law in the narrower sense and international law. Under this scheme, international law has primacy over national law in the narrower sense but not over national law in the wider sense (Ibid., pp. 632–634).

[83] Andrew Clapham in Cryer 2005, p. 982.

a "was"'.[84] In other words, while it is true that States gave life to international law, international law has gradually acquired a life of its own, making a sharp distinction between 'State authority to rule over a territory and State autonomy to behave inside and outside that territory'.[85] However, States often use sovereignty as a synonym for immunity,[86] an interpretation which, when followed by States, unavoidably leads to a totally symbolic significance of international law. This is perhaps most evident with respect to international criminal law, whose main goal, the fight against impunity,[87] will be severely undermined if international criminal law provisions were to be based exclusively upon State sovereignty considerations.

1.4.2 Procedural and Substantive Issues of the Relationship Between State Sovereignty and International Criminal Law

The interplay between State sovereignty and international criminal law is first and foremost present in the technical-procedural aspects of the function of the ICC. On the one hand, the complementary jurisdiction of the ICC might indicate that States do not wish to limit their State-centric prerogatives and go too far with respect to prosecutions of international crimes.[88] At a first glance, the ICC's complementarity regime is strong evidence that States desire to move away from developing international criminal law in substantive terms towards a more 'adjective (complementary) international criminal law'.[89] In this respect, Bassiouni is right in viewing the ICC 'as an extension of national criminal jurisdictions' which does not infringe on State sovereignty.[90] On the same grounds, Cryer holds that the complementary jurisdiction of the ICC actually encourages the legislative and adjudicative sovereignty of States by rendering their national courts capable fora for the promotion of international criminal law.[91]

[84] Ibid., p. 981.

[85] Broomhall 2003, p. 59.

[86] Henkin 1999–2000, p. 13: '…immunity from law, immunity from scrutiny, immunity from justice…'.

[87] Rome Statute, above n. 2, Preamble, paras 4–5.

[88] Broomhall 2003, p. 31.

[89] Brown 2008, p. 84.

[90] Bassiouni 2003, p. 181.

[91] Cryer 2005, p. 986.

On the other hand, it is clear that the ICC will exercise external oversight over the judicial processes of its States Parties[92] with the risk that their legitimacy be called into question. It will affect State sovereignty of both States Parties and non-Parties especially in case of a Security Council referral[93] or a *proprio motu* investigation of the Prosecutor. Moreover, and judging from its current practice, the ICC seems to follow a rather interventionist and dynamic approach in adjudicating for international crimes. As will be demonstrated in Chap. 2, the ICC tends to prioritise the international prosecution of offenders rather than encourage its States Parties to conduct national prosecutions. Therefore, it becomes evident that the legislative and adjudicative sovereignty of States Parties as well as the sovereignty of non-Parties (in case of a Security Council referral or a *proprio motu* investigation by the ICC Prosecutor) is affected by the ICC, which, despite its complementary function, is definitely much more than a mere extension of national criminal jurisdictions.

The fact that the ICC is not meant to function as a mere substitute of national criminal jurisdictions is also obvious from the interplay between State sovereignty and international criminal law in terms of substance. While the authority of the ICC to prosecute international crimes is granted by its States Parties, which, by their consent, declare that in the name of a common end, they are willing to confer a part of their adjudicative jurisdiction to the ICC, States Parties appear unwilling to show the same vigor in maximising the effectiveness of international criminal law by formulating definitions that give due weight to State sovereignty as well as cosmopolitan concerns. This becomes apparent from the negotiations in Rome regarding the definitions of international crimes. On the one hand, it could be argued that the inclusion of the crime of genocide as well as the crimes against humanity into the jurisdiction of a permanent international criminal court results in delimiting State sovereignty with respect to how a State should behave towards its citizens within the boundaries of its own territory.[94] Sadat goes even further and argues that 'the Rome Conference represented a Constitutional Moment in international law…suggest[ing] an important shift in the substructure of international law'[95] and that the definition process at Rome was a 'quasi-legislative event that produced a criminal code for the world'.[96] In the *Kupreškic* case of the International

[92] Ibid., p. 985. See Articles 18 and 19 of the Rome Statute; ICC, *Prosecutor v Muthaura and ors* (Situation in the Republic of Kenya), 30 August 2011, Case No. ICC-01/09-02/11; ICC, *Prosecutor v Katanga and ors,* Reasons for the Oral Decision on the Motion Challenging the Admissibility of the Case, 16 June 2009, Case No. ICC-01/04-01/07.

[93] See UNSC 2005, adopted under Chapter VII of the UN Charter, above n. 5, with which the Security Council referred the situation in Darfur to the ICC Prosecutor. While Sudan had signed the Rome Statute on September 2000, it has not yet ratified it and cannot be considered as a State Party. However, Sudan has been treated as such, not by its consent but as a result of UNSC 2005, which is binding to all UN Members.

[94] Cryer 2005, p. 985.

[95] Sadat 2002, p. 279.

[96] Ibid., p. 263.

Criminal Tribunal of the Former Yugoslavia, the Trial Chamber opined that the Rome Statute reflects 'the *opinio juris* of a great number of States' and constitutes an 'authoritative expression of [their] legal views…'.[97] However, and while recognising the comprehensive and authoritative character of the definitions of crimes as given in the Rome Statute, it is hard to overlook that the detailed definitions also serve 'ulterior purposes' in the name of the *nullum crimen sine lege* principle.[98] The specificity of definitions, especially where such definitions are complemented by lists of prohibited acts,[99] leaves 'as little discretion as possible in the interpretation and application of substantive criminal law' to the ICC.[100] Even Sadat admits that the lists of crimes in the Rome Statute were 'the lowest common denominator'[101] of acts acceptable by States that can be prosecuted by an international criminal court. Recognising that the *nullum crimen sine lege* principle is a fundamental element of the rule of law, in international criminal law it can constitute a serious limitation in the suppression of future criminal conduct.[102] In this respect, Pellet questions the strict application of the *nullum crimen sine lege* principle in international criminal law seeing it as an obstacle in the administration of international criminal justice:

> Unfortunately, men's criminal imagination appears unlimited and, by enclosing the definition of the crimes in narrow, punctilious formulations, they have forbidden the judges in advance to suppress future malevolent inventions of the human spirit; all the more so, and this is undoubtedly the most serious weakness of the Statute, because, in practice, they have excluded any realistic prospect of amendment.[103]

Therefore, the relationship between State sovereignty and international criminal law is not limited to procedural issues of 'who can have jurisdiction over what' but also extends to substantive issues of what it is exactly that the ICC should have jurisdiction over. Moreover, the tenuous and sometimes conflicted relationship between the State-centric and the cosmopolitan theory is not only reflected into the definitions of crimes included into the Rome Statute but also in the omission of certain crimes from the ICC's jurisdiction. Aggression and terrorism, the former included into the Statute but not defined in Rome and the latter neither the one nor the other, are both crimes with strong implications for State sovereignty. Thus, it is

---

[97] ICTY, *Prosecutor v Furundžija*, Judgment, 10 December 1998, Case No. ICTY-95-17/1-T, para 227.

[98] Cryer 2005, p. 990.

[99] Articles 7–8 of the Rome Statute, above n. 2, provide lists of prohibited acts considered as crimes against humanity and war crimes respectively.

[100] Brown 2008, p. 113.

[101] Sadat 2002, p. 267.

[102] Shahabuddeen argues that 'the principle of *nullum crimen sine lege* does not bar development of the law' provided however that 'the resultant development is consistent with the essence of the offence and could reasonably be foreseen.' (Shahabuddeen 2004, p. 1017).

[103] Pellet 2002, pp. 1058–59.

exactly these implications that have caused (and still cause) so much debate about whether these crimes should fall into the ICC's jurisdiction and be defined for international criminal law purposes.

1.5 The Architecture of the Book: The Interplay Between State Sovereignty Theories and Cosmopolitanism on the Process of Criminalisation and Definition of Aggression and Terrorism

Before examining the interplay between State sovereignty considerations and cosmopolitanism in the criminalisation and definition of aggression and terrorism, it is important first to become familiar with the content and scope of these two poles. To this end, Chap. 2 will provide an analysis of the State-centric and cosmopolitan theories and will show how these theories interact with international law in general and the function of the ICC in particular. Firstly, the content and scope of these theories will be examined in order to highlight their relevance and influence in the field of international law. After putting the theories in context, it will be shown how they are both reflected into the ICC project: the idea behind its establishment was based on universal jurisdiction, which is consistent with cosmopolitan goals. On the other hand, the complementary nature of the ICC reflects the fact that State sovereignty considerations have to be taken into account with respect to the adjudication of international crimes. To this end, the third section of Chap. 2 examines the details of the interaction of the complementarity regime with State sovereignty considerations. It will analyse how complementarity should work in principle according to the Rome Statute provisions, how it has worked in practice so far and how it will work with respect to the crime of aggression. The analysis of the interplay between State sovereignty considerations and cosmopolitanism in the context of the function of the ICC is important in order to comprehend the role these two theories have played and still play in the development of international criminal law and the adjudication of international crimes.

Moving on to Chap. 3, the process of defining and criminalising aggression reveals the need for balance between State sovereignty considerations and cosmopolitan theory in order to push forward the development of international criminal law. Therefore, Chap. 3 will first demonstrate that State-centric and cosmopolitan ideals have been of relevance throughout the history of outlawing, criminalising and defining aggression, from the League of Nations period until the adoption of the Rome Statute. Chapter 4 will further discuss the outcome reached in Kampala under the light of State sovereignty and cosmopolitan considerations, in an attempt to show whether a desired balance between the two has been achieved. The conclusions of this analysis will serve as lessons to be learnt in the process of defining and criminalising international terrorism, which is what constitutes one of the overarching purposes of this study.

After having examined how the crime of aggression was shaped for international criminal law purposes under the light of both State sovereignty considerations and cosmopolitanism, Chap. 5 will shift the centre of attention to the concept of terrorism. Specifically, it will firstly analyse further (i) how the inclusion of terrorism into the ICC's jurisdiction can contribute to the improvement of the current extradition system which is provided for by many international anti-terrorist instruments and fill gaps in its implementation and (ii) why its transnational character does not and should not automatically impede its international criminalisation and inclusion into the ICC's jurisdiction. However, even if terrorism is to be characterised as an international crime, it needs to be defined; therefore, Chap. 5 will subsequently analyse how some recent definitional frameworks for terrorism have been influenced by the two theories under examination. The definitional frameworks chosen for this analysis reflect either the State-centric theory and thus, prioritise the respect for State sovereignty over international criminal justice purposes, or the cosmopolitan theory and the need to serve cosmopolitan purposes despite State sovereignty considerations. Both approaches however, as it will be shown, are bound to have weaknesses and ultimately be ineffective, since they fail to achieve the delicate synthesis required between the theories they advocate.

Finally, Chap. 6 will focus on the question of how to achieve this delicate balance in the search of an international definition for terrorism. It will look into existing definitions of terrorism provided by international, regional and domestic instruments as well as the UN Draft definition as provided for in the UN Draft Convention on Terrorism[104] and the recent Appeals Chamber's decision of the UN Special Tribunal for Lebanon.[105] This comparative analysis will reveal the common ground on which definitions of terrorism are based as well as the points of contention between the abovementioned instruments. The conclusions drawn by this analysis will lead to the second section of the chapter, which will examine the most commonly accepted elements of international terrorism in the context of State sovereignty considerations and cosmopolitan purposes and propose how this context will help resolve the major definitional problems surrounding terrorism. It is the author's opinion that not only can defining terrorism be a realistic prospect but also that it can be effectuated in such a manner so as to meaningfully develop international law in the field and eliminate impunity without disregarding respect to State sovereignty.

---

[104] UNGA 2002.

[105] STL, *Interlocutory Decision on the Applicable Law: Terrorism, Conspiracy, Homicide, Perpetration, Cumulative Charging*, 16 February 2011, Case No. STL-11-01/1.

References

Ambos K, Timmermann A (2014) Terrorism and Customary International Law. In: Saul B (ed) Research Handbook on International Law and Terrorism. Edward Elgar, Cheltenham, pp 20–38

Assembly of States Parties to the Rome Statute of the International Criminal Court (2009), Report of the Bureau on the Review Conference, ICC Doc. ICC-ASP/8/43

Assembly of States Parties to the Rome Statute of the International Criminal Court (2013), Report of the Working Group on Amendments, ICC Doc. ICC-ASP/12/44

Bassiouni MC (1974) An Appraisal of the Growth and Developing Trends of International Criminal Law. Revue Internationale de Droit Penal 45:405–433

Bassiouni MC (1996) International Extradition: United States Law and Practice, 3rd edn. Oceana Publications, Dobbs-Ferry, New York

Bassiouni MC (1999) The Source and Content of International Criminal Law: A Theoretical Framework. In: Bassiouni MC (ed) International Criminal Law Vol I: Crimes, 2nd edn. Transnational Publishers, Inc., Ardsley, New York, pp 3–126

Bassiouni MC (2003) The Permanent International Criminal Court. In: Lattimer M, Sands P (eds) Justice for Crimes Against Humanity. Hart Publishing, Oregon, pp 173–217

Bennoune K (2002) "Sovereignty vs Suffering"? Re-Examining Human Rights through the Lens of Iraq. EJIL 13(1):243–262

Boister N (2003) Transnational Criminal Law? EJIL 14(5):953–976

Boister N (2009) Treaty Crimes, International Criminal Court? New Crim L Rev 12:341–365

Broomhall B (2003) International Justice and the International Criminal Court: Between Sovereignty and the Rule of Law. Oxford University Press, Oxford

Brown BS (2008) Depoliticizing Individual Criminal Responsibility. In: Sadat LN, Scharf MP (eds) Theory and Practice of International Criminal Law: Essays in Honor of M. Cherif Bassiouni. Martinus Nijhoff, Leiden, pp 81–126

Cassese A (1998) On the Current Trends towards Criminal Prosecution and Punishment of Breaches of International Humanitarian Law. EJIL 9:2–17

Cassese A (1999) The Statute of the International Criminal Court: Some Preliminary Reflections. EJIL 10:144–171

Cassese A (2001) Terrorism is also Disrupting some Legal Categories of International Law. 12 (5) EJIL 12(5): 993–1001

Cassese A (2003) A Big Step Forward for International Justice. Crimes of War Project. http://www.crimesofwar.org. Accessed 14 April 2013

Creegan E (2010–11) A Permanent Hybrid Court for Terrorism. Am U Int'l L Rev 26:237–313

Cryer R (1996) The Security Council and Article 39: A Threat to Coherence? J Armed Conflict L 1:161–195

Cryer R (2005) International Criminal Law vs State Sovereignty: Another Round? EJIL 16 (5):979–1000

Cryer R, Wilmshurst E (2010) Introduction: What is international criminal law? In: Cryer R and ors (eds) An Introduction to International Criminal Law and Procedure, 2nd edn. Cambridge University Press, Cambridge, pp 3–21

Damaska M (2008) What is the Point of International Criminal Justice? Chi-Kent L Rev 83: 329–365

de Londras F (2010) Terrorism as an International Crime. In: Schabas W, Bernaz N (eds) Routledge International Book of Criminal Law. Routledge, London, pp 169–180

Fletcher GP (2005) Parochial versus Universal Criminal Law. JICJ 3:20–34

Freeland S (2008) The "Effectiveness" of International Criminal Justice. ALTA Law Research Series 16. www.austlii.edu.au/au/journals/ALRS/2008/16.html. Accessed 18 January 2017

Gaeta P (2009) International criminalization of prohibited conduct. In: Cassese A (ed) The Oxford Companion to International Criminal Justice. Oxford University Press, Oxford, pp 63–74

Henkin L (1999–2000) That “S” Word: Sovereignty, and Globalization, and Human Rights, et cetera. 68 Fordham L Rev 68:1–14

Henley K (2011) Sovereignty. In: Chatterjee DK (ed) Encyclopedia of Global Justice. Springer Science and Business Media B V, Dordrecht, pp 1025–1027

Kelsen H (1959–1960) Sovereignty and International Law. The Georgetown L J 48(4):627–640

Klabbers J (1998) Clinching the Concept of Sovereignty: Wimbledon Redux. ARIEL 3(3):345–367

Kress C (2008) International Criminal Law. In Wolfrum R (ed) The Max Planck Encyclopedia of Public International Law, online edn. Oxford University Press, Oxford

Krohne SW (1997) The United States and the World Need an International Criminal Court as an Ally in the War Against Terrorism. Ind Int'l & Comp L Rev 8:159–188

Mégret F (2013) Cour pénale internationale et colonialism: au-delà des évidences (The International Criminal Court and Colonialism: Beyond the Obvious). http://ssrn.com/abstract=2221424. Accessed 18 January 2017

Morris M (2004–2005) Terrorism: The Politics of Prosecution. Chic J Int'l L 5:405–422

Nagle LE (2010) Should Terrorism Be Subject to Universal Jurisdiction? 8 Santa Clara J Int'l L 8:87–100

Norberg N (2010) Terrorism and International Criminal Justice: Dim Prospects for a Future Together. Santa Clara J Int'l L 8:11–50

O'Keefe R (2004) Universal Jurisdiction, Clarifying the Basic Concept. JICJ 2:735–760

Pellet A (2002) Applicable Law. In: Cassese A and ors (eds) The Rome Statute of the International Criminal Court, A Commentary, vol 2. Oxford University Press, Oxford, pp 1051–1084

Plachta M (2001) The Lockerbie Case: The Role of the Security Council in Enforcing the Principle aut dedere aut judicare. EJIL 12(1):125–140

Proposal submitted by Algeria, India, Sri Lanka and Turkey on Article 5 (1998) UN Doc. A/CONF.183/C.1/L.27

Report of the Policy Working Group on the United Nations and Terrorism (2002) UN Doc. S/2002/875 Annex to A/57/273. http://www.globalsecurity.org/security/library/report/2002/un-wrkng-grp-terrorism.htm. Accessed 18 January 2017

Sadat LN (2002) The International Criminal Court and the Transformation of International Law: Justice for the New Millennium. Transnational Publishers, Ardsley New York

Sailer TM (1999) The International Criminal Court: An Argument to Extend its Jurisdiction to Terrorism and a Dismissal of U.S. Objections. Temp Int'l & Comp L J 13:311–346

Saul B (2008) Defining Terrorism to Protect Human Rights. Sydney Law School Research Paper No 08/125. http://papers.ssrn.com/sol3/papers.cfm?abstract_id=1292059. Accessed 18 January 2017

Schabas W (2016) International Criminal Law. Encyclopaedia Britannica. www.britannica.com/topic/international-criminal-law. Accessed 18 January 2017

Secretary-General (2004) Report of the High-Level Panel on Threats, Challenges and Change: A More Secure World: Our shared responsibility. UN Doc. A/59/565

Shahabuddeen M (2004) Does the principle of legality stand in the way of progressive development of law? JICJ 2:1007–1017

Ssenyonjo M (2009) The International Criminal Court and the Warrant of Arrest for Sudan's President Al-Bashir: A Crucial Step Towards Challenging Impunity or a Political Decision? Nordic J Int'l L 78:397–431

Tiefenbrun S (2002–2003) A Semiotic Approach to a legal definition of Terrorism. 9 ILSA J Int'l and Comp L 9:357–390

UNGA (1998a) Diplomatic Conference of Plenipotentiaries on the Establishment of an International Criminal Court UN Doc. A/CONF 183/13

UNGA (1998b) Final Act of the United Nations Diplomatic Conference of Plenipotentiaries on the Establishment of an International Criminal Court UN Doc. A/CONF.183/10

UNGA (2002) Report of the Ad Hoc Committee established by UNGA Res 51/210 of 17 December 1996 UN Doc. Supp No 37 (A/57/37)

UNSC (1992) Resolution 748 UN Doc. S/RES/748

UNSC (1993) Statute of the International Criminal Tribunal for the Former Yugoslavia, UN Doc. S/RES/827

UNSC (1994) Statute of the International Criminal Tribunal for Rwanda, UN Doc. S/RES/955

UNSC (1999) Resolution 1269 UN Doc. S/RES/1269

UNSC (2001a) Resolution 1368 UN Doc. S/RES/1368

UNSC (2001b) Resolution 1373 UN Doc. S/RES/1373

UNSC (2005) Resolution 1593 UN Doc. S/RES/1593

Wilson P (2009) Aggression, Crime and International Security: Moral, Political and Legal Dimensions of International Relations. Routledge, London

Zeidan S (2004) Desperately Seeking Definition: The International Community's Quest for Identifying the Specter of Terrorism. Cornell Int'l L J 36:491–496

Chapter 2
State Sovereignty, Cosmopolitanism and the International Criminal Court

Abstract The overarching argument of this book is that a definition of international terrorism in an international criminal law context will not be functional nor serve the purposes of international criminal justice unless it balances properly State sovereignty considerations and cosmopolitan ideals. The State-centric theory of international law on the one hand, and cosmopolitanism on the other, treat the concept of State sovereignty from different perspectives, with the former emphasising sovereign interests, sometimes at the expense of international criminal justice purposes, and the latter prioritising cosmopolitan aspirations over the respect for State sovereignty. The crime of aggression and international terrorism present aspects that can be addressed in either a pro-State sovereignty or a pro-cosmopolitan context. This chapter will focus at this differentiation of the treatment of State sovereignty in the context of the UN Charter and the Rome Statute frameworks, focusing on the regime of complementarity enshrined in the latter and contributing thus to our understanding of the differentiated approaches that the Security Council and the ICC follow on issues that touch upon State sovereignty. The effectiveness of the definitions of international crimes as provided into the Rome Statute, and for the purposes of this book, the definition of the crime of aggression and possibly terrorism, will ultimately be determined by whether they will be successful in promoting the cosmopolitan ethos that the ICC represents in an international system of sovereign States which might feel threatened by that ethos.

Keywords Cosmopolitanism · Cosmopolitan theory · State sovereignty · State-centric theory · UN Charter · Rome Statute · Complementarity

Contents

S. Margariti, *Defining International Terrorism*, International Criminal Justice Series 15, DOI 10.1007/978-94-6265-204-0_2

2.1 Introduction

This chapter will first discuss the relationship between State sovereignty and international law in light of the State-centric and cosmopolitan theories. It will analyse the position that sovereignty holds in these theories, highlighting the role they have played in the development of the concept of sovereignty in international law. The analysis of these theories will be complemented by an examination of how the UN Charter,[1] as the most fundamental international law instrument, treats State sovereignty and balances it with the international rule of law. While the UN Charter enshrines cosmopolitan aspirations, such as the respect for human rights, the promotion of peace and the prohibition of the use of force, the function of the UN up to date has shown a particular sensitivity to State sovereign interests, mainly those of the Members of the Security Council and consequently their allies. In the subsequent chapters, it will be shown that situations pertaining to aggression/use of force and international terrorism, have been addressed by the Security Council in a way that prioritised national security interests (at least those of the most powerful States) often at the expense of cosmopolitan purposes, the promotion of international criminal justice included. For the purposes of this chapter, it will suffice to highlight this contradistinction between the preference the Security Council has shown to the State-centric theory, with the pro-cosmopolitan basis on which the ICC[2] is meant to function. The establishment of a permanent international criminal court can be viewed as an offset to the sovereignty-based concessions the Security Council has made in this respect and can constitute a genuine cosmopolitan effort in the fight against impunity, even despite State sovereign concerns. However, and since the overarching argument of the book focuses on the need for balance, the final part of this chapter will examine to what extent the complementarity regime of the ICC can achieve a desired balance between its cosmopolitan ethos and the sovereign priorities of its States Parties. While there is no explicit obligation for the States Parties to adopt the Rome Statute[3] definitions verbatim in their national law, the current

[1] Charter of the United Nations, opened for signature 26 June 1945, 1 UNTS XVI (entered into force 24 October 1945) (UN Charter).

[2] UNGA 1998.

[3] Rome Statute of the International Criminal Court, opened for signature 17 July 1998, 2187 UNTS 90 (entered into force 1 July 2002) UN Doc. A/CONF. 183/9 (Rome Statute).

practice of the ICC has shown that possible differentiation between the range of offences as charged against an individual accused by national courts and the ICC Prosecutor might result in a case being admissible before the ICC, something that is not strictly envisioned by the Rome Statute. Thus, the chapter will finally conclude with an analysis of the complementarity regime of the ICC, looking at different but interrelated aspects of it: (i) how complementarity interacts with State sovereignty under Article 17 of the Rome Statute[4] which provides for the criteria of inadmissibility of a case before the ICC, and notably with the concept of State inability to prosecute, (ii) what the current practice of the ICC has shown with respect to whether States have the implicit obligation to adopt the Rome Statute definitions in order to avoid being considered unable to conduct national proceedings and finally (iii) to what extent complementarity will allow the ICC to achieve the required balance, when it confronts cases of aggression and, perhaps, terrorism.

2.2 The Two Theories

2.2.1 The Traditional State-Centric Theory About the Relationship Between Sovereignty and International Law

The traditional State-centric theory rests upon the original and etymological meaning of the word sovereignty, that of supremacy.[5] A State being sovereign means it is supreme and, legally speaking, that its legal authority (or national order) is superior to any other.[6] In this sense, if a State recognises international law as binding for its organs, then international law becomes part of its national legal order.[7] Thus, one can regard sovereignty as a system of norms that does not derive its validity from any other supreme order,[8] whereas international law is a system of norms which gains validity only when recognized by the sovereign State. Complementing this idea, Brus views sovereign States as the backbone of world

[4] The conditions of inadmissibility of a case as provided by Article 17(1) of the Rome Statute are: '(a) The case is being investigated or prosecuted by a State which has jurisdiction over it, unless the State is unwilling or unable genuinely to carry out the investigation or prosecution; (b) The case has been investigated by a State which has jurisdiction over it and the State has decided not to prosecute the person concerned, unless the decision resulted from the unwillingness or inability of the State genuinely to prosecute; …'.

[5] Kelsen 1959–1960, p. 627.

[6] For an elaboration on the concept of sovereignty and its historical development see Henley 2011, pp. 1025–1027.

[7] This is also in accord with Kelsen's monistic theory, where he argues that 'international law and national law form a unity' which can be achieved with the primacy of the one over the other (Kelsen 1959–1960, p. 629). See also text to n. 78.

[8] Ibid., 630.

order, as 'creators and enforcers' of international law.[9] This view is also to be found in the Grotian tradition of international law which holds that international order should be regulated through States; either by creating State responsibility mechanisms or by rendering States the enforcement arm of international law.[10] Finally, according to Bodin, the essential manifestation of sovereignty is the law-making power, suggesting that those who make laws (the sovereign States) cannot be bound by the laws they create and consequently, they are above the (international) law.[11] This theory, or rather this attitude towards sovereignty views the surrender of sovereignty as a necessary precondition for the development of international law.

As a result, it becomes obvious that the State-centric theory views sovereignty as a system of norms incompatible with the idea of subjection to another superior normative order.[12] Being sovereign means to have no other supreme order to account to, and thus, Cassese contends that 'either one supports the international rule of law or one supports State sovereignty'.[13] However, the gradual developments of the post-World War II (WWII) period, the emergence of new, decolonised States and the end of the Cold War era changed the centre of gravity of the concept of sovereignty. Instead of the State, sovereignty moved towards the people; it took the new dimension of self-determination of peoples and became a synonym of sovereign independence from the colonial State who exercised territorial sovereignty.[14] This notion is also manifest in the UN Charter, which starts with the phrase 'We the Peoples of the United Nations determined…'.[15] Sovereignty as self-determination means that the people are the ultimate source of sovereignty, who authorise the State, as their organ, to exercise sovereign powers.[16] Thus, the newly-developed idea was that State sovereignty has to include authority derived from the people of that State, in the absence of which this new 'people's sovereignty' remains incomplete or even violated.[17] In this sense, the modern, post-WWII manifestations of sovereignty come in tension with the traditional State-centric ideas,[18] and this tension could not but be reflected in the relationship between State sovereignty and international law that was to be formed with the

[9] Brus 2002, p. 3.

[10] Mégret 2001, p. 257.

[11] Jennings 2002, p. 27.

[12] Kelsen 1959–1960, p. 627.

[13] Broomhall 2003, p. 56 commenting on Cassese 1998, pp. 11–17.

[14] Jennings 2002, p. 29.

[15] UN Charter, above n. 1, Preamble. See also Articles 1(2) and 55.

[16] Nagan and Hammer 2004, p. 171. While the principle of national self-determination as a manifestation of the sovereignty of the people was asserted from the French revolution, it lost ground during the Cold War era but regained its validity after the demise of the bi-polar model of balance of power (in Pavković and Radan 2003, p. 4).

[17] That a State exercises public powers within a territory does not necessarily mean that these powers are sovereign if this happens contrary to the will of the people. In this case, one can talk about violation of the sovereignty of the people. See also Sarooshi 2005, pp. 9–10.

[18] Broomhall 2003, p. 52.

establishment of the UN and the emergence of decolonised States gradually leading to the further development of the international legal order.

2.2.2 *Cosmopolitan Theory and International Law*

While it can be argued that cosmopolitan thinking was born together with the idea of democracy, the cosmopolitan tradition in international law can be traced back into the Enlightment era and in particular into the ideas of Kant,[19] whose theory will be briefly analysed as an example of traditional cosmopolitanism; by the same token, the views of some modern cosmopolitan theorists will be examined and compared with the views of Kant, in an attempt to demonstrate the development of cosmopolitan thought in international law. Taking Kant's cosmopolitanism as the point of departure, Kant's vision of a cosmopolitan society moves into a middle passage between 'a world State' model and the traditional, sovereignty-based Westphalian model.[20] Kant was critical of both the absolute State sovereignty supremacy on the international plane and the creation of a world republic, in which States would have lost all their sovereign prerogatives and would have to surrender their sovereignty to coercive international institutions.[21] Instead, he envisaged a model that would mostly resemble a federation of States which would be bound by 'a commonly accepted international right.'[22] While he supported the establishment of international institutions, he was against their interference in States' constitution and government[23] and viewed the domestic administration of justice as the first necessary step for the creation of a cosmopolitan order.[24]

Kant's approach of the interrelationship between States and international law can be summarised in the following statement: States have a central role to play in international institutions, there are systems of checks and balances developed in order to limit State sovereignty according to the conditions prescribed by international law instruments, while, at the same time, there is no international sovereign to enforce any duties on States or to oblige them to participate in international organisations and sign international treaties.[25] The Kantian approach of the structure of international law bears significant resemblances with the structure that general international law took after the establishment of the UN and that of international criminal law after the establishment of the ICC. Therefore, one could argue that the ICC seems to bring Kantian cosmopolitanism in its modernity:

[19] Cabrera 2011, p. 209.

[20] Brown 2005, pp. 497–98.

[21] Ibid., p. 501.

[22] Kant 1793 in Reiss 1970, pp. 61–92.

[23] Gregor 1996, p. 96.

[24] Brown 2005, p. 501.

[25] Teson 1992, pp. 86–7.

cosmopolitanism is no more an 'intellectual ethos' but 'a vision of global political consciousness...generated and sustained by international institutions',[26] the ICC included.

While Kant's vision of cosmopolitanism seems reconcilable with the current ICC system, the same cannot be said for the modern version of cosmopolitanism, at least as envisaged by some cosmopolitan theorists. For example, Jürgen Habermas and Hans Kelsen radicalise the Kantian vision of cosmopolitanism in a manner incompatible with the current structure and function of the ICC. While in the Kantian system States do not lose their place in the international plane, both Habermas and Kelsen envisage an international system where a 'world State' would have absorbed all State sovereign prerogatives and separate national legal systems and where the centralisation of power would be the only means to secure a peaceful international order.[27] Similarly, according to Pogge's idea of what he calls 'institutional cosmopolitanism', State sovereignty should not be concentrated at a single level (the State) but should be dispersed in a vertical manner among several units—at least domestically—which will be 'sovereign' on their own right and manifest the traditional characteristics of State.[28] That does not mean that Pogge is in favour of the establishment of a world State, which he sees as a repetition of the 'State sovereignty model' only at a global level.[29] However, he is in favour of this vertical distribution of sovereignty in some fields of international law, such as international peace and security, for which he proposes a central decision-making mechanism, whose function would not depend on State voluntary cooperation and which would have the ability to enforce its decisions to States and thus, to violate their sovereignty.[30]

Despite the differences between the Kantian theory of cosmopolitanism and the modern ones, a concept of relevance to international law that is strongly attached to all, is the concept of morality. For Kant, morality becomes of relevance for international law because he views it as a means to promote moral behaviour through legal institutions which would impose penalties for conduct falling outside the scope of that morality.[31] More recent theorists like Archibugi held that cosmopolitan law is not based on coercion but rather on moral authority,[32] something that is also underpinned by Finch's assertion that, before WWII, the weaknesses of international law were not based on the lack of enforcement mechanisms but on the absence of 'an international moral sense'.[33] Concerning international law developments in general and the ICC in particular, Koller has argued that international

---

[26] Cheah 2006, p. 486.

[27] Zolo 1999, p. 437; Zolo 1998, p. 310.

[28] Pogge 1992, p. 58.

[29] Ibid.

[30] Ibid., pp. 61–62.

[31] Wacks 2005 in Fouladvand 2012, p. 30.

[32] Archibugi 1995, p. 443.

[33] Finch 1979, p. 37.

lawyers believe that any development of international law will bring us closer to the establishment of 'first an international community and then a cosmopolitan community' in which 'all individuals are accorded equal moral status'.[34]

Therefore, the concept of morality is not far from the essence of law, and in particular from international law. The recognition of diversity between States constitutes a legal innovation which allows States to apply their own understanding to judge international events, promoting thus the ultimate goal of Kantian cosmopolitanism, the perpetual peace.[35] Thus, States have a place in the moral discourse, firstly as central actors in international relations and secondly through their domestic legal systems[36] which regulate the lives of their citizens through coercive mechanisms requiring a moral justification.[37]

Therefore, for a coercive legal system, be it national or international, to be legitimate, there has to be a moral justification as a basis for its establishment. In the case of the ICC, its moral justification is already declared in the Preamble of the Rome Statute, when it affirms that 'the most serious crimes of concern to the international community as a whole must not go unpunished' and when it makes reference to the millions of victims of 'unimaginable atrocities that deeply shock the conscience of humanity'.[38] This moral basis of the ICC's establishment is actually the door that, it can be argued, potentially opens the transition from international law to cosmopolitan law, in the sense that the rights of an individual are now protected irrespective of his or her nationality or the territory they happened to be in, an idea equivalent to Kant's cosmopolitan right. By the same token, the ICC's moral basis also justifies the applicability of coercive international criminal law to persons that violate that cosmopolitan right irrespective of their nationality or the place where the conduct happens to occur. This cosmopolitan model—called by Feldman minimalist legal cosmopolitanism—aims at eliminating any 'law-free' zones, any chance where an individual could evade prosecution either because no jurisdiction could reach him or her or because the applied jurisdiction would fall short of the basic moral standards that the ICC is meant to promote.[39]

However, the model of minimal legal cosmopolitanism is not to be performed solely by an international institution—the ICC in this case—but instead, it holds a central place for States. It is not meant to erode the concept of State sovereignty; to the contrary, it is meant to give primacy to domestic legal systems to protect the cosmopolitan right not just of their own nationals but of everyone whose cosmopolitan right is violated. The essence of that model is not that universal jurisdiction should apply everywhere but that some jurisdiction should be applicable

[34] Koller 2008, p. 1050.
[35] Archibugi 1995, p. 443.
[36] Fouladvand 2012, p. 40.
[37] Feldman 2007, p. 1045.
[38] Rome Statute, above n. 3, Preamble paras 2 and 4.
[39] Feldman 2007, pp. 1065–1069.

everywhere to avoid the creation of legal vacuums.[40] This concept matches perfectly the complementarity regime of the ICC, which attempts to reconcile cosmopolitan morality, legitimate coercive international criminal law mechanisms and respect for State sovereignty.

Before moving on to examine the interplay between the concept of State sovereignty and the Rome Statute, it will be important to examine first to what extent the UN Charter, as the most fundamental international legal instrument, has laid the legal basis on which State sovereignty and international law can co-exist. As it will be argued in Chap. 5, the Security Council has taken a rather pro-sovereignty approach in addressing issues that relate to the use of force/aggression and international terrorism. This pro-sovereignty response to conducts whose definitions are the main focus of this study, is founded on UN Charter provisions which clearly favour sovereign prerogatives—at least of the five permanent members of the Security Council and their allies—over cosmopolitan purposes. Instead, the definition of aggression for the purposes of the ICC and the formulation of a definition for international terrorism for international criminal law purposes focus, or will focus, primarily on the cosmopolitan aspirations enshrined by international criminal law. Therefore, it is important to show this antithesis of the treatment of State sovereignty in the context of firstly, the UN Charter and subsequently, the Rome Statute frameworks. This differentiation of approaches towards State sovereignty will help understand the Security Council's pro-sovereignty practice in addressing use of force/aggression and international terrorism issues and the ICC's pro-cosmopolitan mandate in responding to the commission of the crime of aggression, and hopefully international terrorism.

2.3 Sovereignty and International Law: The UN Charter Provisions

According to Kelsen's theory[41] concerning the primacy of international law over national legal orders, there is a distinction between the concept of sovereignty that is excluded under international law and the concept of sovereignty that can be limited or controlled by international law. The type of sovereignty that is excluded by international law is the one advocated by the traditional State-centric theory, i.e. the absolute supremacy of national law over the international. On the other hand, the type of sovereignty that can be regulated by international law is that of sovereignty as freedom of action by the State, namely unlimited competence of its legal order. The latter is not automatically rejected by international law but can be subject to regulations and norms, prescribed by an international organisation. Whether one views international law as superior to national legal orders or as a

[40] Ibid., p. 1067.

[41] Kelsen 1959–1960, p. 636.

body of law that is part of that order and thus, inferior to it, sovereignty can still be subject to international normative regulations.[42]

In this respect, when a State recognises international law when adhering to an international organisation or becoming a party to an international treaty, it becomes bound to international legal regulations, irrespective of which legal order it regards as superior, the national or the international. International law is valid in both cases, either as supreme to a national legal order or as a part of that legal order which binds the sovereign State. In both cases, State sovereignty can be restricted and regulated and thus, an international organisation which will have the competence of regulating a State's sovereignty is always possible. The extent to which a State's sovereignty can be restricted and regulated by international law, according to Kelsen, has always to do with the content of international law and not with the concept of sovereignty itself.[43]

It can be said that State sovereignty is the fundamental principle upon which the UN system is based; the UN is composed of sovereign States. Whether it can function only as a sum of sovereign States or it can have a broader capacity that surpasses the boundary of the accumulation of several State sovereignties is a question of politics. However, the provisions of the UN Charter can provide some insight of how the principle of State sovereignty is understood and tackled at an international level and how its concept has been formed by the State-centric and the cosmopolitan theory.

In the first place, being a sovereign State is the *sine qua non* condition of membership to the UN.[44] This precondition alone is indicative of the fact that a State's capacity of sovereignty pre-exists or exists independently of its membership to an international organisation. In this sense, a State does not need the recognition of its sovereignty to be conferred by a supreme authority but this State quality exists *a priori*. Furthermore, Article 2(7) of the UN Charter provides for the non-interference in the internal affairs of a Member State,[45] a provision that can be said to formulate a statement very close to a definition of State sovereignty.[46] Ultimately, one of the core articles of the UN Charter, Article 2(4), protects in an unequivocal way the territorial integrity and the political independence of its Member States.[47] In this respect, the UN Charter appears to respect at least the core

---

[42] Ibid. However, it is obvious that these two types of sovereignty, the absolute supremacy of national order and the unlimited competence of a State to act (inside or outside its territory) are two sides of the same coin. What Kelsen is trying to argue with this distinction is that, although the absolutist view about sovereignty is in any respect antithetical to international law, a State's freedom of action is not, if conditioned upon certain rules.

[43] Ibid., p. 637.

[44] UN Charter, above n. 1, Article 3.

[45] Ibid., Article 2(7): 'Nothing contained in the present Charter shall authorize the United Nations to intervene in matters which are essentially within the domestic jurisdiction of any state or shall require the Members to submit such matters to settlement under the present Charter; but this principle shall not prejudice the application of enforcement measures under Chapter VII.'

[46] Nagan and Hammer 2004, p. 25.

[47] UN Charter, above n. 1, Article 2(4).

aspects of State sovereignty and to recognise and protect a State's ruling and behavioural autonomy within its own territory.

However, this conclusion, which is in harmony with the traditional State-centric theory of the concept of sovereignty, is not fully supported by other provisions of the UN Charter which refer to the obligations of its Member States and to the authority of the UN organs over them. Article 1 of the UN Charter states that the Members of the UN should honour their Charter obligations and should always seek pacific means for the settlement of their disputes.[48] Article 4 continues by adding another precondition for acquiring a UN membership status, namely that a State should be 'peace-loving' and willing and able to accept all Charter obligations.[49] Regarding the scope of authority of the UN organs over their Member States, the decision-making mechanisms of the UN Charter give the General Assembly the competence to give rise to any issue that falls within the scope of the Charter and make it a matter of international discussion.[50]

Despite these cosmopolitan elements in the function of the UN and the formulation of some UN Charter provisions, the UN cannot in any case be characterised as a pro-cosmopolitan institution. The competences and prerogatives that its primary organ, the Security Council, enjoys, go far beyond the individual State sovereign prerogatives of the other Member States of the UN and have been characterised by some as super sovereign powers.[51] The power of veto of the five permanent members of the Security Council,[52] the competence of the Security Council to enforce its decisions even by the use of force under Chapter VII of the UN Charter,[53] its primary responsibility for the protection of international peace and security[54] and its power to determine the existence of threats to the peace, breaches of the peace or acts of aggression[55] constitute powers that severely favour the most powerful States (and their allies) sometimes at the expense of other, smaller States' sovereign interests or at the expense of cosmopolitan purposes. Moreover, the Security Council, when acting under Chapter VII, is not bound by any international legal obligations, apart from respecting the UN Charter.[56] Consequently, the Members of the Security Council enjoy a latitude that can

[48] Ibid., Article 1.

[49] Ibid., Article 4.

[50] Ibid., Article 10.

[51] Nagan and Hammer 2004, p. 26; Goodrich and ors 1969, pp. 290–309.

[52] UN Charter, above n. 1, Article 27(3). The power of veto is not explicitly mentioned in the UN Charter, however Article 27(3) requires the concurring votes of the five permanent members of the Security Council for the adoption of resolutions that concern non-procedural matters (regulated by Article 27(2)), permitting thus any permanent Member to block the proceedings.

[53] Ibid., Article 42.

[54] Ibid., Article 24.

[55] Ibid., Article 39.

[56] UN Charter, above n. 1, Article 24(2): 'In discharging these duties [concerning its responsibility for the maintenance of international peace and security] the Security Council shall act in accordance with the Purposes and Principles of the United Nations…'. See also Kelsen 1950, pp. 294–95.

possibly be used to serve political exigencies without due regard to cosmopolitan considerations enshrined in the UN Charter, such as protection and respect for human rights, promotion of peace or the prohibition of the use of force. In the subsequent chapters, it will be shown that more often than not, at least with respect to the use of force/aggression and international terrorism, the Security Council has mostly prioritised State-centric concerns pertaining to these issues rather than cosmopolitan aspirations.

Turning now to the relationship between sovereignty and the UN Charter, it seems that, under the UN Charter provisions, the concept of sovereignty is transformed into meaning independence in the sense of non-interference.[57] Sovereignty has retained its external characteristics under Article 2(7) referring to the domestic jurisdiction of Member States but has been subject to restrictions and control by the UN Charter and its organs. The international legal order established by the UN requires a transfer of aspects of sovereignty in areas such as international security and the use of force to the UN organs as well as a convergence of the individual interests of the Member States.[58] By the same token, the development of international criminal law, as reflected in the establishment of the ICC, requires from States the relinquishment to it, even if only on a subsidiary basis, of legal-judicial aspects of sovereignty in the area of prosecution of international crimes. However, it has to be noted that compliance with the international legal order is often mostly determined by factors that are little related to the cosmopolitan principles promoted by the UN or international criminal justice, but related to political pressure or national interests.[59] If one looks at the examples of the ad hoc military tribunals of the Former Yugoslavia and Rwanda (ICTY and ICTR respectively), one will draw the conclusion that the political context in each of these examples played a significant role in whether the affected States would cooperate with the tribunals.[60] In

[57] Brus 2002, p. 8.

[58] Broomhall 2003, p. 58.

[59] Ibid., p. 61.

[60] Broomhall 2003, pp. 152–54. In the case of the ICTR, two incidents are worth noticing: in the first one, while the newly-formed Rwandan government invited the Security Council to establish the tribunal and engaged to cooperate, it then voted against the resolution adopting its Statute, on the basis of the temporal jurisdiction of the tribunal (post-genocide revenge killings by the Tutsis would fall into its jurisdiction) and of its failure to apply the death penalty. The second one involves an order of the ICTR Appeals Chamber to release a suspect whose rights of fair trial had been violated. In response, the Rwandan government promised to suspend its cooperation with the tribunal. The Prosecutor applied for a review of the decision for release and finally the Chamber reversed its initial decision. In the case of the ICTY, Croatia was mostly unwilling to extradite its nationals to the tribunal or to provide evidence. It finally agreed to surrender to the tribunal Tihomir Blaskić and Zlatko Aleksovski, after the US's threats to block international loans. In the Report of the International Tribunal for the Prosecution of Persons Responsible for Serious Violations of International Humanitarian Law Committed in the Territory of the Former Yugoslavia since 1991 (1999), the ICTY stated that there was 'a pattern of non-compliance, including the failure to defer to the competence of the Tribunal, failure to execute warrants, failure to provide evidence and information and the refusal to permit the Prosecutor and her investigators into Kosovo', paras 91–99.

principle, there is no reason to believe that this will not be the case as far as the ICC is concerned. Despite the existence of a sufficient framework of obligations for cooperation in the Rome Statute,[61] the ICC will not be able to function effectively without the goodwill and favourable legislative frameworks of its States Parties. The extent to which States will respond (if at all) to violations of international criminal law or decide to cooperate with the ICC depends highly on politics and any enhanced normative infrastructure promoted by the ICC in terms of State obligations will only temper, but not replace, the role international politics play in the enforcement of international law.[62] Therefore, adhering to a treaty regime and to the definitions of crimes contained therein will have consequences that pertain to sovereignty.

What follows next is an assessment of how the ICC deals with the concept of State sovereignty. The ICC has given flesh and blood to some extent to the principle of universal jurisdiction[63] for international crimes and the Rome Statute constitutes a body of international law the violation of which bears severe consequences for its States Parties. The introduction of a permanent international criminal law enforcement mechanism into the international legal order constitutes a novelty for the community of sovereign States, which might feel threatened by it due to its more direct effect on—at least the judicial—aspects of their sovereignty. As was noted above, in contrast to the Security Council, whose function and approach towards international security matters relies heavily on State-centric considerations (at least of its Member States and its allies), the ICC is meant to function on a more pro-cosmopolitan basis, prioritising cosmopolitan concerns despite State considerations in the adjudication of international crimes, including those that pertain to international security matters, such as aggression. Eventually, the success of the Rome Statute definitions will highly rely on their ability to promote and defend cosmopolitan ideals in a system of States which might be very distrustful or even hostile towards those ideas. As such, the complementarity regime of the ICC is meant to work towards this direction.[64]

---

[61] Rome Statute, above n. 3, Articles 86–102.

[62] Broomhall 2003, p. 61.

[63] It is more accurate to speak of a qualified or quasi-universal jurisdiction. Article 12(2) of the Rome Statute provides that the ICC may exercise its jurisdiction when the territorial State or the State of nationality of the accused (or both) are Parties to the Statute or have accepted its jurisdiction ad hoc. However, this jurisdictional link with the territorial or nationality State is not required in case of a Security Council referral of a situation to the ICC Prosecutor under Chapter VII of the UN Charter (Rome Statute, above n. 3, Articles 12 and 13). Besides, some of the crimes of the Rome Statute, such as the grave breaches of the Geneva Conventions (Rome Statute, above n. 3, Article 8(2a)), are subject to universal jurisdiction anyway. On the other hand, some national legislations relating to the implementation of the Rome Statute provisions either adopt the jurisdictional bases explicitly referred to in the Rome Statute or clearly establish universal jurisdiction. On national implementation of the Rome Statute substantive law see Kleffner 2003, p. 86.

[64] Philippe 2006, p. 375, where he argues that the principle of complementarity is the means through which to enforce universal jurisdiction for international crimes.

2.4 Sovereignty and International Law: The Rome Statute and the Principle of Complementarity

If, for the reasons analysed above, one views the Security Council as a mostly State-centric organ driven by political exigencies and State sovereignty concerns, the ICC can be seen as an offset, an international criminal justice mechanism whose principal purposes rely on cosmopolitanism, the respect for the rule of law and the fight against impunity. While a definition for aggression, and aggression as an international crime in its own right, have ultimately found their place among the other crimes of Article 5 of the Rome Statute,[65] the same cannot be said with respect to international terrorism and it may take a long time before international criminal justice is allowed to play a role in such cases. However, the paradigm of the ICC as a permanent international court that could potentially exercise jurisdiction, cannot go without examination as to the extent to which it can achieve the desired balance between State sovereignty and cosmopolitanism in the adjudication of international crimes. Therefore, this section has as its focus the ICC's complementary mandate and will examine (i) whether the criterion of State inability as a ground of admissibility of cases before the ICC can be seen as an implied obligation for States to adopt the Rome Statute definitions in national legislations, (ii) whether the current practice of the ICC manifests that States are compelled to follow the Rome Statute definitions even if there is no explicit obligation under the Rome Statute to do so and (iii) how the complementarity regime in general might work when the ICC confronts a case of aggression and possibly, terrorism. While in principle, complementarity strikes a certain degree of balance between the respect for State sovereignty and the cosmopolitan goal of fighting impunity in the adjudication of international crimes, complementarity in practice has revealed an ICC which sometimes appear to be pro-cosmopolitan, in the sense of stepping in circumstances not clearly envisioned by the Rome Statute. Since the author's view is that the balance between State sovereignty concerns and cosmopolitan ideals should not be limited to the definition of international crimes but should extend to their criminalisation and modalities of prosecution, it has to be noted early on that an ICC with an overly pro-cosmopolitan orientation might constitute a disincentive for States to eventually extend its jurisdiction over a crime of international terrorism or define it for that purpose.

---

[65] As was also noted in Chap. 1, the international crimes under the ICC's jurisdiction (genocide, war crimes, crimes against humanity and the crime of aggression) will be hereinafter referred to as Article 5 crimes.

2.4.1 Complementarity in Principle

2.4.1.1 Conditions of Inadmissibility: Article 17

According to Article 17(1), there are four conditions that have to be met for a case to be declared inadmissible before the ICC[66]: (i) the case is being investigated or prosecuted by a State which has jurisdiction over it, (ii) the case has been investigated by a State with jurisdiction but that State decided not to prosecute the individual concerned, (iii) the individual concerned has already been tried for the same conduct by a State[67] and (iv) the case is not of sufficient gravity in order to fall within the ICC's jurisdiction. In this respect, it has to be noted that the fourth condition is a condition of admissibility as well as one of jurisdiction, according to the Article 1 formulation of 'the most serious crimes of concern'. If a case is not of sufficient gravity, it will not fall into the ICC's jurisdiction anyway, even if the State of jurisdiction is not investigating or has not investigated the case or prosecuted the concerned individual(s). On the other hand, if a case is of sufficient gravity, it still needs to be checked whether any of the other three conditions is not met, before a case is declared admissible. In other words, for a case to be admissible before the ICC the condition of sufficient gravity does not suffice on its own but it has to be coupled with the absence of any of the other conditions mentioned in the provision.

However, even if one of the first three conditions is met, a case may still be deemed admissible before the ICC. Article 17 provides some exceptions regarding the first three conditions of inadmissibility. For conditions (i) and (ii), a case can still be declared admissible if the State of jurisdiction is 'unwilling' or 'unable' to 'genuinely' carry out proceedings against a concerned individual.[68] For the third condition, a similar exception also applies and it is formulated in Article 20(3), where it states that the proceedings conducted by the State of jurisdiction should not have had as their purpose to 'shield' the accused from justice and that they should have been carried out independently and impartially 'in accordance with the norms of due process recognised by international law'.[69] Article 17(2) gives some further guidelines regarding the context of the terms 'unwillingness' and 'inability' as used in the provision: namely, for a State to be deemed unwilling to 'genuinely' carry out proceedings it has to be shown that the national proceedings were carried out with

---

[66] Rome Statute, above n. 3, Article 17.

[67] This third condition complements Article 20(3) of the Rome Statute, concerning the *ne bis in idem* principle.

[68] Rome Statute, above n. 3, Article 17(1): '(a) The case is being investigated or prosecuted by a State which has jurisdiction over it, unless the State is unwilling or unable genuinely to carry out the investigation or prosecution; (b) The case has been investigated by a State which has jurisdiction over it and the State has decided not to prosecute the person concerned, unless the decision resulted from the unwillingness or inability of the State genuinely to prosecute;…'.

[69] Rome Statute, above n. 3, Article 20(3).

the purpose of shielding the accused from justice or carried out with unjustified delay 'inconsistent with an intent to bring the person concerned to justice' or that they are not or have not been carried out independently or impartially, again 'inconsistent with an intent to bring the person concerned to justice'.[70] Concerning the term 'inability', a State is unable to carry out proceedings when its national judicial system is partly or totally collapsed or unavailable and thus, the State cannot 'obtain the accused or the necessary evidence and testimony or [is] otherwise unable to carry out its proceedings.'[71]

2.4.1.2 'Inability' as Lack of Compatible Domestic Legislation

The language of the above-mentioned provisions is meant to cover two possible situations that the ICC wishes to avoid with respect to the administration of international justice: firstly, to avoid the possibility that a State conducts sham trials, a problem foreseen when the ICTY was established and secondly, to avoid the possibility that a State will not conduct any proceedings at all due to the unavailability of its national judicial system, as was the case with the ICTR's creation.[72] The criterion of 'unwillingness', contrary to that of 'inability', raised a number of objections from States during the negotiations[73] due to its subjectivity. In particular, it was feared that the ICC gains too much discretion in deciding in which cases a State is unwilling to try an alleged offender, with the risk of functioning as a court of appeal and potentially overruling judgments of national judicial systems.[74] Moreover, since a State's unwillingness shall be measured by 'the principles of due process recognised by international law',[75] this can be said to give an extra discretion to the ICC to also determine what these principles of due process are and if they are complied with by the concerned State. However, most States at the negotiation conference seemed willing enough to give priority to the promotion of international criminal justice over their need to protect their judicial sovereignty, at least in this respect, and the criterion of 'unwillingness' was finally introduced.

As an objective criterion, inability presumably applies to States which suffer from a breakdown of their national institutions or are plagued by chaos due to civil war or any other public disorder.[76] All the three deficiencies mentioned in Article

---

[70] Ibid., Article 17(2).

[71] Ibid., Article 17(3).

[72] Trahan 2012, pp. 581–82.

[73] Ibid.

[74] Ibid. See also Gurulé 2001–2002, p. 30.

[75] Rome Statute, above n. 3, Article 17(2): 'In order to determine unwillingness in a particular case, the Court shall consider, having regard to the principles of due process recognized by international law, whether one or more of the following exist, as applicable…'.

[76] Benzing 2003, p. 613. According to Article 17(3) of the Rome Statute, inability is determined by three factors: whether, due to a total or substantial collapse or unavailability of its national judicial system the State is (i) unable to obtain the accused, (ii) unable to obtain the necessary

17(3), the inability to obtain the accused, necessary evidence and testimony and the inability to otherwise carry out the proceedings, have to be a result of collapse or unavailability of the national judicial system.[77] In this respect, it is unclear whether a State can be deemed unable to carry out national proceedings in cases where the national legislation either does not include the crimes under the jurisdiction of the ICC or does not penalise them to the same extent as the Rome Statute. As is the case with the rest of the Article 5 crimes, it is always questionable whether an eventual inclusion, and for this reason, formulation of a definition for international terrorism for the purposes of the Rome Statute, will equal to a subsequent obligation for States to enshrine this same definition into their national legal frameworks.

It has to be noted at first that the Rome Statute creates criminal liability for the crimes under the jurisdiction of the ICC only at an international and not at a national level. Thus, an act committed by an individual that can be categorised as an international crime under Article 5 of the Rome Statute does not automatically fall into the same category for the national criminal justice system concerned, unless the State has introduced in its domestic penal legislation the definitions of the Article 5 crimes of the Rome Statute.[78] In the opposite case, it is possible that such an act might be prosecuted and punished as an 'ordinary crime'.[79] To the extent that the scope of 'unavailability of the national judicial system' includes the absence of compatible penal legislation from domestic judicial systems, a State can be seen as

(Footnote 76 continued)

evidence and testimony or (iii) otherwise unable to carry out its proceedings. In the ICC, *Prosecutor v Saif Al-Islam Gaddafi and Abdullah Al-Senussi*, Decision on the admissibility of a case against Saif Al-Islam Gaddafi, 31 May 2013, Case No. ICC-01/11-01/11-344-Conf (*Gaddafi* Admissibility Decision) para 200, the Pre-Trial Chamber held that the ability of a State to genuinely carry out proceedings 'must be assessed in the context of the relevant national system and procedures… [and] in accordance with the substantive and procedural criminal law applicable in Libya'.

[77] Rome Statute, above n. 3, Article 17(3).

[78] The relationship between national and international legal orders has been divided into three, principal theories: (i) the monistic view which advocates the supremacy of national law over the international, (ii) the dualistic view which advocate that international law and national law are 'independent of each other in their validity' (Kelsen 1959–1960, p. 629) and therefore can be valid simultaneously and (iii) the monistic view which places international law above the various national legal systems. The dualistic theory started to lose ground after the second half of the 20th century and in its place, the monistic theory of international law supremacy over national legal systems started to emerge. The Vienna Convention on the Law of Treaties, (opened for signature 23 May 1969, 1155 UNTS 331, entered into force 27 January 1980) under Article 27, provides that a State party to a treaty cannot invoke national legislation as justification for non-compliance with its treaty obligations. Also, Article 88 of the Rome Statute provides that the national legal systems of its States Parties shall have in place procedures which allow all forms of cooperation, as envisaged by Part 9 of the Rome Statute, for the purposes of the ICC. The incorporation in domestic legislations of international rules as such is also another manifestation of the monistic theory of the primacy of international law over national legal orders. For a thorough analysis of these theories see Cassese 2005, pp. 213–237.

[79] Benzing 2003, p. 614.

'otherwise unable to carry out its proceedings' if it has not incorporated the definitions of the Article 5 crimes.[80]

However, even when such legislation exists, a State can be still deemed 'unable' if the national legislation is assessed as inadequate by the ICC Prosecutor.[81] In the context of definitions of crimes, inadequacy might entail the recategorisation of a conduct being an international offence under the Rome Statute, to an ordinary offence under a State's national legislation.[82] Thus, provided that international terrorism becomes an offence under the Rome Statute, a State Party with absent or incompatible national legislation concerning terrorist offences might not satisfy the complementarity requirements of Article 17, increasing the number of cases related to terrorism that can be found admissible before the ICC. This interpretation of unavailability might provide an additional reason for States to be wary of any extension of the ICC's jurisdiction over a crime of international terrorism and consequently, of the formulation of an international criminal law definition. While Article 17 of the Rome Statute clearly shows a preference for domestic prosecutions of international crimes, State sovereignty has been rendered conditional,[83] in that (and as it will also be shown in the next section) the ICC is provided with the pro-cosmopolitan competence of exercising external oversight over the national proceedings for the commission of international crimes of its States Parties.

While there are views which support that in this case State sovereignty is undermined under the Rome Statute,[84] it should be pointed out that one of the aims of complementarity is to urge States to exercise their criminal jurisdiction for the commission of international crimes and remind them that it is first and foremost their duty to enforce international law.[85] If an obligation to introduce compatible penal legislation to domestic laws would undermine aspects of State sovereignty, then the absence of this obligation would clearly undermine the overall purpose of the complementarity principle, as the ICC would not be able to rely on national prosecutions for international crimes.[86] While not explicitly required by the Rome Statute, the harmonisation of national legislation concerning international crimes

[80] Doherty and McCormack 1999, p. 152; Kleffner 2003, p. 89. However, Colombia opposed to this interpretation. See also Declaration of Colombia upon ratification of the Rome Statute (1998) that 'the word "otherwise" […] refers to the obvious absence of objective conditions necessary to the conduct of trial' and that 'none of the provisions of the Rome Statute alters the domestic law applied by the Colombian judicial authorities in exercise of their domestic jurisdiction within the territory of the Republic of Colombia'.

[81] Ibid.

[82] Kleffner 2003, p. 95. In the *Gaddafi* Admissibility Decision, above n. 76, para 88, the Pre-Trial Chamber held that domestic prosecutions under the category of ordinary crimes can be considered sufficient provided though that the case covers the same conduct as the one to be charged by the ICC Prosecutor. A discussion on the 'same person, same conduct' test as has been applied by the ICC will follow in the next section.

[83] McAuliffe 2014, p. 273; Robinson 2010, p. 96.

[84] Benzing 2003, p. 616.

[85] Rome Statute, above n. 3, Preamble paras 4, 6.

[86] Kleffner 2003, p. 93.

with the Rome Statute definitions seems to be the only way that allows the ICC to really function on a complementary basis and not as a replacement of national judicial systems.[87] An opposite interpretation of complementarity would mean that States Parties would be free to define international offences according to their own understanding, categorising them as ordinary offences or define them more narrowly than the Rome Statute. The legislative gaps resulting from differentiated international and national definitions would most probably increase the number of cases before the ICC, as States Parties would fail to establish their jurisdiction over an Article 5 crime for the purpose of conducting national prosecutions.[88]

As Newton suggests, the reasons why States should criminalise Article 5 crimes and thus, harmonise their national criminal justice systems with ICC standards, are: (i) to ensure the primacy of national jurisdictions over the ICC, (ii) to ensure that the ICC is not overburdened with cases, (iii) to eliminate the creation of safe havens for international criminals trying to flee prosecution and (iv) to strengthen the international criminal justice system by rendering States the 'enforcement arms' of international law, ensuring that there will be no impunity for the commission of international crimes.[89] However, there are several scenarios that can take place in the effort of States to harmonise their domestic penal legislation with the ICC provisions. The first one, which was already mentioned in the previous paragraph, involves the national prosecution of an Article 5 crime under a different criminal formulation, categorised as the 'ordinary crime' of murder for example, a scenario that will most probably result in finding the State of jurisdiction 'unable' to carry out the proceedings. A second scenario would be the verbatim adoption of Article 5 definitions, such as is the case of the UK, with the adoption of the UK International Criminal Court Act 2001.[90] In this case, the mirroring of the ICC provisions into domestic legislation would preclude the finding that a State is unable to carry out national proceedings. However, if the national Prosecutor decides to charge the alleged offenders for different crimes than the ones the ICC Prosecutor would charge, should the trial be conducted before the ICC, then there is the risk that the jurisdictional State be found 'unwilling' to prosecute the perpetrators[91] or that it conducts proceedings for a different range of crimes than the one envisaged by the ICC Prosecutor.[92]

Other practices followed by States in their effort of harmonisation are the adoption of narrower definitions of international crimes or of definitions taken by other international law instruments than the Rome Statute. The example of the Swiss Penal Code is indicative of the first practice. Whereas the reformed Swiss

---

[87] Ibid.

[88] Ibid., p. 94.

[89] Newton 2011, p. 320.

[90] International Criminal Court Act 2001 c 17.

[91] Newton 2011, p. 321.

[92] As was the case with ICC, *Prosecutor v Thomas Lubanga Dyilo*, Case No. ICC-01/04-01/06-8, which will be commented below.

Penal Code includes more precise definitions for war crimes, so far sanctioned only by general reference to international humanitarian law,[93] provisions concerning the crime of genocide and the responsibility of senior officials are less broad than in the Rome Statute.[94] On the other hand, the Extraordinary Chambers of Cambodia, a hybrid international court, which was established however 'within' the Cambodian courts,[95] operates under the 2001 Law on establishment of the Extraordinary Chambers[96] which reproduces in part the provisions of the Rome Statute. In particular, some formulations for crimes against humanity have been taken from the Statute of the International Criminal Tribunal for Rwanda,[97] other acts of crimes against humanity are omitted[98] whereas some others are only mentioned by reference and without definitions.[99]

This selectivity of approaches concerning the harmonisation of definitions under international criminal law with domestic legislation can be paradoxically interpreted to be either in conformity or in conflict with the complementarity regime. On the one hand, a vision of complementarity, based on identical criminal definitions between the Rome Statute and domestic legislations of States Parties, suggests that the main concern of the ICC is not simply whether international criminal justice can be administered by States, but also whether it is administered according to the ICC's own standards of what best constitutes international criminal justice.[100] This universalist approach of complementarity, namely that national prosecutions should be conducted following the definitions provided in the Rome Statute, does not leave much room for tolerance to the pluralism of the national judicial systems of States Parties and suggests that the means of administering international criminal justice

---

[93] Hirondelle News Agency 2008.

[94] Article 259(1bis) of the Swiss Criminal Code, 21 December 1937 (status as of 1 May 2013) provides that public provocation to commit genocide is prosecutable only when genocide has taken place in whole or in part in Switzerland without criminalising incitement to commit genocide abroad. Also Article 264k(1) provides that a superior could be held responsible only for crimes he was aware that a subordinate has committed or will commit and failed to act. The Rome Statute establishes liability for superiors also in cases where a superior 'should have known' that the forces under his or her command have committed or will commit Article 5 crimes (Article 28(a)(i)).

[95] Report of International Federation of Human Rights 2006.

[96] Law on the Establishment of Extraordinary Chambers in the Courts of Cambodia for the Prosecution of Crimes Committed during the period of Democratic Kampuchea, 10 August 2001, amended 27 October 2004 (2001 Law).

[97] The chapeau of the definition of crimes against humanity (Article 5 of 2001 Law) is taken from the UNSC 1994, Article 3.

[98] Report of International Federation of Human Rights 2006, p. 21. Article 5 of the 2001 Law, above n. 96, omits some material acts included in Article 7 of the Rome Statute, above n. 3: enforced disappearances, sexual violence other than rape and the crime of apartheid.

[99] Ibid. Article 5(2) of 2001 Law, above n. 96, includes extermination, enslavement, deportation, persecutions and other inhumane acts as constitutive elements of crimes against humanity without any definition of these terms. The crime of torture is defined, not according to Article 7 of the Rome Statute, above n. 3, but according to Article 500 of the 1955 Cambodian Criminal Code (Article 3 of the 2001 Law, above n. 96).

[100] Mégret 2011, p. 363.

matter as much as the end. In fact, it is argued that this approach runs counter to the very essence of the complementarity regime,[101] which dictates primacy of national jurisdictions and the respective national definitions they entail.

On the other hand, it can be argued that States Parties have an implied obligation, arising from the Rome Statute, to include Article 5 crimes into domestic legislation. This obligation can be derived from both a contextual and a teleological interpretation of the Preamble of the Rome Statute. According to the preambular para 6,[102] States Parties have a duty to prosecute international crimes, meaning that they cannot impede the administration of international justice for any reason, including the lack of appropriate legislation or non-criminalisation of a particular conduct which is criminalised under the Rome Statute. A teleological interpretation would support that conclusion, in that the ultimate purpose of the ICC, the fight against impunity, will not be achieved if States Parties have not fully criminalised the conduct which is punishable under the Rome Statute, weakening thus the deterrent effect of national prosecutions.[103] Since (i) the object and purpose behind the establishment of the ICC is the fight against impunity, (ii) preambular para 4 provides that effective prosecutions 'must be ensured by taking measures at the national level'[104] and (iii) practically, not all cases concerning international crimes can be prosecuted by the ICC, the harmonisation of domestic definitions for international crimes with the international ones is necessary, in order to both prevent States from being exposed to the ICC and, at the same time, promote a common understanding regarding the content and scope of international crimes recognised by, at least, the States Parties to the Rome Statute.

All in all, the applicability of the test of a State's unwillingness and inability is characterised as a judicial tightrope,[105] since the balance between a too narrow and a too broad interpretation of the terms is quite tenuous. On the one hand, too broad an interpretation may lead to criticisms that the ICC exceeds its powers in being too intrusive into national judicial systems. On the other hand, if the ICC follows too narrow an approach for the concepts of 'unwillingness' and 'inability', it may attract criticism for being too lenient towards State sovereign prerogatives. The term 'genuinely' tries to strike that balance by adding a standard, that of genuine State action to investigate or prosecute, in order to assess its unwillingness or inability. However, the practice of the ICC has not offered any further elaboration of these terms in its current case law; on the contrary, it seems that it has taken a different, broader approach with respect to the admissibility of cases. This broader approach, while in line with a pro-cosmopolitan model of international criminal justice, might have an adverse effect on the degree of States willingness towards an eventual definition and criminalisation of international terrorism for the purposes of the

[101] Ibid.

[102] Rome Statute, above n. 3, Preamble.

[103] Kleffner 2003, p. 93.

[104] Rome Statute, above n. 3, Preamble para 4.

[105] Benzing 2003, p. 603.

Rome Statute. The following section will show to what extent the ICC, as it has been revealed by its practice to date, has walked away from a strict application of the complementarity regime, risking the delicate balance achieved by the Rome Statute provisions between the respect for State sovereignty and the ICC's cosmopolitan aspirations.

2.4.2 Complementarity in Practice

Turning now to the current practice of the ICC relating to the complementarity regime, there is not so far much development in case-law concerning further elaboration of the terms of unwillingness or inability on the part of a concerned State; from the ten situations that have reached the ICC at the time of writing, five of them have reached it through self-referrals, two through Security Council referrals and three situations have been brought before the ICC through investigations conducted *proprio motu*.[106] So far, the role of the ICC seems to go beyond the one prescribed in the Rome Statute at least for the five self-referred situations, in that the vision of a complementarity regime which would strengthen and encourage States to conduct national prosecutions is far from reality.[107] Instead, the concepts of unwillingness and inability seem to have been replaced in practice by unavailability or inactivity.[108] So far, it has been shown that, in most cases, the ICC has intervened where the concerned State showed no intention to prosecute.[109] This lack of intention for national prosecutions does not indicate that there is genuine unwillingness on the part of the State (if the situation is referred to the ICC by the concerned State itself) or genuine inability (because the national judicial system might be perfectly in place) but it shows State unavailability or inaction. However, according to the Preamble of the Rome Statute, it is the duty of States Parties primarily to prosecute international crimes and only in cases of unwillingness and inability, can jurisdiction be relinquished. Having the ICC conducting trials for international crimes in cases where the jurisdictional States are both willing (in the sense that they wish that justice be done) and able to do so, does not equal to a proper use of complementarity but rather to a waiver of it. This pro-cosmopolitan interventionist policy, which circumvents aspects of the concerned State's judicial sovereignty, seems to prioritise the goal of ending impunity in The Hague over the goal of encouraging States to conduct national prosecutions, a function that goes beyond the initial vision of complementarity as envisaged by the States Parties.[110] The ICC's judicial dynamism, though in conformity with a cosmopolitan model of

[106] ICC, Situations under investigation 2017.

[107] McAuliffe 2013, p. 215.

[108] Mégret 2011, p. 376.

[109] Ibid.

[110] McAuliffe 2013, p. 215.

international criminal justice, might have adverse effects with respect to States' willingness to potentially expand the ICC's jurisdiction over an international crime of terrorism (and define it for that purpose), should the ICC continues to follow this broader approach with respect to the admissibility of cases.

2.4.2.1 The *Lubanga* and *Katanga* Precedents: An Intrusive ICC?

Examples from the current practice of the ICC have demonstrated that the ICC avails itself of a more interventionist approach to initiate proceedings even in circumstances not necessarily envisioned by the drafters of the Rome Statute. The *Prosecutor v Lubanga Dyilo* was the first case that was made admissible through self-referral by the Democratic Republic of Congo (DRC). Although the Pre-Trial Chamber recognised that the Congolese judicial system 'had undergone certain changes' and was 'able' to prosecute the case under Article 17, admissibility was granted on grounds that the accused was not being prosecuted by the national authorities for the same offences as were to be charged with by the ICC Prosecutor.[111] When the ICC Prosecutor sought an arrest warrant against Lubanga in January 2006, the accused was already in the custody of the DRC since March 2005, being charged with, among other things, genocide and crimes against humanity.[112] The Prosecutor based his application for arrest on allegations that the accused committed the war crimes of recruiting, conscripting, and enlisting child soldiers[113] and argued that the case should be declared admissible, because the DRC government had stated that it was not able to prosecute crimes under the jurisdiction of the ICC, and thus, it was deemed 'unable' under Article 17.[114] The Pre-Trial Chamber I rejected inability as a ground of admissibility but declared the case admissible, because 'for a case arising from the investigation of a situation to be inadmissible, national proceedings must encompass both the person and the conduct which is the subject of the case before the Court'.[115] The Congolese authorities were conducting proceedings against Lubanga for a different range of offences than those presented by the ICC Prosecutor, thus the case, according to a strict interpretation of Article 17(1a), which should involve both the same person and the same criminal conduct, was not being prosecuted at all.

The Pre-Trial Chamber I introduced a third ground of admissibility of a case before the ICC: apart from a genuine State 'unwillingness' or inability', State inactivity can constitute a ground of admissibility. The Pre-Trial Chamber found

---

[111] ICC, *Prosecutor v Thomas Lubanga Dyilo*, Under Seal Decision of the Prosecutor's Application for a Warrant of Arrest, Article 58, 10 February 2006, Case No. ICC-01/04-01/06-8 (*Lubanga* decision) paras 35–37.

[112] Ibid., para 33.

[113] Ibid., para 38.

[114] Ibid., para 34.

[115] Ibid., para 37.

that 'the DRC cannot be said to be acting in relation to the specific case before the Court'[116] and held that the 'case would be admissible only if those States with jurisdiction over it have remained inactive in relation to that case or are unwilling or unable' under Article 17.[117] While this holding went unchallenged by the defence,[118] this irregular application of Article 17 gave rise to criticism that the ICC sidestepped the complementarity spirit of the Rome Statute. Instead of supporting the national primacy of the DRC to conduct proceedings against the accused and encouraged confidence in the Congolese criminal justice system to enforce implementation of the Rome Statute provisions,[119] it preferred to supersede a national trial and rushed to assume as much responsibility as possible.[120] This type of judicial activism walks away from the initial vision of complementarity which was destined to protect the judicial aspects of State sovereignty from a court which would intervene on grounds other than unwillingness and inability.[121] In this particular case, it also had the awkward effect of the ICC's conducting its first trial for offences less serious than the ones pursued by the authorities of the DRC.[122]

Similarly, in *Prosecutor v Katanga*,[123] the ICC took a broader approach with respect to the admissibility of cases than the one provided in the Rome Statute. In June 2005, the Prosecutor sought an arrest warrant against Germain Katanga on grounds that he was allegedly responsible for a number of war crimes and crimes against humanity committed in February 2003 in a village in the DRC.[124] The arrest warrant was granted by the Pre-Trial Chamber, even though the accused had already been arrested and detained since March 2005 by the authorities of the DRC.[125] However, the Pre-Trial Chamber found the case admissible because, as in the *Lubanga* case, the domestic proceedings against Katanga did not 'encompass the same conduct' as the Prosecutor's application for arrest. The defence challenged the validity of the so-called 'same conduct' test, arguing that it was a flawed precedent and that it departed from a proper interpretation of Article 17.[126] The Trial Chamber rejected the defence motion without however providing any elaboration on the proper applicability of the 'same conduct' test; rather, it held that the

[116] Ibid., para 39.

[117] Ibid., para 29.

[118] Schabas 2008a, p. 757.

[119] Jurdi 2011, p. 264.

[120] Schabas 2008b, pp. 32–33.

[121] McAuliffe 2013, pp. 220–21.

[122] Schabas 2008a, p. 743.

[123] ICC, *Prosecutor v Germain Katanga*, Case No. ICC-01/04-01/07-4.

[124] ICC, *Prosecutor v Germain Katanga*, Decision on the Evidence and Information Provided by the Prosecution for the Issuance of a Warrant of Arrest for Germain Katanga, 6 July 2006, Case No. ICC-01/04-01/07-4, paras 3, 10.

[125] Ibid., para 18.

[126] ICC, *Prosecutor v Germain Katanga and Mathieu Ngudjolo Chui*, Motion Challenging the Admissibility of the Case by the Defence of Germain Katanga, pursuant to Article 19(2)(a) of the Statute, 11 March 2009, Case No. ICC-01/04-01/07-949 paras 31–37.

case was admissible before the ICC because the DRC was deemed 'unwilling' to prosecute the accused under Article 17. According to the Trial Chamber's decision, an 'unwilling' State can be also a State

> which may not want to protect an individual, but, for a variety of reasons, may not wish to exercise its jurisdiction over him or her…[t]he Chamber considers that a State which chooses not to investigate or prosecute a person before its own courts, but has nevertheless every intention of seeing that justice is done, must be considered as lacking the will referred to in Article 17.[127]

This pro-cosmopolitan attitude of the ICC in the implementation of the 'same conduct' test might send the message to its States Parties that it interprets its mandate in a way that it is much more than a complementary international court. In the context of defining and making international terrorism an offence under the Rome Statute, a potential differentiation between the range or content of the offence as charged by a State against an individual accused and the ICC Prosecutor might equal to a sufficient ground on which a case can be made admissible before the ICC. While a textual approach of the complementarity regime seems to privilege State sovereignty[128] in that the jurisdiction of the ICC is only subsidiary and is exercised only when a State's unwillingness or inability becomes manifest, in practice it seems that the ICC has applied the 'same conduct' test in a self-serving way.[129] It remains to be seen whether this self-serving use of complementarity is explained by the urgency that the ICC might have felt in the early days of its establishment to pursue cases[130] and thus justify its existence or is meant to be its standard practice in the future. What remains true however, is that the more sovereignty-conscious States, which have already opposed to the idea of international terrorism's inclusion into the Rome Statute based on sovereignty-based concerns as was shown in Chap. 1, will have an additional reason to remain opposed, should this pro-cosmopolitan understanding of the complementarity regime predominates over the pro-sovereignty one.

So far, it has been shown that, while on paper the complementarity regime seems to be able to do justice to both State sovereignty concerns relating to their judicial primacy and to cosmopolitan purposes relating to the fight against impunity, in practice the ICC has departed—at least in part—from this vision of complementarity which regards States and international law as mutually constituted.[131] As such, it becomes obvious that the required balance between sovereignty and law is not only to be searched for in the definitions of international crimes but also in the

---

[127] ICC, *Prosecutor v Germain Katanga and Mathieu Ngudjolo Chui*, Reasons for the Oral Decision on the Motion Challenging the Admissibility of the Case, 16 June 2009, Case No. ICC-01/04-01/07, para 77.

[128] On how international institutions practically function in a privileging way towards State sovereignty see Kahn 2000, p. 10.

[129] Nouwen 2011, pp. 212–214.

[130] Schabas 2011, p. 156. However, he notes further that this over-intrusiveness was rather welcome by the DRC since prosecutions were targeted against enemies of the official government. In this respect see also Schabas 2010; Tiemessen 2014, p. 444.

[131] Mégret 2006, pp. 49–51.

modalities of their prosecution. Regardless of whether a criminal definition is construed in a way that rightly weighs the respect for State sovereignty and the need for justice, if the administration of this justice is imbalanced, then the overall effectiveness of an international crime definition will be undermined and ICC's credibility severely compromised.

In this respect and since this study focuses on the crime of aggression and international terrorism, the analysis of complementarity should be concluded with an examination of the challenges that the ICC will face when it confronts an aggression case. Since the ICC has not as yet acquired jurisdiction over aggression cases, an analysis of how the complementarity regime will work is only speculative; however, the conclusions drawn will shed some light on several sovereignty-pertaining issues that might be raised which can also be of relevance when and if terrorism finds its place among the international crimes with its own international definition. For this reason, the next section will attempt to give an insight on how the complementarity regime will work for cases of aggression and how the adjudication of aggression cases by an international court may implicate with issues of State sovereignty. This examination will bring us closer to understand why State sovereignty often functions as an obstacle to the further development of international criminal justice and how this obstacle can be overcome if sovereign interests are to be properly weighed against the purposes of international criminal justice.

2.4.3 The Applicability of the Complementarity Regime on Cases of Aggression

Before examining the development and finalisation of the definition of aggression for the purposes of the Rome Statute in Chaps. 3 and 4, it is worth making some remarks on how it raises, among other issues, some jurisdictional questions under the existing framework of the complementarity regime. Using Article 17 as a starting point for the following analysis, a case is inadmissible before the ICC when a State, *which has jurisdiction over it*, is investigating or prosecuting or has investigated or prosecuted the case concerned.[132] The question that arises from this provision is obviously which State has, or better *can* have jurisdiction over a case of aggression. Since a case of aggression will involve at least two States, one aggressor and one victim State, the bases of jurisdiction that can unequivocally be invoked are the territoriality and the nationality principles.[133] However, the provision does not make clear whether a third State, exercising universal jurisdiction,

[132] Rome Statute, above n. 3, Article 17.

[133] Rome Statute, above n. 3, Article 12(2): '[…] (a) The State on the territory of which the conduct in question occurred or, if the crime was committed on board a vessel or aircraft, the State of registration of that vessel or aircraft; (b) The State of which the person accused of the crime is a national.'

can prosecute a case of aggression if either the aggressor or the victim State, or both, are unwilling or unable to do so. Under the 'Princeton Principles on Universal Jurisdiction', a State can exercise universal jurisdiction over an individual for serious crimes under international law, such as, among others, crimes against peace,[134] the post-WWII equivalent for aggression. Some authors also argue that national courts of third States can try cases of aggression under the principle of universality.[135] Nevertheless, setting aside the precedents of the Nuremberg and Tokyo trials, the principle of universal jurisdiction has not been invoked since for the crime of aggression, showing that State practice in this respect casts doubts on the existence of universal jurisdiction for this crime. Besides, the 1996 Draft Code of Crimes against the Peace and Security of Mankind of the International Law Commission, in its Article 8 provides that jurisdiction on aggression can rest only with an international court or a State whose national is the alleged offender.[136] From this formulation, two conclusions can be drawn with respect to how the crime of aggression was viewed, at least before the establishment of the ICC: firstly, that aggression was different from the rest of the international crimes of the Draft Code, in that universal jurisdiction was not supported for it and secondly, that the only State that could exercise jurisdiction was the State of nationality of the accused, a view not shared by the Rome Statute and inconsistent with the regime of complementarity enshrined in it.[137] On the other hand, domestic prosecutions for the crime of aggression are nowhere to be exempted in the Kampala Resolution, and therefore the principle of the Rome Statute Preamble that it is the duty of national courts to try those responsible for the commission of international crimes applies also to the crime of aggression once the Kampala Resolution enters into force.[138] Moreover, the jurisprudence of the famous *Lotus* case,[139] where France questioned the jurisdiction of Turkey to prosecute a French sailor for criminal manslaughter when a French vessel ran into a Turkish one on the high seas, causing a number of deaths of Turkish citizens, advocates that the exercise of extraterritorial jurisdiction is valid and that it was on France to prove that Turkey's exercising jurisdiction violated a prohibitive rule of international law.[140] In light of this principle, it has been argued that the exercise of domestic universal jurisdiction is valid, unless the party questioning this jurisdiction can demonstrate that there is a generally accepted rule in international law which would prohibit the exercise of such jurisdiction.[141]

[134] Princeton Project on Universal Jurisdiction 2001, Principle 2(1).

[135] Dinstein 2005, p. 145; Brotóns 2005, p. 16 quoted in Wrange 2010, p. 600.

[136] International Law Commission 1996, Article 8: '…Jurisdiction over the crime set out in Article 16 shall rest with an international court. However, a State referred to in Article 16 is not precluded from trying its nationals for the crime set out in that article.'

[137] Clark 2011, p. 726.

[138] Scharf 2012, p. 364.

[139] PCIJ, *SS Lotus (France v Turkey)*, Judgment, 1927, PCIJ Series A No. 10.

[140] Ibid., para 46.

[141] Scharf 2012, p. 380.

Since, under the complementarity regime of the Rome Statute, cases of aggression will most probably be adjudicated by either the aggressor or the victim State (and only if they should fail, will the ICC step in) it remains to be seen to what extent the national courts of either the victim or the aggressor State are competent to adjudicate such cases. While the Special Working Group on the Crime of Aggression, during the negotiations held in Kampala for the incorporation of aggression in Article 5 of the Rome Statute, decided to treat aggression similarly to the other Article 5 crimes, it seems that there are distinguishing features that make aggression not well-suited for the complementarity regime.[142] Firstly, and generally speaking, there is the question of whether national judiciaries could function independently and impartially with respect to so politically-charged crimes such as aggression. Of course, this argument can be equally valid for the conduct of trials concerning the other core crimes under the ICC jurisdiction, which can also have political aspects. However, as was pointed out above, the crime of aggression would involve at minimum two States, whereas so far, the ICC practice has shown that the crimes that have been or are being prosecuted by the ICC, have been committed in the territory of one State. Without excluding a scenario where crimes against humanity or war crimes are committed in a context where more than one State is involved, the involvement of at least two States in a national trial concerning aggression will exacerbate the already disturbed relations of the States concerned with the risk of further aggravating an already intense situation. Corollary to this is also the high risk of having States conducting trials which lack independence and impartiality and have the intention to shield the accused from justice, in which case of course, the ICC can intervene and invoke the provisions of Article 17(2c) that the State appears 'unwilling' to try the accused due to such lack. At the same time, even in cases where the victim State and not the State of nationality of the accused is to conduct a highly politicised trial, it is possible that the national courts will appear 'all too willing' to prosecute, and thus, issues of fair trial and due process might be raised.[143] While due process considerations do not constitute *per se* a ground of admissibility, there might be instances where overzealous national authorities might indefinitely detain the accused for purposes different from conducting a trial (such as extracting information). The ICC's primary role is to function as an anti-impunity mechanism[144] and ensure that judicial proceedings take place, be it national or international. In this respect, it is likely that where judicial proceedings do not occur, a case might be deemed admissible before the ICC (given also the so far interventionist practice it has adopted regarding the conditions of admissibility), not due to the commission of human rights violations against the accused but due to the lack of intention of the national authorities to

[142] Trahan 2012, p. 587.

[143] For a discussion concerning over-zealous national prosecutions see Trahan 2012, pp. 594–601.

[144] Mégret and Samson 2013, p. 573.

conduct a trial.[145] As such, it is highly likely that States which have been directly involved in an aggression case would be deemed by the ICC as either unwilling or unable to genuinely carry out the investigation or prosecution, resulting in the subsequent ICC's intervention.

Secondly, the attribution of individual liability for the crime of aggression goes beyond the individual himself and implicates directly the State on behalf of which he acted.[146] There is a direct implication of a State's action with the commission of the individual crime of aggression, which is absent from the other Article 5 crimes. This implication is also reflected into the definition for aggression as formulated in the Kampala negotiations, where the act of aggression, committed by a State, forms an express element of the offence.[147] Thus, a national judiciary that will sit in judgment for a case concerning the crime of aggression will have to assess the legality of another State's decision to use force,[148] a competence which is primarily reserved to the Security Council under its Chapter VII powers.[149]

With these implications in mind, it is still questionable whether national courts can be seen as appropriate fora to conduct aggression trials.[150] But even if the jurisdiction-related considerations are set aside, there is still a number of theoretical and procedural issues that have to be addressed when a State acquires jurisdiction over a case of aggression. Firstly, it comes as a logical conclusion that, if a case of aggression falls under a State's jurisdiction, then the jurisdictional filters that are in place for the ICC to exercise the same jurisdiction, will not be in place for the national court, unless specifically provided by the domestic legislation.[151] In other words, when a case of aggression is referred to the ICC by a State or in case of a *proprio motu* initiation of proceedings, the Prosecutor shall seek the Security Council's determination of the existence of an act of aggression or, in the absence of it, he or she shall turn to the Pre-trial Division.[152] These mechanisms will be absent if a national court adjudicates over a case of aggression, meaning that the concerned State will have to make a determination on the existence of an act of

[145] Ibid., p. 586. About Rome Statute's safeguards concerning due process protection see Fry 2012.

[146] Morris 2001, pp. 14–15.

[147] Resolution RC/Res. 6, Annex I, Amendments to the Rome Statute of the International Criminal Court on the Crime of Aggression, 11 June 2010 (Kampala Resolution) Article 8*bis*: 'For the purpose of this Statute, "crime of aggression" means the planning, preparation, initiation or execution, by a person in a position effectively to exercise control over or to direct the political or military action of a State, of an act of aggression which, by its character, gravity and scale, constitutes a manifest violation of the Charter of the United Nations.'

[148] Van Schaack 2012, p. 149.

[149] UN Charter, above n. 1, Article 39: 'The Security Council shall determine the existence of any threat to the peace, breach of the peace, or act of aggression…'.

[150] Among the authors that are sceptical about the application of the complementarity regime to cases of aggression are: Trahan 2012; Wrange 2010; Van Schaack 2012.

[151] Van Schaack 2012, p. 151.

[152] Kampala Resolution, above n. 147, Article 15*bis* (6) and (8).

aggression allegedly committed by itself or another State, something that is contrary to Article 39 of the UN Charter, which confers this power primarily to the Security Council, and also contrary to the principle of the sovereign equality of States.

Apart from these issues that will probably arise when aggression cases are to be adjudicated nationally, there are also some sovereignty-related questions that may come into play in the adjudication of both aggression and terrorism cases. In the first place, the issue of immunities, which will most certainly arise in cases of aggression since the crime of aggression is established as a 'leadership crime', might also arise in cases of terrorist crimes which involve a State's high political or military officials. The framework provided by the Rome Statute does not recognise immunity statuses[153]; however, this renunciation of immunities will likely not be applied before national jurisdictions.[154] Domestic immunities are often in place in a State Party's national legislation and protect its officials from being tried before their own courts. Amending immunity-related domestic legislation to accommodate the ICC's requirements for national prosecutions pursuant to the complementarity principle or for surrender to the ICC might be seen as an infringement into a State's sovereignty.[155] But even if States Parties amend their relevant domestic legislation to allow the surrender or national prosecution of their own nationals, the situation is different with respect to requests for surrender of non-nationals. In this latter case, the ICC will have to decide whether States Parties, in agreeing to limit immunity before the ICC (Article 27), are deemed to have done so with respect to one another or that States Parties cannot arrest or surrender officials of another State Party, without a waiver of their immunity, according to Article 98(1).[156]

Another challenge that is to be faced when States adjudicate on cases of aggression and even more so on cases of international terrorism, is the fragmentation and differentiation of their domestic penal codes in the very definition of the crimes. The ICC, as with the rest of the crimes under its jurisdiction, applies a uniform legal framework for all the States Parties, which contain thoroughly negotiated elements; in contrast, a State which is going to incorporate or has already incorporated domestic provisions related to aggression, might pick and choose among the definitional elements of the crime, something that will give way to incoherence in the applicability of the legal framework for international crimes as

---

[153] Rome Statute, above n. 3, Article 27.

[154] Wrange 2010, p. 594; Mégret 2011, p. 383 where he argues that immunity laws might be a legitimate reason for non-prosecution on a horizontal plane and between States but not before an independent international institution. See also Rome Statute, above n. 3, Article 98(1) where it states that without a waiver of immunity by the State whose national is being accused, the Court cannot proceed with a request for surrender or assistance.

[155] Broomhall 2003, p. 140. France and Germany have dealt with this issue by making amendments which either allow the surrender to the ICC but not the domestic prosecution of a person entitled to immunities (France) or allow both the surrender and prosecution after authorisation of the parliament (Germany).

[156] Ibid., pp. 141–45.

accepted by the Assembly of States Parties (ASP).[157] As it was already shown by the 'same conduct' test that the ICC applied in *Lubanga* and considered in *Katanga*, it is highly likely that differentiation between the range of offences (and possibly their definitions) against an accused that are brought before national courts and before the ICC, will favour heavily the ICC's intervention. Besides, the incorporation of domestic provisions related to aggression is somewhat discouraged by the Understandings regarding the amendments to the Rome Statute of the International Criminal Court on the crime of aggression.[158] Understanding 5 provides that the Kampala Resolution does not create any right or obligation for States to exercise jurisdiction over an act of aggression committed by another State, implying (i) that the incorporation of related legislation should not be seen as mandatory and probably is not even seen as desirable by the negotiators[159] and (ii) that the reference 'by another State' means that the exercise of jurisdiction by a State whose nationals are being accused was considered as less problematic.[160] This Understanding was adopted due to US concerns that States Parties to the Rome Statute will finally incorporate a definition of aggression into their domestic laws ('particularly one we believe is flawed')[161] expanding principles of jurisdiction and resulting in officials' being prosecuted for aggression in foreign courts. The US opposition against such a development is based on the view that international customary law does not recognise an existing right for States to exercise universal jurisdiction over aggression.[162] As a result, the effect of Understanding 5 will be to discourage,[163] but not to preclude States from harmonising their national criminal laws with the Kampala provisions. However, it has been argued that this Understanding could at least ensure that States Parties could not invoke the Kampala Resolution to support the exercise of jurisdiction over the crime of aggression committed by non-nationals.[164] With respect to terrorism, the problem of differentiation of national legislations is even more acute; the divergence of views regarding core elements of the definition of international terrorism are such[165] that they have not allowed so far the formulation of a universally accepted definition and, as was also mentioned in Chap. 1, the sovereignty-related

[157] As emphasised by Van Schaack, a national definition for aggression might for example reject the 'leadership requirement' of the crime or the threshold of 'manifest violation' or even permit the prosecution of 'attempted aggression', issues that have been decided upon after careful and rigorous negotiations by the ASP. Van Schaack 2012, p. 152.

[158] Kampala Resolution, above n. 147, Annex III 'Understandings regarding the amendments to the Rome Statute of the International Criminal Court on the crime of aggression'.

[159] Van Schaack 2012, p. 155.

[160] Ibid., p. 160.

[161] Koh 2010.

[162] Scharf 2012, p. 365.

[163] Kress and von Holtzendorff 2010, p. 1216.

[164] Van Schaack 2012, p. 161.

[165] A thorough examination of the major points of contention on the core elements of an international definition for terrorism will follow in Chaps. 5 and 6.

implications of agreeing on an international definition of terrorism have heavily obstructed its inclusion into the ICC.

All in all, it seems that the complementarity model prescribed for the rest of the international crimes under the ICC's jurisdiction is not appropriate for cases of aggression and might not be for cases of international terrorism as well. The very thin practice of States exercising universal jurisdiction on cases of aggression, the high risk of politicisation of national courts that will adjudicate over such cases and the absence of jurisdictional filters that are in place for the ICC but not for national courts make it clear that complementarity might not be applied in the same way to aggression as it is with the other Article 5 crimes. Finally, the controversial nature of aggression as an international crime touches upon challenges which may also come into play should terrorism become an international crime (under the jurisdiction of the ICC or any other international tribunal), such as the immunity statuses of high-ranking officials and the risk of fragmentation of the definition of the crime in domestic penal codes. All these challenges, however, reveal a common denominator which will inevitably determine the effectiveness of international crimes definitions to contribute to the fight against impunity: State sovereignty. The crucial question to be asked is what place and content State sovereignty should hold in the modern international criminal justice system in order to comply with the current exigencies of international law.

2.5 Conclusion

This chapter has demonstrated how the concept of State sovereignty in light of the State-centric and the cosmopolitan theories has been influencing international law in general and international criminal law in particular, as embodied in the Rome Statute of the ICC. State sovereignty considerations are reflected into the function of the ICC and specifically into its provisions regarding the complementarity regime under which it operates. The establishment of the complementary role of the ICC is the means through which the Rome Statute attempts to strike the balance between the respect for State sovereignty on the one hand and the promotion of cosmopolitan purposes, in the form of international criminal justice, on the other. To this end, the chapter has analysed the details of this complementary function, and specifically how a State's failure to harmonise its national law definitions of crimes with the Rome Statute ones can be understood as State inability to genuinely carry out proceedings, how complementarity has worked in practice as to whether the application of the 'same conduct' test means that States Parties are compelled to follow the ICC's definitions (or the ICC prosecutorial agenda) in order not to be characterised as unable and how the adjudication of aggression and perhaps, terrorism cases raise jurisdictional issues that other Article 5 crimes do not. It was shown that to date, the ICC has to some extent failed to implement complementarity as it was envisioned by the drafters of the Rome Statute, by overstretching its jurisdictional mandate to the maximum allowed for the purpose of declaring cases admissible even in circumstances not clearly envisioned by the Rome Statute.

The last part of this chapter analysed the reasons why the crime of aggression should not be treated in the same way under the complementarity regime of the Rome Statute as the rest of the Article 5 crimes. The implications on State sovereignty in cases of aggression render States a less appropriate forum for the prosecution of this crime by national courts whereas an international forum appears more suitable for this purpose. The strong political dimension of the crime of aggression was what had hampered its definition and criminalisation for so long, leaving room for States to prioritise their national interests over the need to push forward the development of international law to this direction. Therefore, the next chapter will attempt to show in a historical perspective the dynamics that shaped the concept of aggression and finally led to its definition and criminalisation under the Rome Statute. The analysis of these dynamics will contribute in our comprehension of the role that State sovereignty considerations and cosmopolitan ideals have played in this process, underlying the position they hold in the formation of international criminal law as it stands today.

References

Archibugi D (1995) Immanuel Kant, Cosmopolitan Law and Peace. EJIL 1(4): 429–456

Benzing M (2003) The Complementarity Regime and the International Criminal Court: International Criminal Justice between State Sovereignty and the Fight Against Impunity. Max Planck Yrbk UN L 7: 591–632

Broomhall B (2003) International Justice and the International Criminal Court: Between Sovereignty and the Rule of Law. Oxford University Press, Oxford

Brotóns AR (2005) Aggression, Crime of Aggression, Crime without Punishment. Working Paper No 10 (Fundación para las Relaciones Internacionales y el Diálogo Exterior (FRIDE): 1–17. http://fride.org/download/WP10_CrimeCastig_ENG_jun05.pdf. Accessed 3 February 2017

Brown GW (2005) State Sovereignty, Federation and Kantian Cosmopolitanism. Eur J Int Relat 11 (4): 495–522

Brus M (2002) Bridging the Gap between State Sovereignty and International Governance: The Authority of Law. In: Kreijen G (ed) State, Sovereignty and International Governance. Oxford University Press, Oxford, pp 3–24

Cabrera L (2011) Cosmopolitanism. In: Chatterjee DK (ed) Encyclopedia of Global Justice. Springer Science and Business Media B V, Dordrecht, p 209

Cassese A (1998) On the Current Trends towards Criminal Prosecution and Punishment of Breaches of International Humanitarian Law. EJIL 9:2–17

Cassese A (2005) International Law, 2nd edn. Oxford University Press, Oxford

Cheah P (2006) Cosmopolitanism. Theory, Culture & Society 23: 486–496

Clark R (2011) Complementarity and the Crime of Aggression. In: Stahn C, El Zeidy M (eds) The International Criminal Court and Complementarity: From Theory to Practice, vol 1, Cambridge University Press, Cambridge, pp 721–744

Declaration of Colombia upon ratification of the Rome Statute (1998). www.icrc.org/ihl/NORM/909EEAAE157FBD43412566E100542BDE?OpenDocument. Accessed 2 February 2017

Dinstein Y (2005) War, Aggression and Self-Defence, 4th edn. Cambridge University Press, Cambridge

Doherty KL, McCormack TLH (1999) "Complementarity" as a Catalyst for Comprehensive Domestic Penal Legislation. U C Davis J Int'l L & Pol'y 5: 147–180
Feldman N (2007) Cosmopolitan Law? Yale L J 116: 1022–1070
Finch JD (1979) Introduction to Legal Theory, Sweet & Maxwell, London
Fouladvand S (2012) Complementarity and Cultural Sensitivity: Decision-Making by the ICC Prosecutor in relation to the Situations in the Darfur region of the Sudan and the Democratic Republic of the Congo (DRC). DPhil thesis, University of Sussex, 30. http://sro.sussex.ac.uk/38540/. Accessed 1 February 2017
Fry E (2012) Between Show Trials and Sham Prosecutions: The Rome Statute's Potential Effect on Domestic Due Process Protections. Crim L F 23: 35–62
Goodrich LM and ors (1969) Charter of the United Nations; commentary and documents, 3rd edn. Columbia University Press, New York
Gregor MJ (1996) Kant: The Metaphysics of Morals. Cambridge University Press, Cambridge
Gurulé J (2001–2002) United States Opposition to the 1998 Rome Statute Establishing an International Criminal Court: Is the Court's Jurisdiction Truly Complementary to National Jurisdictions? 35 Cornell Int'l L J 35: 1–45
Henley K (2011) Sovereignty. In: Chatterjee DK (ed) Encyclopedia of Global Justice. Springer Science and Business Media B V, Dordrecht, pp 1025–1027
Hirondelle News Agency (2008) Swiss prepares bill to harmonise laws with ICC. www.hirondellenews.com/fr/icc/320-collaboration-with-states/21877-en-en-090508-swissicc-swiss-prepares-bill-to-harmonise-laws-with-icc1092810928. Accessed 2 February 2017
ICC, Situations under investigation. www.icc-cpi.int/en_menus/icc/situations%20and%20cases/Pages/situations%20and%20cases.aspx. Accessed 1 February 2017
International Law Commission (1996) Draft Code of Crimes against the Peace and Security of Mankind. UN Doc. A/CN4/L532
International Tribunal for the Former Yugoslavia (1999) Report of the International Tribunal for the Prosecution of Persons Responsible for Serious Violations of International Humanitarian Law Committed in the Territory of the Former Yugoslavia since 1991, UN Doc. A/54/187
Jennings R (2002) Sovereignty and International Law. In: Kreijen G (ed) State, Sovereignty and International Governance. Oxford University Press, Oxford, pp 27–44
Jurdi NN (2011) The International Criminal Court and National Courts: A Contentious Relationship. Routledge, London
Kahn P (2000) Speaking Law to Power: Popular Sovereignty, Human Rights, and the New International Order. Chi J Int'l L 1: 1–18
Kant I (1793) On the Common Saying: This May be True in Theory, but it does not Apply in Practice. In: Reiss HS (ed) (1970) Kant's Political Writings. Cambridge University Press, Cambridge, pp 61–92
Kelsen H (1950) The Law of the United Nations: A Critical Analysis of its Fundamental Problem. The Lawbook Exchange Ltd, New Jersey
Kelsen H (1959–1960) Sovereignty and International Law. The Georgetown L J 48(4):627–640
Kleffner J (2003) The Impact of Complementarity on National Implementation of Substantive Criminal Law. JICJ 1: 86–113
Koh HH, Legal Adviser, US Department of State (2010) Statement at the Review Conference of the International Criminal Court. www.state.gov/s/l/releases/remarks/142665.htm. Accessed 9 August 2015
Koller D (2008) The Faith of the International Criminal Lawyer. 40 NYU Journal of International Law and Politics 40: 1019–1069
Kress C, von Holtzendorff L (2010) The Kampala Compromise on the Crime of Aggression. JICJ 8: 1179–1217
McAuliffe P (2013) Transitional Justice and Rule of Law Reconstruction. Routledge, London
McAuliffe P (2014) From Watchdog to Workhorse: Explaining the Emergence of the ICC's Burden-Sharing Policy as an Example of Creeping Cosmopolitanism. Chinese JIL 13: 259–296
Mégret F (2001) Epilogue to an Endless Debate: The International Criminal Court's Third Party Jurisdiction and the Looming Revolution of International Law. EJIL 12 (2): 247–268

Mégret F (2006) Why Would States Want to Join the ICC? A Theoretical Exploration Based on the Legal Nature of Complementarity. In: Kleffner J, Kor G (eds) Complementary Views on Complementarity. TMC Asser Press, The Hague, pp 1–51
Mégret F (2011) Too much of a good thing? Implementation and the uses of complementarity. In: Stahn C, El Zeidy M (eds) The International Criminal Court and Complementarity: From Theory to Practice, vol 1. Cambridge University Press, Cambridge, pp 361–390
Mégret F, Samson MG (2013) Holding the Line on Complementarity in Libya: The Case for Tolerating Flawed Domestic Trials. JICJ 11: 571–589
Morris M (2001) High Crimes and Misconceptions: The ICC and Non-Party States. Law & Contemp Probs 64(1): 13–66
Nagan WP, Hammer C (2004) The Changing Character of Sovereignty in International Law and International Relations. Colum JIL 43: 141–187
Newton MA (2011) The quest of constructive complementarity. In: Stahn C, El Zeidy M (eds) The International Criminal Court and Complementarity: From Theory to Practice, vol 1. Cambridge University Press, Cambridge, pp 304–340
Nouwen S (2011) Fine-tuning Complementarity. In: Brown BS (ed) Research Handbook of International Criminal Law. Edward Elgar, Cheltenham, pp 206–231
Pavković A, Radan P (2003) In Pursuit of Sovereignty and Self-Determination: Peoples, States and Secession in the International Order. Macquarie LJ 3: 1–12
Philippe X (2006) The principles of universal jurisdiction and complementarity: how do the two principles intermesh? Int'l Rev Red Cross 88 (862): 375–398
Pogge T (1992) Cosmopolitanism and Sovereignty. Ethics 103: 48–75
Princeton Project on Universal Jurisdiction (2001) The Princeton Principles on Universal Jurisdiction.
Reiss HS (ed) (1970) Kant: Political Writings. Cambridge University Press, Cambridge
Report of the International Federation for Human Rights (2006) International Criminal Court, Implementation of the Rome Statute in Cambodian Law. No 443/2
Robinson D (2010) The Mysterious Mysteriousness of Complementarity. Crim L F 21(1): 67–102
Sarooshi D (2005) International Organisation and their exercise of Sovereign Powers. Oxford University Press, Oxford
Schabas W (2008) "Complementarity in Practice": Some Uncomplimentary Thoughts. Crim L F 19(1): 5–33
Schabas W (2008) Prosecutorial Discretion v. Judicial Activism at the International Criminal Court. JICJ 6: 731–761
Schabas W (2011) The Rise and Fall of Complementarity. In: Stahn C, El Zeidy M (eds) The International Criminal Court and Complementarity: From Theory to Practice, vol 1. Cambridge University Press, Cambridge, pp 150–164
Schabas W (2012) The International Criminal Court: Struggling to Find its Way. In: Cassese A (ed) Realizing Utopia: The Future of International Law. Oxford University Press, Oxford, pp 250–260
Scharf M (2012) Universal Jurisdiction and the Crime of Aggression. Harv Int'l L J 53(2): 357–389
Teson FR (1992) The Kantian Theory of International Law. Colum L Rev 92: 53–102
Tiemessen A (2014) The International Criminal Court and the Politics of Prosecution. The International Journal of Human Rights 18(4–5): 444–461
Trahan J (2012) Is Complementarity the right approach for the International Criminal Court's Crime of Aggression? 45 Cornell Int'l L J 45: 569–601
UNGA (1998) Diplomatic Conference of Plenipotentiaries on the Establishment of an International Criminal Court. UN Doc. A/CONF 183/13
UNSC (1994) Statute of the International Criminal Tribunal for Rwanda. UN Doc. S/RES/955
van Schaack B (2012) Par in parem imperium non habet, Complementarity and the Crime of Aggression. JICJ 10: 133–164
Wacks R (2005) Understanding Jurisprudence: An Introduction to Legal Theory. Oxford University Press, Oxford

Wrange P (2010) The Crime of Aggression and Complementarity. In: Bellelli R (ed) International Criminal Justice: Law and Practice from the Rome Statute to Its Review. Ashgate, Farnham, pp 591–607

Zolo D (1998) Hans Kelsen: International Peace through International Law. 9 EJIL 9: 306–324

Zolo D (1999) A Cosmopolitan Philosophy of International Law? A Realist Approach. Ratio Juris 12(4): 429–444

Chapter 3
The Paradigm of Aggression: State-Centric and Cosmopolitan Approaches in the Effort to Outlaw and Criminalise Aggression

Abstract The theories of State sovereignty and cosmopolitanism have played their own, distinctive part in the formation of the Rome Statute regime and especially in the establishment of the complementary role of the ICC in the adjudication of international crimes. It has been demonstrated that the discrepancy between how complementarity should work according to the provisions of the Rome Statute and how it has worked so far in practice has resulted in sovereignty-related implications for the States Parties. As the role of State sovereignty in the development of international criminal law has now been established, this chapter will focus on the concept of aggression itself, using it as a paradigm of how the same theories of State sovereignty and cosmopolitanism have influenced its development. The 'State sovereignty versus cosmopolitanism' debate has been relevant throughout the history of outlawing, criminalising and defining aggression, from the League of Nations period until its inclusion in the Rome Statute and the formulation of the definition of the crime of aggression in the Review Conference held in Kampala in 2010. The driving forces that shaped this development are manifest in the outcome reached in the Kampala Resolution and what can be learnt from this outcome concerning whether and how State sovereignty concerns and cosmopolitan ideals can be properly balanced is what will be discussed in the next chapter.

Keywords League of Nations · Aggression · Nuremberg Charter · Tokyo Charter · Crimes Against Peace · Act of Aggression · UNGA Resolution 3314

Contents

S. Margariti, *Defining International Terrorism*, International Criminal Justice Series 15, DOI 10.1007/978-94-6265-204-0_3

3.1 Introduction

This chapter is separated into three sections. The first section examines the Covenant of the League of Nations (1919)[1] and the collective security system it established, which, despite its cosmopolitan intentions, failed to achieve its primary goal of world peace due to the emphasis given on sovereign interests. The second section moves on to the Nuremberg and Tokyo Trials and the provisions of the Nuremberg and Tokyo Charters that first introduced 'crimes against peace'.[2] This first legal and judicial precedent of holding individuals accountable for waging aggressive war will be analysed as the first cosmopolitan effort,[3] although not without criticism, made to criminalise and define aggression (as a 'crime against peace'). Subsequently, the third section passes to the UN era and examines the State-centric character of the UN Charter[4] provisions related to the prohibition on the use of force and especially the role attributed to the Security Council. In particular, the discussion will focus on Article 39 and the powers of the Security Council in deciding upon international peace and security matters as well as the

[1] Covenant of the League of Nations, opened for signature 28 April 1919, [1919] UKTS 4 (entered into force 10 January 1920) (Covenant of the League of Nations).

[2] Charter of the International Military Tribunal, opened for signature and entered into force 8 August 1945, 82 UNTS 279 (Nuremberg Charter) and Charter of the International Military Tribunal for the Far East, opened for signature and entered into force 19 January 1946, (Tokyo Charter) Article 6a: 'Crimes against peace: namely, planning, preparation, initiation or waging of a war of aggression, or a war in violation of international treaties, agreements or assurances, or participation in a common plan or conspiracy for the accomplishment of any of the foregoing'. The provision reads almost the same in Article 5a of the Tokyo Charter except for two changes: '… waging of a declared or undeclared war of aggression…' and '…or a war in violation of international law, treaties, agreements…'.

[3] The first step to this direction was taken with Articles 225 and 227 of the Treaty of Versailles, which arraigned Kaiser Wilhelm II for committing 'a supreme offence against the international morality and the sanctity of treaties'. Though the Kaiser was never brought before a court to account for this international offence, this provision is the first official recognition that individuals (and not 'abstract entities' as Chief Justice Stone will say several years later) can be responsible for the commission of international crimes, and especially the initiation of an unlawful war. See Treaty of Peace Between the Allied and Associated Powers and Germany (Treaty of Versailles) opened for signature 28 June 1919, 225 CTS 188, (entered into force 10 January 1920).

[4] Charter of the United Nations, opened for signature 26 June 1945, 1 UNTS XVI (entered into force 24 October 1945) (UN Charter).

definition of aggression as provided in the UNGA Resolution 3314[5] and its limited legal value and effect on the Security Council's discretionary powers.

All of these instances in international legal history make manifest that, in the effort to make war unlawful as a means for settling inter-State disputes, to criminalise 'crimes against peace', to unequivocally prohibit the threat or use of force and to finally formulate a definition for aggression, both State sovereignty interests and cosmopolitan aspirations had to be taken into account in order to reach an outcome that would sufficiently respond to the need of developing international law in this direction. In this respect, the aim of this chapter is to show in a historical perspective how the community of States treated the balancing of these two potentially antithetical considerations—the protection of State interests and the promotion of cosmopolitan ideas—in the effort to fight and/or define aggression. This analysis will ultimately bring us closer to the main subject of this book, which is to argue that the achievement of due balance between State sovereignty concerns and cosmopolitan ideals reflected in definitions of international crimes, eventually enhances their effectiveness and contributes to the success of international prosecutions for their commission. It is the author's view that it is exactly this due balance that constitutes the key for the successful criminalisation and prosecution of international terrorism, a subject that will be analysed in detail in Chaps. 5 and 6.

3.2 The Covenant of the League of Nations: A Cosmopolitan Idea with a State-Centric Application

After World War I, the need for a new global collective security system became apparent, a system which would give priority to universal moral values relating to peace rather than the traditional ideas of the system of balance of powers.[6] A proposal made to US President Woodrow Wilson by Colonel House in 1914 concerning an agreement between the US and the States of South America for mutual guarantees of political independence and territorial integrity, inspired President Wilson to extrapolate this cosmopolitan model to Europe and the rest of the world.[7] Article 10 of the Covenant of the League of Nations reflected this core value of the new collective security system, stating that

> [t]he Members of the League undertake to respect and preserve as against external aggression the territorial integrity and existing political independence of all Members of the League. In case of any such aggression or in case of any threat or danger of such aggression the Council shall advise upon the means by which this obligation shall be fulfilled.[8]

[5] UNGA 1974.

[6] Wilson 2009, p. 19.

[7] Seymour 1926, p. 216.

[8] Covenant of the League of Nations, above n. 1, Article 10.

It has been argued that the Article expressed only a moral and not a legal obligation for the Member States of the League to consider aggression unlawful,[9] however this was the first time that this general principle was unequivocally stated. The term aggression was used as such, but it seemed that there was no intention on the part of the drafters to include a definition, as it was thought that the emphasis put on the moral value of peace by the Member States would be enough for them to recognise aggression in practice.[10]

However, during the negotiations of the drafting of the Covenant, the great powers were mostly wary of the extent of the obligations assumed towards the smaller States under Article 10 and the restraints posed on the more powerful.[11] Britain was reluctant to assume positive obligations to protect the smaller States in light of Article 10, whereas France was looking to extend these obligations to any type of aggression, not only that related to political independence and territorial integrity.[12] On the American side, the US Senate was more concerned with the power of the League to interfere with US actions,[13] which was ultimately what prevented the US from becoming a member of the League.[14]

As a compromise to reconcile the opposing views of the major powers, the US added the second part of Article 10 which conferred the power to the Executive Council of the League to actually decide how these obligations would be fulfilled. The political compromise of the Article, namely the assumption of only negative obligations by the Members on the one hand, and the power of the Council to give advice upon the means used for the fulfilment of these obligations on the other, is indicative of the then major powers' willingness to take cosmopolitan steps for the prevention of war but in a rather modest way. Firstly, the Covenant did not specify whether the Members of the League were obliged to follow the Council's advice or whether they were free to ignore it (in which case Article 10 was practically worthless).[15] Secondly, the formulation of the Article suggested that the political and territorial *status quo* of the Members of the League was 'just and expedient'[16] since the Members had the obligation not only to respect but also 'to preserve' from aggression 'the territorial integrity and existing political independence of all Members of the League'.[17] Under this interpretation, it could be possible that the

---

[9] Brownlie 1981, p. 63.

[10] Wilson 2009, p. 22.

[11] Ibid., p. 26.

[12] Ibid., p. 23.

[13] Ibid., pp. 23–25.

[14] Ibid., p. 26.

[15] Ibid., p. 33. This criticism was formulated by Canada in an attempt to propose amendments for Article 10.

[16] Ibid.

[17] Ibid. It is also suggested that the fact that Germany was 'humiliated' after the end of World War I by the Treaty of Versailles, which, among other things, deprived Germany of any territorial annexations or colonies, contributed to her initiating 'aggressive warfare' against the Allies of

obligation 'to preserve' would lead States to war in an effort to fulfil this guarantee enshrined in Article 10.[18]

Nonetheless, subsequent articles of the Covenant did not refer to 'aggression' but to 'war', 'threat to war' (Article 11)[19] and 'act of war' (Article 16).[20] This discrepancy in terminology should not be seen as signifying that the context of 'aggression' and that of 'war' were different at the time. Although war could be normally defined as an official state of armed conflict, aggression was nowhere defined in the Covenant, and the use of the term was only limited to Article 10, the cornerstone of the new security system. The flexibility of the term was seen as desirable at the time of drafting,[21] in that it did not *a priori* restrict the types of acts that could constitute aggression or war. However, in practice, there were instances where this lack of definition led States to avoid obligations assumed under the Covenant, by denying the existence of a war-like situation in their territories,[22] thus obstructing the interference of the League in situations where it would have been totally justified.

Be that as it may, if read in conjunction with Articles 12, 13 and 15,[23] Article 10 attributed to aggression a dimension that it did not have until that time. These Articles obliged the Members of the League to submit any 'dispute likely to lead to a rupture' to arbitration or judicial settlement.[24] Thus, they provided a general basis by which to define the aggressor State, namely by the extent to which it complies with its obligations to use mechanisms of pacific dispute settlement as provided by

(Footnote 17 continued)
World War I (Winks 2003, p. 209). Article 10 of the Covenant actually 'freezes' the territorial status quo as was formed by the Treaty.

[18] Brownlie 1981, p. 62.

[19] Covenant of the League of Nations, above n. 1, Article 11(1): 'Any war or threat of war, whether immediately affecting any of the Members of the League or not, is hereby declared a matter of concern to the whole League…'.

[20] Ibid., Article 16: 'Should any Member of the League resort to war in disregard of its covenants under Articles 12, 13 or 15, it shall ipso facto be deemed to have committed an act of war against all other Members of the League…'.

[21] Brownlie 1981, p. 55.

[22] During the conflict between China and Japan from 1937 to 1941, all the involved States refused to recognise that there was a war going on in the area. See Ibid., p. 60.

[23] Covenant of the League of Nations, above n. 1, Article 12: 'The Members of the League agree that, if there should arise between them any dispute likely to lead to a rupture they will submit the matter either to arbitration or judicial settlement or to enquiry by the Council…'; Article 13: 'The Members of the League agree that whenever any dispute shall arise between them… they will submit the whole subject-matter to arbitration or judicial settlement.'; Article 15: 'If there should arise between Members of the League any dispute likely to lead to a rupture, which is not submitted to arbitration or judicial settlement in accordance with Article 13, the Members of the League agree that they will submit the matter to the Council….'.

[24] In particular, Article 12 provides for an obligation not to resort to war 'until three months after the award by the arbitrators or the judicial decision, or the report by the Council…'.

the Covenant.[25] Obliging States to use pacific means of dispute settlement indicates a hesitant but important step towards a cosmopolitan perspective of combatting aggression in light of the conservative collective security system as established by the League of Nations.

In practical terms, Article 10 was successfully invoked in few cases. While it was successfully invoked in the Greco-Bulgarian dispute (1925) and in the dispute of Ethiopia against Britain and Italy (1926), it did not find successful application in the case of Manchuria (1931–33) and the second Ethiopian dispute against Italy (1935–36).[26] It was not invoked at all in the case of Poland against Lithuania (1919–1920), Turkey against Armenia (1920), France against Germany (1923–25), Soviet Union against Finland (1939) and in the case of Germany's rearmament (1935).[27] In the case of the dispute between Ethiopia against Britain and Italy, the concept of aggression was interpreted widely to include economic aggression as well.[28] However, in the majority of cases where Article 10 could have been invoked, the political dynamics of the period did not allow any further involvement of the League security system, leading unavoidably to a further disturbance of world peace. Indicative of this state of affairs was the refusal of some small States, neighbouring Germany, to invoke Article 16 of the Covenant against Germany, after its invasion in Czechoslovakia in 1938, for fear of being exposed to German animosity themselves.[29]

Overall, the contribution of the Covenant, despite the lack of its practical value, consists of the direct recognition that aggression was now a matter of international concern.[30] However, the efforts to submit States to an international institution with cosmopolitan goals related to world peace did not compensate for the States' willingness to continue defending their sovereign interests at all costs. The League system failed, not the least due to the political climate of the period but also due to the overreliance on the individual members' appreciation of whether and to what extent they should fulfil their Covenant obligations.[31] In the subsequent years, the prohibition of the use of force would reappear in several international legal documents[32] reflecting on the one hand, the need to create firmer foundations than those

[25] Brownlie 1981, p. 57.

[26] Wilson 2009, pp. 37–42.

[27] Ibid.

[28] In the dispute between Ethiopia against Britain and Italy, aggression was conceived in political and economic terms rather than military, since the League found that the financial agreement that was concluded in 1926 between the three States constituted an indirect threat to Ethiopia's territorial integrity. See Wilson 2009, p. 38.

[29] Brownlie 1981, p. 59.

[30] Covenant of the League of Nations, above n. 1, Article 11(1).

[31] Brownlie 1981, p. 60.

[32] Draft Treaty of Mutual Assistance 1924, World Peace Foundation Pamphlet Series 480; League of Nations Protocol for the Pacific Settlement of International Disputes, opened for signature 2 October 1924 (Geneva Protocol); Treaty between the United States and other Powers providing for the renunciation of war as an instrument of national policy, opened for signature 27 August 1928, 94 LNTS 57 (entered into force 24 July 1929) (Kellogg-Briand Pact). The first two

created by the Covenant and on the other, the fear that a possibility of a second large-scale war was imminent. The League security system failed to take into account the cosmopolitan aspirations enshrined in the Covenant and the sovereign interests of its great powers in a balanced way, and thus left the door open for further efforts towards this end.

3.3 A Cosmopolitan Approach: 'Crimes Against Peace' Under the Nuremberg and Tokyo Charters

Cosmopolitan aspirations shaped dynamically the development of international law after the end of World War II (WWII), with the establishment of the International Military Tribunals of Nuremberg and Tokyo (IMTs). The IMTs, established to try individuals for the commission of crimes against peace, war crimes and crimes against humanity, put the foundations for the establishment of the ICC and the further development of international criminal law.[33] As the first legal and judicial precedents of holding individuals accountable for international crimes,[34] it is fair to characterise the Nuremberg and Tokyo trials as the genesis of international criminal law and 'crimes against peace' the predecessor of the newly-born crime of aggression.[35]

The significance of the Nuremberg legacy with respect to the concept of aggression is twofold. Firstly, and for the first time, international tribunals implemented the concept of individual criminal liability for 'crimes against peace'. Secondly, 'crimes against peace' were actually defined. Therefore, it is necessary to examine which factors facilitated the transition from the mere renunciation of war as a means of national policy, a principle enshrined in Article 1 of the Kellogg-Briand Pact,[36] which came into force during the inter-war years, to the establishment of individual criminal liability for, among other crimes, the waging of such a war.

In 1943, when the Allies first launched the United Nations War Crimes Commission, their intention was to prosecute the German leaders only for the

(Footnote 32 continued)

instruments used the term aggression as such but without ever coming into force, whereas the Kellogg Briand Pact has survived until today.

[33] Rome Statute of the International Criminal Court, opened for signature 17 July 1998, 2187 UNTS 90 (entered into force 1 July 2002) UN Doc. A/CONF.183/9 (Rome Statute).

[34] Admittedly, the trial of Peter Von Hagenbach in 1474 has been considered as the first prosecution before an international criminal tribunal for charges related to systematic violence against civilians, and especially rape as a war crime. See Durham 2012, p. 257; Gordon 2013.

[35] For an analysis of the impact of the IMTs on international criminal law see Heller 2011.

[36] Kellogg-Briand Pact, above n. 32, Article 1: 'The High Contracting Parties solemnly declare… that they condemn recourse to war…'.

commission of war crimes, a concept which was well established by that time.[37] However, within a year, the Allies authorised the tribunals to prosecute the Nazi leaders on the basis of crimes against peace, war crimes and crimes against humanity,[38] with the first category acquiring in the final judgment of the Nuremberg Tribunal the title of the 'supreme international crime'.[39] The incorporation of 'crimes against peace' into the subject-matter jurisdiction of the Tribunal was a bold legal innovation since it extended the scope of individual liability to violations of *jus ad bellum* for the first time. This legal innovation of the Tribunal to act both as a legislator and a judge[40] gave rise to much controversy among jurists and academics[41] and constituted the legal basis for the defence of the accused. The defence argued that the principle of *nullum crimen sine lege*, which prohibits retroactive criminal prosecutions,[42] 'derives from the recognition of the fact that any defendant must needs [*sic*] consider himself unjustly treated if he is punished under an *ex post facto* law'.[43] Specifically, the three main arguments of the defence were that (i) aggressive war was not criminal in 1939, when WWII began; (ii) it did not carry individual criminal responsibility and (iii) there was no international court with potential jurisdiction to try the defendants.[44] These arguments were also complemented by the lack of legal grounds for Germany's sanctions, since Germany had withdrawn from the League before the beginning of the war and the League system had already failed to counteract German aggression.[45] Thus, the great powers could not claim that Germany had violated commitments under the League Covenant.

However, in his opening speech, the Chief Prosecutor of the United States, Justice Jackson, held that the illegality of aggressive war was established by the Kellogg-Briand Pact and that in any case the outlawry of aggressive war was one of the 'generally accepted rules of international law'[46] which were part of the German Law under the Weimar Constitution. Moreover, concerning the legal basis of prosecuting the accused on crimes against peace, the Tribunal held that the *nullum crimen sine lege* principle was relative, being subject to exceptions, and could not apply for the defendants since they 'must have known that they were acting in

37 Schabas 2004, p. 17.

38 Ibid.

39 International Military Tribunal (Nuremberg) 1947, p. 186.

40 Overy 2003, p. 2.

41 Senator Robert A Taft of Ohio characterised the judgment in Nuremberg as a 'miscarriage of justice' and held that 'the idea of justice in Europe might have been discredited for the years to come' (in Mignone 1946–1947, p. 476). See also Overy 2003, p. 15. For an opposite view see Kelsen 1947, p. 165.

42 Affirmation of the *nullum crimen sine lege* principle can be found in many human rights treaties as well as in the Universal Declaration of Human Rights, opened for signature 10 December 1948, UNGA Resolution 217 A (III), Article 11(2).

43 IMT 1947, pp. 168–170.

44 Wilson 2009, p. 55.

45 Ibid.

46 International Military Tribunal 1946, p. 39.

defiance of all international law when in complete deliberation they carried out their designs of invasion and aggression.'[47]

Regardless of these arguments however, the prosecution knew that these trials did not absolutely conform to principles of legality[48] and for that reason the Tribunal tried to emphasise the evolving character of international law[49] and the fact that it was trying to fill a gap in international criminal procedure.[50] Nevertheless, if one tries to trace the reasons why the great powers found that this war was different from the previous ones, in a way that required the establishment of individual liability for the waging of it, one will be confronted mainly with cosmopolitan considerations.[51] The Kellogg-Briand Pact renounced the use of force as a means of national policy but did not establish individual liability for an unlawful use of force. The reasons for this transition from the outlawing to the criminalisation of aggression were based on cosmopolitan considerations and have to be sought in the actual nature of WWII.[52] Firstly, Germany was waging wars for the mere purpose of enslavement of people and annexation of territories,[53] without any justification of self-defence. Secondly, the war had a strong ideological character and the supporters of this ideology committed grave crimes against other ethnic or racial groups.[54] The commission of crimes that stems from ideological motives, such as the Holocaust, although constituting national policy, was not regarded as a pure act of State by the Tribunal. The individuals involved in the commission of these crimes bore their own separate responsibility since they could have chosen not to become part of this ideology and consequently, to abstain from committing crimes in the name of it. Thus, it can be said that they made the moral choice to engage in such actions, disregarding universal values, such as the peace, security and well-being of the individuals they chose to victimise. For these reasons, the Nuremberg trials were the first occasion in the history of international law

[47] Schabas 2012, p. 49.

[48] 'The Tribunal was not to conform to existing principles in international law but to establish new rules of international conduct and agreed boundaries in the violation of human rights.' in Overy 2003, p. 23. See also Brownlie 1981, p. 173, for the opinion of Judge Pal of India of the Tokyo Tribunal.

[49] 'The law is not static, but by continual adaptation follows the needs of a changing world', abstract from the Nuremberg Judgment as found in Mignone 1946–1947, p. 481.

[50] Brownlie 1981, p. 169.

[51] It has been argued however that, at least on the US part, an important consideration for the conduct of criminal trials against the Nazi leaders was to create a show for the American public. See Brunner 2002; Peterson 2007, p. 257.

[52] 'If aggressive warfare in violation of treaty obligation is a matter of international cognizance, the preparations for it must also be of concern to the international community' in Jackson 1946.

[53] Boeving 2004–2005, p. 565.

[54] However, these arguments cannot be invoked in the case of the Japanese war criminals. Japanese efforts for regional domination were generally supported and there seemed to be no clear pattern of conduct or ideology during the war but rather opportunism. Besides, Japan used a range of means to promote Japanese domination apart from wars of conquest (such as the installation of puppet regimes) which could not be characterised as aggression (Wilson 2009, pp. 64–66).

where individuals were brought to the fore of the international arena, both as alleged offenders but also as victims, with the criminalisation of violations of international law committed against individuals. The Nuremberg trials shifted the focus and application of international law to the individual, giving thus priority to cosmopolitan purposes, such as the fight against impunity, protection of all human beings and prevention from the commission of grave crimes that can put the peace, security and well-being of the world at serious peril, over sovereignty concerns of the State involved.

All in all, the Nuremberg trials were innovative when they established individual criminal responsibility for the commission of crimes against peace, the forerunner of the crime of aggression. Their contribution to the introduction of 'crimes against peace' in an international criminal law context cannot be underestimated. The Nuremberg trials were the starting point of a new era for international criminal law and procedure, an era where war criminals, regardless of their status and potential to claim immunity, could and should be prosecuted and punished for their acts. However, apart from this cosmopolitan-oriented development of the attribution of individual criminal liability for aggression, the newly established UN condemned and prohibited the use of force using a more State-oriented approach, by putting more emphasis on the protection of State sovereign interests rather than cosmopolitan purposes.

3.4 A State-Centric Approach: 'Act of Aggression' Under the UN Charter and UNGA Resolution 3314

3.4.1 The Discretionary Powers of the Security Council Under UN Charter Article 39

On 26 June 1945, the same day that the proposal to make waging a war of aggression a crime under international law was submitted to the London Conference, the UN Charter outlawed the use of force in San Francisco.[55] The UN Charter framework on the prohibition of the use of force can be summarised as such: Article 2(4) of the UN Charter provides that

> [a]ll Members shall refrain in their international relations from the threat or use of force against the territorial integrity or political independence of any State, or in any other manner inconsistent with the Purposes of the United Nations.

This statement has been accepted as constituting a prohibition under customary law and thus, it is legally binding for all States (even for the few non-Members of

[55] Schabas 2004, pp. 27–28.

the UN).[56] Furthermore, Article 24 complements Article 2(4) by conferring primary responsibility to the Security Council for the maintenance of international peace and security[57] and Article 39 confers to the Security Council the power to determine any 'threat of the peace, breach of the peace or act of aggression.' These Articles introduced a number of concepts which are complementary to aggression and therefore, it is necessary to examine to what extent they attributed to it new features independent of the ones acquired at Nuremberg. The UN Charter, unlike the Nuremberg one, created obligations for States to abstain from the use of force without any particular role attributed to individuals. It should be remarked that the creation of the collective security system established through the UN came as a necessary complement to the attribution of individual liability in the effort of the outlawing of war. However, this new collective security system, with the Security Council in the centre of its function, takes a more conservative, State-centred approach in the fight against aggression. While the UN Charter explicitly prohibits the use or threat of force by States, it also safeguards absolute discretion for the members of the Security Council to determine on a case-by-case basis whether a violation of Article 2(4) has occurred. To this end, Article 39 provides some further explanations on the manifestations of 'a threat or use of force', by naming the circumstances under which the Security Council can take action against a State in order to restore international peace and security.

Article 39 authorises the Security Council to determine whether a threat to the peace, a breach of the peace or an act of aggression have been committed. The Security Council has full discretion in determining what specific actions can fall into one of the three abovementioned circumstances.[58] However, it has been argued that generally, a threat to the peace is conceived of as a State's warning to use force or a State's active preparation for hostilities.[59] Article 1(1) of the UN Charter refers to the 'prevention and removal of threats to the peace', signifying that the term 'threat' is possibly used in its literal sense.[60] However, the Security Council practice has not been consistent regarding the criteria of when a situation constitutes a threat to the peace[61] and the term has been employed in situations ranging from

[56] ICJ, *Case Concerning Military and Paramilitary Activities in and against Nicaragua (Nicaragua v USA)*, Merits, 27 June 1986, ICJ Rep 14 paras 188–90; ICJ, *Case Concerning Armed Activities on the Territory of the Congo (Democratic Republic of the Congo v Uganda)*, Judgment, 19 December 2005, ICJ Rep 168. The former decision has been criticised however for its scarce citation of State practice and *opinio juris* and the fact that it did not take into account contrary State practice (in Charlesworth 1984–1987, pp. 18–22 and 28).

[57] UN Charter, above n. 4, Article 24(1): 'In order to ensure prompt and effective action by the United Nations, its Members confer on the Security Council primary responsibilityfor the maintenance of international peace and security…'.

[58] Goodrich and Hambro 1946, p. 156; Cryer 1996, p. 163.

[59] McDougall 2013, p. 67. See UNSC 1977, referring to South African military build-up and acquisition of arms as a threat to the peace.

[60] McDougall 2013, p. 66.

[61] See generally Cryer 1996.

actual uses of inter-State armed force,[62] internal conflicts[63] and mass violations of international humanitarian or human rights law[64] to acts of terrorism.[65] This ample use of the term probably signifies that a determination of an act as a threat to the peace is the least offensive one that the Security Council can make about a State's use of force.[66] Therefore, by implication, one could argue that the three circumstances of Article 39 are placed in order of progressive severity.[67] Concerning the concept of a breach to the peace, it has been argued that this circumstance consists of all actual hostilities of inter-State armed forces[68] and finally the term 'act of aggression' is theoretically reserved for the commission of grave breaches of the peace.[69] In practice, there have been a few occasions in which the Security Council has classified conduct as aggression since 1945.[70] However, the term was employed in a rather ambiguous way, usually appearing in the preamble of the relevant resolution and used as an adjective rather than a noun.[71] Moreover, the permanent members of the Security Council occasionally abstained in these determinations,[72] enforcing the idea that the characterisation of a State's actions as acts of aggression bears the gravest implications for the concerned State. The finding of an act of aggression was left entirely to the discretion of the Security Council and no definition was provided in the UN Charter. However, it was felt that further clarification of what exactly constitutes an act of aggression was required, a need that was fulfilled almost 30 years later, with the UNGA Resolution 3314.

[62] See eg UNSC 1974, concerning the Turkish invasion in Cyprus.

[63] UNSC 1991a, concerning the military action against the Kurds in Northern Iraq; UNSC 1991b, on the situation in the Former Yugoslavia; UNSC 1994, on the situation in Rwanda; more recently UNSC 2014a, on the situation in the Central African Republic.

[64] UNSC 1992b, on the situation in Bosnia-Herzegovina; UNSC 1993, referring to violations of international humanitarian law and 'ethnic cleansing' as a threat to international peace and security.

[65] UNSC 1992a, affirming the right of States 'to protect their nationals from acts of terrorism that constitute threats to international peace and security'; UNSC 2014b.

[66] McDougall 2013, p. 66.

[67] Ibid., p. 67; Boeving 2004–2005, p. 566.

[68] Wright 1956, p. 524; McDougall 2013, p. 67.

[69] Frowein and Krisch 2002, p. 722; Meron 2001, p. 11.

[70] UNSC 1976b concerning acts of aggression committed by South Africa against Angola; UNSC 1973 (Southern Rhodesia).

[71] In UNSC 1976a (acts of aggression committed by Southern Rhodesia against Mozambique) and UNSC 1982 (acts of aggression by South Africa against Lesotho) a reference is made in the preamble to 'provocative' or 'premeditated aggressive acts'.

[72] UNSC 1985 (US abstention on resolution about Israeli attack against PLO headquarters); UNSC 1988 (US abstention on resolution about Israel assassination in Tunisia).

3.4.2 *The UNGA Resolution 3314: A Poor Legal Precedent*

The first attempt to define aggression for the purposes of the UN Charter was made by the International Law Commission (ILC), which held that aggression cannot be specifically defined and consequently, every conflict should be considered on its merits.[73] However, the ILC included aggression as a crime in the 1954 Draft Code of Offences against the Peace and Security of Mankind,[74] but did not provide a definition for an 'act of aggression'.[75] Generally, aggression was considered as any use of armed force that does not fall into the two exceptions provided for by the UN Charter, namely the use of force for the purpose of self-defence or after Security Council authorisation.[76] The General Assembly felt that a clearer picture of what constituted aggression was needed and thus, appointed the first Special Committee on the Question of Defining Aggression in 1952.[77] After four Special Committees and over 20 years of deliberations, the General Assembly passed Resolution 3314 in 1974 with a definition of aggression. The definition is comprised of two parts, a generic definition and an indicative list of acts that can possibly amount to acts of aggression.

Article 2 of Resolution 3314 introduces two principles that should be taken into account by the Security Council when it exercises its powers under Article 39 to determine an act of aggression: the priority and the *de minimis* principles. According to the priority principle, a use of armed force is *prima facie* evidence of an act of aggression if it is the first use of force committed between the belligerent States.[78] In this respect, it could be presumed that, by implication, the first use of armed force can fall into the scope of Article 2 of Resolution 3314, if it is not carried out in self-defence or under Security Council authorisation, a finding which would require further interpretation, considering that a State will always use some type of legal justification when it decides to use armed force against another State.[79] The provision continues however with the incorporation of the *de minimis*

---

[73] ILC 1951.

[74] ILC 1954.

[75] ILC Special Rapporteur Spiropoulos argued that defining aggression would be a 'waste of time' and that, even though aggression could be recognisable to anyone, it was impossible to be comprehensively defined. (ILC 1950, p. 262 as found in McDougall 2013, p. 4).

[76] UNGA 1956.

[77] Ferencz 1972, p. 494.

[78] UNGA 1974, Article 2: 'The first use of armed force by a State in contravention of the Charter shall constitute *prima facie* evidence of an act of aggression although the Security Council may, in conformity with the Charter, conclude that a determination that an act of aggression has been committed would not be justified in the light of other relevant circumstances, including the fact that the acts concerned or their consequences are not of sufficient gravity.'

[79] See for example, the opinion of ICJ Judge, Christopher Greenwood regarding the war against Sadam Hussein, that 'the war was legal by reason of SC Resolution 678' and the arguments made by Serbia concerning genocide in the ICJ, *Use of Force cases*, Provisional Measures, 2 June 1999, Rep 136, paras 34–35 and in the ICJ, *Application of the Convention on the Prevention and*

principle, stating that an act of aggression or its consequences should be of sufficient gravity in order to be characterised as such by the Security Council. This principle acquires particular importance when examined in conjunction with Article 3, which provides an indicative list of the acts that can amount to acts of aggression. The characterisation of these acts as acts of aggression is not automatic and has to be justified 'in light of other relevant circumstances',[80] including that they are of sufficient gravity. In this respect, Article 2 gives the Security Council the discretion to minimise the list of acts provided in Article 3. Similarly, Article 4 allows the Security Council to add to the list other acts that can constitute acts of aggression, stating that the list in Article 3 is not exhaustive.[81] Consequently, the overall effect of the main provisions of Resolution 3314 is to guarantee full discretion for the Security Council to make determinations under Article 39 of the UN Charter by (i) allowing the Security Council to add and detract acts that can qualify as acts of aggression from the list of Article 3, (ii) keeping the threshold of seriousness of a potential act of aggression undefined and (iii) refraining from providing any distinction between the terms used in Article 39.

As a general remark, the drafting of Resolution 3314 was not the result of a search by UN Member States to find an accurate and functional definition for aggression, but rather of their need 'to maximise the value of the definition to themselves as an instrument to be invoked in support of their own political objectives, or to minimise its value as an instrument invoked by others against themselves'.[82] Resolution 3314 does not in any way affect the scope of the Security Council's powers in determining an act of aggression, entrenching the sovereign interests of its Members States.[83] As an international instrument, it was drafted by the General Assembly, which has no power to restrain the Security Council's discretion.[84] In this respect, its legal value is minimised in relation to the use of force provisions of the UN Charter.[85] In any case, the purpose for which Resolution 3314 was drafted, as manifested by its Preamble, was to be used only as a guideline for the Security Council when exercising its powers under Article 39, without imposing any legal limitations to it or any legal obligations to the Member States of the UN.[86]

(Footnote 79 continued)

Punishment of the Crime of Genocide (Bosnia and Herzegovina v Serbia and Montenegro), Judgment, 26 February 2007, Rep 43, para 278.

[80] UNGA 1974, Article 2.

[81] Ibid., Article 4.

[82] Stone 1977a, pp. 147–48.

[83] Stone 1977b, p. 228.

[84] Mc Dougall 2013, p. 77.

[85] Stone 1977b, p. 225.

[86] UNGA 1974, Preamble, para 4: '…Calls the attention of the Security Council to the Definition of Aggression, as set out below, and recommends that it should, as appropriate, take account of that Definition as guidance in determining, in accordance with the Charter, the existence of an act of aggression.'

3.5 Conclusion

The interplay between State sovereignty and cosmopolitan concerns was present in all efforts to outlaw, criminalise or define aggression but did not end with the establishment of the UN and the prohibition of the use of force. Looking back, the cosmopolitan basis on which the League of Nations was meant to function aimed at the enforcement of the will of the majority of States, but it did not take into account that it was the great powers of that period that had to enforce that will.[87] On the other hand, the new collective security system established by the UN was structured in such a way so as to assert that the great powers will have a mechanism through which to promote their own State interests, the Security Council.[88] It has been argued that in 1945 it was perfectly understood that the League system was 'too democratic and too liberal' and thus, it was preferable to establish a new collective security system that might 'weaken certain universalistic principles and compromise the effective response to possible transgressions where a large nation was involved, but that was a lot better than no security system at all'.[89] With the UN Charter operating on a State-centred basis and the Security Council enjoying full discretion in making determinations of aggression, there was no development in the field of international criminal law with respect to cases of aggression. The cosmopolitan legacy of the Nuremberg precedent was not used to the direction of formulating a definition for aggression. This could have only been achieved with the establishment of an international criminal court with explicit jurisdiction over the crime of aggression which, while avoiding the criticisms of its Nuremberg predecessor, would push forward the development of international criminal law in the field. This development could only be effectuated by taking all the relevant parameters into account, as set out by the UN Charter and its provisions related to aggression and the use of force.

In this respect, the next chapter will turn to the Rome Statute regime and the definition of the crime of aggression as formulated in the Kampala Resolution.[90] The definition formulated therein contains aspects which pertain to the 'State sovereignty versus cosmopolitanism' debate and it is precisely these aspects that will demonstrate whether and to what extent the definition of aggression achieves the delicate balance required between these two opposing dynamics. Their influence on the Kampala definition forms an essential part of this study, as it will make a valuable contribution on the discussion of how an international definition for terrorism should be approached for the purposes of international criminal justice under the prism of these same dynamics.

---

[87] Anderson 2009, p. 354.

[88] Ibid. The UN Charter ensured that no P-5 State would ever be charged with aggression or a breach of the peace by the Security Council, given the veto provisions. See Forsythe 2012, p. 484.

[89] Kennedy 2006, pp. 27–28.

[90] Resolution RC/Res. 6, Annex I, Amendments to the Rome Statute of the International Criminal Court on the Crime of Aggression, 11 June 2010, Article 8*bis*.

References

Anderson K (2009) The Rise of International Criminal Law: Intended and Unintended Consequences. EJIL 20(2): 331–358

Boeving JN (2004–2005) Aggression, International Law and the ICC: An Argument for the Withdrawal of Aggression from the Rome Statute. Colum J Transnat'l L 43: 557–612

Brownlie I (1981) International Law and the Use of Force by States, 2nd edn. Clarendon Press, Oxford

Brunner J (2002) American Involvement in the Nuremberg War Crimes Trial Process. Michigan Journal of History 1(2). https://michiganjournalhistory.files.wordpress.com/2014/02/brunner_joseph.pdf. Accessed 7 February 2017

Charlesworth HCM (1984–1987) Customary International Law and the Nicaragua Case. Australian Yrbk of Int'l L 11: 1–32

Cryer R (1996) The Security Council and Article 39: A Threat to Coherence? Journal of Armed Conflict Law 1: 161–195

Durham H (2012) Women and International Criminal Law: steps forward or dancing backwards. In: Boas G and ors (eds) International Criminal Justice, Legitimacy and Coherence. Edward Elgar, Cheltenham, pp 254–268

Ferencz B (1972) Defining Aggression: Where it stands and where it's going. AJIL 66: 491–508

Forsythe DP (2012) Political Trials? The UN Security Council and the Development of International Criminal Law'. In: Schabas W and ors (eds) The Ashgate Research Companion to International Criminal Law: Critical Perspectives. Ashgate, Farnham, pp 475–498

Frowein J, Krisch N (2002) Article 39. In: Simma B and ors (eds) The Charter of the United Nations, 2nd edn. Oxford University Press, Oxford, pp 701–806

Goodrich LM, Hambro EI (1946) Charter of the United Nations, Commentary and Documents. World Peace Foundation, Boston

Gordon G (2013) The Trial of Peter Von Hagenbach, Reconciling History, Historiography and International Criminal Law. In: Heller KJ and Simpson G (eds) The Hidden Histories of War Crimes Trials. Oxford University Press, Oxford, pp 13–49

Heller KJ (2011) The Nuremberg Military Tribunals and the Origins of International Criminal Law. Oxford University Press, Oxford.

ILC (1950) Report by Mr J Spiropoulos, Special Rapporteur. Yrbk of the International Law Commission, vol II. UN Doc. A/CN.4/SER.A/1950/Add.1

ILC (1951) Second report by Mr J Spiropoulos, Special Rapporteur, Chapter II entitled 'The Possibility and Desirability of a Definition of Aggression'. Yrbk of the International Law Commission vol II. UN Doc. A/CN.4/44

ILC (1954) Draft Code of Offences Against the Peace and Security of Mankind. UN Doc. Supp No 9 (A/2693)

IMT (1946) The Trial of German Major War Criminals. Opening Speeches of the Chief Prosecutors. HMSO, London

IMT (1947) Motion adopted by all Defence Council, 19 November 1945. In: The Trial of the Major War Criminals Before the International Military Tribunal. International Military Tribunal, Nuremberg, pp 168–170

IMT (Nuremberg) (1947) Judgment and sentences. AJIL 41: 172–333

Jackson R (1946) Opening Address for the United States. In: Nazi Conspiracy and Aggression, vol I. United States Government Printing Office, Washington, pp 114–174

Kelsen H (1947) Will the Judgment in the Nuremberg Trial Constitute a Precedent in International Law? ILQ 1: 153–171

Kennedy P (2006) The Parliament of Man: The Past, Present and Future of the United Nations. Random House, New York

McDougall C (2013) The Crime of Aggression under the Rome Statute of the International Criminal Court. Cambridge University Press, Cambridge

Meron T (2001) Defining Aggression for the International Criminal Court. Suffolk Transnat'l L Rev 25: 1–16

Mignone F (1946–1947) After Nuremberg, Tokyo. Texas L Rev 25: 475

Overy R (2003) The Nuremberg Trials: International Law in the making. In: Sands P (ed) From Nuremberg to the Hague, The Future of International Criminal Justice. Cambridge University Press, Cambridge, pp 1–29

Peterson J (2007) Unpacking Show Trials: Situating the Trial of Saddam Hussein. Harv Int'l L J 48(1): 257–292

Schabas W (2004) Origins of the Criminalization of Aggression: How Crimes Against Peace Became the "Supreme International Crime". In: Politi M, Nesi G (eds) The International Criminal Court and the Crime of Aggression. Ashgate, Farnham, pp 17–32

Schabas W (2012) Unimaginable atrocities: Justice, Politics, and Rights at the War Crimes Tribunals. Oxford University Press, Oxford

Seymour C (1926) Intimate Papers of Colonel House, vol 1. Ernest Benn Ltd, London

Stone J (1977) Conflict Through Consensus: United Nations Approaches to Aggression. Johns Hopkins University Press, Baltimore

Stone J (1977) Hopes and Loopholes in the 1974 Definition of Aggression. AJIL 71: 224–246

UNGA (1956) Report of the Special Committee on the Question of Defining Aggression. UN Doc. Supp No 16 (A/3574)

UNGA (1974) Resolution 3314 (XXIX) UN Doc. A/RES/3314

UNSC (1973) Resolution 326 UN Doc. S/RES/326

UNSC (1974) Resolution 353 UN Doc. S/RES/353

UNSC (1976) Resolution 386 UN Doc. S/RES/386

UNSC (1976) Resolution 387 UN Doc. S/RES/387

UNSC (1977) Resolution 418 UN Doc. S/RES/418

UNSC (1982) Resolution 527 UN Doc. S/RES/527

UNSC (1985) Resolution 573 UN Doc. S/RES/573

UNSC (1988) Resolution 611 UN Doc. S/RES/611

UNSC (1991) Resolution 688 UN Doc. S/RES/688

UNSC (1991) Resolution 713 UN Doc. S/RES/713

UNSC (1992) Resolution 731 UN Doc. S/RES/731

UNSC (1992) Resolution 771 UN Doc. S/RES/771

UNSC (1993) Resolution 808 UN Doc. S/RES/808

UNSC (1994) Resolution 918 UN Doc. S/RES/918

UNSC (2014) Resolution 2134 UN Doc. S/RES/2134

UNSC (2014) Resolution 2178 UN Doc. S/RES/2178

Wilson P (2009) Aggression, Crime and International Security: Moral, Political and Legal Dimensions of International Relations. Routledge, London

Winks R (2003) Europe 1890–1945: Crisis and Conflict. Oxford University Press, Oxford

Wright Q (1956) The Prevention of Aggression. AJIL 50: 514–532

Chapter 4
The Paradigm of Aggression: The Kampala Definition and Lessons Learnt for the Purpose of Defining International Terrorism

Abstract The criminalisation of aggression under the Rome Statute is an effort to counter-balance the State-oriented approach taken on the prohibition of the use of force, by holding individuals, and in particular, political and military leaders, criminally responsible. The shift, once again after the Nuremberg trials, turns to the individual responsible and not to the State: the crime of aggression can be committed by the leadership of a State, having been implicated in the commission of an act of aggression. However, during the Rome Conference, it seemed impossible to arrive at any widely accepted definition. After the entering into force of the Rome Statute, the Assembly of States Parties established the Special Working Group for the Crime of Aggression (SWGCA), whose work resulted in the Resolution adopted during the Kampala Conference, which introduced a definition and the conditions of the exercise of the ICC's jurisdiction. Some aspects of this definition and the conditions introduced are significant examples of how the definition and prosecution of international crimes can raise concerns that pertain to the 'State sovereignty versus cosmopolitanism' debate. This chapter, therefore, aims at demonstrating how cosmopolitan purposes, in the form of international criminal justice, and sovereign interests, in the form of Security Council powers, were balanced in the case of aggression. The analysis of the connection between the definition and prosecution of aggression with the State-centric and cosmopolitan theories will pave the way for the following chapter, which will discuss how similar concerns have been raised by some current efforts of defining and criminalising international terrorism.

Keywords Crime of Aggression Article 8*bis* · Leadership Requirement · Act of Aggression · Manifest Violation · Article 15*bis*

S. Margariti, *Defining International Terrorism*, International Criminal Justice Series 15, DOI 10.1007/978-94-6265-204-0_4

Contents

4.1 Introduction

Chapter 3 has demonstrated that the need for protection of State sovereign interests and the effort to promote cosmopolitan aspirations both clearly influenced the development of international law in the field of outlawing, criminalising and finally defining aggression. While the first collective security system ever made was founded upon the cosmopolitan idea of world peace and the fight against aggression, it soon became obvious that these ideals could not find practical implementation in a security system where States had absolute discretion whether or not to assume their obligations under the League of Nations Covenant. The Nuremberg and Tokyo trials, though not without criticism, were a welcome cosmopolitan development in that they brought the protection of individuals from international crimes to the centre of international attention. The Nuremberg trials sought and found the responsibility of one of the most, if not the most, criminal wars in European history, not in the abstract concept of 'State' but in particular individuals who had carried out particular criminal acts, with criminal intent. Complementary to this judicial effort to criminalise aggression, came a political one, with the establishment of the UN collective security system and the prohibition on the use of force. While the UN Charter prohibits the use of force for practically all States, it does indeed preserve a special place for the members of the Security Council in its decision-making mechanisms, as they are empowered to determine whether aggression has occurred, who can qualify as the aggressor State and ultimately what aggression actually consists of. These wide discretionary powers do not come without severe implications for the development of international law in the fight against aggression, by rendering this fight selective, undermining the protection of individuals from the commission of aggressive acts and finally ensuring that the arm of the UN Charter regime will not reach the sovereign interests of—at least the permanent—Security Council members.

Article 8*bis* of the Resolution RC/Res.6 adopted in the Review Conference in Kampala defines the crime of aggression for the purposes of the Rome Statute and reads as follows:

1. For the purpose of this Statute, 'crime of aggression' means the planning, preparation, initiation or execution, by a person in a position effectively to exercise control over or to direct the political or military action of a State, of an act of aggression which, by its character, gravity and scale, constitutes a manifest violation of the Charter of the United Nations.
2. For the purpose of para 1, 'act of aggression' means the use of armed force by a State against the sovereignty, territorial integrity or political independence of another State, or in any other manner inconsistent with the Charter of the United Nations. Any of the following acts, regardless of a declaration of war, shall, in accordance with United Nations General Assembly resolution 3314 (XXIX) of 14 December 1974, qualify as an act of aggression:...[1]

The final text of the definition, complemented by the list of acts that can qualify as acts of aggression taken verbatim from Article 3 of the UNGA Resolution 3314 (Resolution 3314), follows a twofold structure. Paragraph 1 defines the individual crime of aggression whereas para 2 repeats the definition of an 'act of aggression', as was formulated in Resolution 3314.[2] This structure serves the purpose of linking the individual crime of aggression to the State act of aggression, a link considered necessary by the delegations during the negotiations of the SWGCA.

Looking at the structure of each one of the paragraphs, we can further discern the constituent elements of both parts of the definition. The definition for the individual crime of aggression is composed by (i) the *actus reus* ('...planning, preparation, initiation or execution...'), (ii) the leadership requirement clause ('...by a person in a position effectively to exercise control over or to direct the political or military action of a State...') and (iii) the threshold clause ('...of an act of aggression which, by its character, gravity and scale, constitutes a manifest violation of the Charter of the United Nations.'). Similarly, the definition for the State act of aggression is composed by (i) a chapeau clause which defines the act of aggression following the definition of Article 1 of Resolution 3314 and (ii) a list of acts that can constitute acts of aggression if they fulfil the requirements of the chapeau clause.

It is not one of the purposes of this chapter to include a discussion on the strengths and weaknesses of each of the particular constituents of the definition. Instead, this chapter will start with an analysis of those elements that are of

---

[1] Resolution RC/Res.6, Annex I, Amendments to the Rome Statute of the International Criminal Court on the Crime of Aggression (11 June 2010) (Kampala Resolution).

[2] The first sentence of para 2 is taken from Article 1 of UNGA 1974. The rest of para 2 is a repetition of Article 3 of the same Resolution which provides a list of acts that may constitute acts of aggression.

relevance to the 'State sovereignty versus cosmopolitanism' debate. To this end, the first section will try to demonstrate how the 'leadership requirement' clause of the definition does in fact enhance the role of cosmopolitanism in an international criminal law context, by bringing individuals of a high political or military status to the fore of the international arena not only as alleged perpetrators of international crimes but also as alleged 'violators' of a State's fundamental rights (sovereignty, territorial integrity, political independence). The second section will discuss the 'manifest violation' threshold and the question of what impact it will have in the admission of aggression cases to the ICC. As was discussed in Chap. 2, the ICC has, at times, shown so far a rather interventionist and dynamic approach in admitting cases concerning the other Article 5 crimes. However, the prevailing view concerning the meaning and role of the 'manifest violation' clause is that it will significantly restrain the ICC's competence of jurisdiction in aggression cases, in that only the most serious and least disputable of them will be able to meet this threshold.[3] Whether this is a desirable or an undesirable consequence requires a lot of discussion but what is of relevance here is the approach that the ICC will follow if it is ever in a position to rule on the admissibility of an aggression case. This approach will indicate whether the ICC is willing to assume an interventionist role, more compatible to the cosmopolitan model, by setting the 'manifest' threshold low, or whether it will set the threshold high and refrain itself from taking a view on controversial, which are also the more frequent, cases that pertain to the unlawful use of force. The third section will then examine the relationship that the Rome Statute regime creates between the ICC competence of adjudicating aggression cases and the Security Council powers to determine the existence of an act of aggression. It will offer an examination of the concerns that framed the issue of balancing the roles of the ICC as a judicial body that seeks to promote a cosmopolitan model and that of the Security Council as a political body that seeks to preserve the sovereign interests of its Member States, and under this perspective, it will discuss the compromise reached in Kampala. Ultimately, the last section is going to discuss the lessons that can be learnt from the Kampala process in the quest of a definition for terrorism. Its focus will lie on how similar concerns can be raised in the context of terrorism and how they should be addressed under the light of the required balance to be achieved between State-centric and cosmopolitan considerations.

[3] Kress 2010, p. 1138; Potter 2008, p. 166; Kress and Holtzendorf 2010, p. 1211; Barriga 2012, p. 29; Sayapin 2014, p. 262.

4.2 The 'Leadership Requirement' Clause

The 'leadership requirement' clause comes directly from the legacy of the Nuremberg trials where crimes against peace, the equivalent of aggression at the time, were considered as policy level crimes[4] and therefore, it has long been linked to the commission of the crime of aggression.[5] It has been argued that this connection is the consequence of the nature of aggression as a 'State crime', which can only be prosecuted and punished through the prosecution and punishment of the leaders of the aggressor State, having acted collectively.[6] The crime of aggression is, by definition, more State-centric comparing to the other Article 5 crimes of the Rome Statute, in that its focus lies on the protection from the use of force against the sovereignty, territorial integrity and political independence of States,[7] rather than the protection of individuals, which is the focus of the criminalisation of genocide, crimes against humanity and war crimes.

As such, the 'leadership requirement' clause of the crime of aggression brings with it a novelty which, although being of a theoretical character, is relevant to the 'State sovereignty versus cosmopolitanism' debate. International law is usually conceived of as a field of law which regulates the disputes of either States versus States (under public international law or the law on State responsibility) or individuals versus individuals, under international criminal law, as it has been applied by international tribunals and the ICC up to date. In both these situations, we will find a State or an individual having committed a violation or a crime under international law against a State or an individual who has suffered the results of this violation or crime. The European Court of Human Rights is an example of how a variation of this 'State versus State' or 'individual versus individual' equation is applied, by allowing individuals to bring claims against States.[8] In this equation, the individual is always to be found on the side of the allegedly wronged person (the 'victim') and the State on the side of the alleged 'wrongdoer'. Nevertheless, the crime of aggression, because of the 'leadership requirement' clause in its definition, is the only occasion in international law that permits an equation where States are on the side of the victim whereas individuals are on the side of the 'wrongdoers' against them. The crime of aggression protects States' fundamental rights against acts of aggression, which although being conceived of as committed by States, are prosecuted and punished through the prosecution and punishment of individuals under the Rome Statute. While cosmopolitan thinking is usually linked to the

---

[4] Heller 2007, p. 488.

[5] McDougall 2013, p. 169; Sayapin 2014, p. 259; Barriga 2012, pp. 22–23. See also ILC Commentary on the Draft Code of Crimes against the Peace and Security of Mankind, which limits responsibility for the crime of aggression to 'leaders' and 'organisers' in UNGA 1996.

[6] Ambos 2010, p. 483.

[7] Heinsch 2010, p. 722.

[8] European Convention on Human Rights, as amended by Protocols No. 11 and 14, opened for signature 4 November 1950, ETS 5 (entered into force 3 September 1953), Articles 34–35.

protection of individuals despite State sovereignty considerations, the protection of State interests against individuals who occupy leadership positions and are in a position to 'plan, prepare, initiate and execute an act of aggression' is a manifestation of cosmopolitanism in reverse. Therefore, the effect of the 'leadership requirement' clause in a criminal definition of aggression is that protection is afforded not only to the individual victims of international crimes but also to States, 'victims' of individuals who are in a position to violate their rights.

Be that as it may, the formulation of the 'leadership requirement' in the Kampala definition does not go without some criticism. It has been argued that the leadership requirement makes the scope of the definition narrow, or at least narrower than the 'leadership requirement' standard that was applicable at the Nuremberg trials.[9] Looking back at the *Industrialist* cases of the IMT and the Nuremberg Military Tribunal (NMT), established by the United States in accordance with Law No. 10, both tribunals held that private economic actors could commit all the acts listed in the definition of crimes against peace, namely the 'planning, preparing, initiating and waging wars of aggression'.[10] Specifically, para 2f of Law No. 10 made it clear that both private economic actors and third-State officials could be convicted for crimes against peace.[11]

Moreover, the NMT Tribunal also adopted the 'shape or influence' standard, as it was demonstrated by the *High Command*[12] and *Ministries*[13] cases. In both cases the Tribunal held that, to establish the policy level of an individual, his or her ability to 'shape or influence' a State's political or military action was sufficient[14] and that

[9] Ambos 2010, p. 483; Heinsch 2010, pp. 722–23; Heller 2007, pp. 478–79. For a contrary opinion see Glennon 2010, p. 100. McDougall argues however that the leadership requirement standard was not applied in a uniform pattern at the Nuremberg and Tokyo trials in the cases concerning the commission of crimes against peace (McDougall 2013, pp. 169–78).

[10] Heller 2007, p. 480. In the *Schacht* and *Speer* cases, both defendants, responsible for Germany's rearmament, were acquitted. In the first case, the prosecution failed to prove that the defendant had any knowledge of Germany's aggressive plans or that he had participated in a common plan to wage aggressive war. In the second case, Speer was acquitted on the grounds that he became responsible for Germany's rearmament long after the initiation of aggressive policies by the Nazis. In this respect, '[h]is activities in charge of German Armament Production were in aid of the war effort in the same way that other productive enterprises aid in the waging of war'. In the *Farben* case, the Tribunal also held that 'in the right circumstances, industrialists could be convicted of any form of participation in aggression'. See ibid., pp. 481–84.

[11] Control Council Law No. 10, 20 December 1945, Article II(2f): 'Any person…is deemed to have committed a crime…if he… (f) held a high political, civil or military (including General Staff) position in Germany or in one of its Allies, co-belligerents or satellites or held high position in the financial, industrial or economic life of any such country.'

[12] NMT, *United States v von Leeb* et al, Judgment, 27 October 1948, United States Military Tribunal Case No. 12 (*High Command* case).

[13] NMT, *United States v von Weizsäcker* et al., Judgment, 11 April 1949, United States Military Tribunal Case No. 11 (*Ministries* case).

[14] 'It's not a person's rank or status, but his power to shape or influence the policy of his State, which is the relevant issue for determining his criminality under the charge of crimes against peace' in *High Command* case, above n. 12, p. 489.

the basis for liability for the commission of aggression cannot be limited only to individuals who can control or direct such action.[15] Despite the SWGCA's view that 'it had been always understood that the leadership clause would reach just as far [to cover industrialists and financiers] and that it had never been limited to heads of [S]tate or individuals in the military' during the 2006 inter-sessional meeting,[16] the 'control or direct' standard does not answer the question of who exactly belongs to the leadership circle.[17] While it has been argued that it covers non-political leaders with sufficient control over State policies[18] and does not exclude *stricto sensu* religious or industrial leaders,[19] the fulfilment of this standard requires that these persons should be in a position to exert sufficient control over or to direct the political or military *action* of a State, a position difficult to be formally occupied by someone outside a State's political or military circle. Even if the term 'in a position to' of the leadership clause is interpreted figuratively, meaning that the perpetrator should *have the ability* to 'control or direct' without necessarily belonging to formal leadership structures, the requirement that he or she must be able to control or direct *the political or military action of a State* signifies that he or she must be in a position 'to control or direct the deeds of the political or military establishments of the State aimed at achieving particular objectives.'[20] Therefore, the 'control or direct' standard does not refer to a general ability to exercise influence over the political or military action of a State but to a specific ability to 'control or direct' political or military organs, designated to achieve specific outcomes.

Nonetheless, and despite the criticisms concerning the formulation of the 'leadership requirement' clause in the Kampala definition, it is due to this clause that international criminal law takes a strong position against the impunity, not only of the executive organs of the political or military structures of States, but also of their leaders. The ICC has already issued arrest warrants against Presidents or former Heads of States in relation to the other Article 5 crimes[21] and it is only a welcome prospect that it will be able to do so with respect to aggression in the

[15] 'In convicting Ernst von Weizsäcker ...the Tribunal rejected the idea that aggression could only be committed by individuals who had the ability to control or direct a State's political or military action,' in Heller 2007, p. 487.

[16] Coalition for the International Criminal Court 2006, pp. 30–31.

[17] Ambos 2010, p. 483.

[18] Ibid.

[19] Heinsch 2010, p. 723.

[20] McDougall 2013, p. 180.

[21] ICC, *Prosecutor v Omar Hassan Ahmad Al Bashir*, Decision on the Prosecution's Application for a Warrant of Arrest against Omar Hassan Ahmad Al Bashir, 4 March 2009, Case No. ICC-02/05-01/09; ICC, *Prosecutor v Laurent Gbagbo*, Warrant of Arrest for Laurent Koudou Gbagbo, 23 November 2011, Case No. ICC-02/11-01/11; ICC, *Prosecutor v Muammar Mohammed Abu Minyar Gaddafi*, Warrant of Arrest for Muammar Mohammed Abu Minyar Gaddafi, 27 June 2011, Case No. ICC-01/11-01/11(terminated upon his death in 22 November 2011). However, it has been argued that prosecutions by the ICC might unite political leaders who fear being prosecuted themselves. See for example African Union statements supporting Al-Bashir in Weisbord 2011, p. 113.

future. The fact that, in practice, only a very small number of persons can fulfil the leadership requirement in order to be characterised as the perpetrators of the crime, should not necessarily be seen as a drawback which will hinder the administration of justice; instead, it could be seen as a borderline that delineates the responsibility of the many, State executive organs who might commit genocide, crimes against humanity and war crimes, with the responsibility of the few, persons who truly are in a position to commit the crime of aggression.

4.3 Act of Aggression: The Threshold Clause

According to the definition of Article 8*bis*, an individual commits the crime of aggression when he or she plans, prepares, initiates or executes an act of aggression, 'which, by its character, gravity and scale, constitutes a manifest violation of the Charter of the United Nations'. The conclusions to be drawn from this formulation are firstly, that apparently not all acts of aggression automatically constitute manifest violations of the UN Charter and secondly, that the determining factors of a manifest violation are the character, gravity and scale of the act.

In order to understand the context and role of the threshold clause, one should look at the Preparatory Commission proposals and SWGCA negotiations, and the intention of the drafters to include such a clause. A German proposal from which the 'manifest' threshold appears to have originated, stated that an armed attack should be criminalised for the purposes of the Rome Statute, when 'this armed attack was undertaken in *manifest* contravention of the Charter of the United Nations' having as object or result the establishment of a military occupation or annexation of the territory of another State or part thereof.[22] Although the threshold clause as incorporated into the definition does not include any reference to the object or result of a particular use of force, the definition retained the term 'manifest'. As was also explained by Germany, the proposal was formulated as such so as to capture any 'obvious and indisputable cases' such as aggression committed by Hitler or Saddam Hussein against Kuwait in 1990 and to exclude legitimate uses of force carried out in conformity with the UN Charter.[23]

Following this interpretation, it has been generally accepted that the threshold of manifest violation serves a dual purpose[24]: as a quantitative threshold, it would exclude border skirmishes and similar small-scale uses of force from the jurisdiction of the ICC, in accordance with the spirit of the Rome Statute that 'only the most

---

[22] Preparatory Commission for the International Criminal Court 1999, p. 24.

[23] Ibid., p. 6.

[24] Kress 2010, p. 1138; Potter 2008, p. 166; Kress and Holtzendorf 2010, p. 1211; Barriga 2012, p. 29; Sayapin 2014, p. 262.

serious crimes of concern to the international community as a whole'[25] fall under the ICC's jurisdiction. On the other hand, the threshold is also qualitative, precluding legally controversial cases from the jurisdiction of the ICC. This second interpretation has been confirmed by the SWGCA negotiations by reference to exclusion of cases 'where there might be a degree of uncertainty (legality of the action)'[26] or cases 'falling within a grey area'.[27] Corresponding to this quantitative-qualitative threshold are also the three determinants of whether a manifest violation has occurred: the gravity and the scale of the act would ensure that only acts of a certain magnitude and with extended consequences will amount to manifest violations of the UN Charter. By the same token, the character of the act would prevent any uses of force of questionable legitimate status from reaching the ICC.[28]

Despite these clarifications as to the proper interpretation of the term 'manifest', according to some commentators,[29] its meaning is still unclear. According to Article 46(2) of the Vienna Convention on the Law of Treaties, a manifest violation under domestic law is a violation 'if it would be objectively evident to any State conducting itself in the matter in accordance with normal practice and in good faith'.[30] According to delegations during the SWGCA negotiations, manifest is either 'an obvious illegal violation' or 'a violation with serious consequences' or both.[31] The Amendments to the Elements of Crimes, as presented into the Kampala Resolution, help little in the clarification of the term by stating only that '[t]he term manifest is an objective qualification',[32] meaning that whether a violation is manifest or not does not depend on subjective opinions, the opinion of the actor included.[33] However, all these approaches prove to be of little help. The definition of Article 46(2) of the Vienna Convention refers only to violations of domestic law where natural criminal law principles are stricter and better established than in international law.[34] What is more, a US proposal during the Review Conference to include an Understanding referring to the definition of 'manifest violation' as

[25] Rome Statute of the International Criminal Court, opened for signature 17 July 1998, 2187 UNTS 90 (entered into force 1 July 2002) UN Doc. A/CONF.183/9 (Rome Statute), Article 1.

[26] SWGCA 2005, p. 3.

[27] SWGCA 2008, p. 4. A list of 'grey areas' relating to the use of force includes 'anticipatory self-defence, forcible reactions to a 'minor' use of force of another state, armed interventions to rescue nationals, the extraterritorial use of force against a massive non-state armed attack, and genuine humanitarian intervention' (Wilmshurst 2007, p. 268).

[28] Kress 2010, p. 1138.

[29] McDougall 2013, p. 160; Paulus 2009, p. 1121.

[30] Vienna Convention on the Law of Treaties, opened for signature 23 May 1969, 1155 UNTS 331 (entered into force 27 January 1980), Article 46(2).

[31] Vyver 2010–2011, p. 25.

[32] Kampala Resolution, above n. 1, Annex II, Amendments to the Elements of Crimes, Introduction, para 3.

[33] Heinsch 2010, p. 727.

[34] Ibid., pp. 725–6.

provided by Article 46(2) of the Vienna Convention, was finally rejected by States in Kampala.[35] Secondly, and in criminal law terms, the evidentiary issue of a violation should not be confused with the substance of the committed crime which is, at least in national criminal law, irrelevant with how 'clear or obvious to the eye'[36] a violation is. Since an evidentiary issue cannot constitute an element of the crime, the essence of 'manifestness' shall be sought elsewhere, namely at the indisputable illegality of a particular use of force.

To this end, the three determinants of whether a manifest violation has occurred might be of assistance. As was mentioned above, the gravity and scale of a use of force will be assessed in order to determine whether the act was a manifest violation in terms of seriousness. However, there does not seem to be any link between these determinants and the assessment of the legality of a particular use of force. For this reason, it follows that the determinant of character will be used to assess whether a particular use of force is of an indisputably illegal nature or falls within a grey area of international law, and thus, it cannot be established as a manifest violation.[37]

Kress argues that the crime of aggression under customary law, as it has evolved from the Nuremberg and Tokyo precedents, covers only the *noyau dur* of the prohibition on the use of force and that this acknowledgment is reflected into the Kampala definition by the incorporation of the 'manifest violation' threshold.[38] In this respect, the qualitative threshold of the 'manifest violation' clause will ensure that the ICC will remain within the confines of customary law when adjudicating cases of aggression and that it will not find itself in a position to decide upon cases that give rise to controversial issues of international norms pertaining to the use of force.[39] Given the scarcity of judicial precedents related to aggression, it is necessary to keep the Rome Statute definition of the crime of aggression within the ambit of customary law and make use of the ICC's jurisdiction over this crime only when the illegality of an act of aggression is found to be incontrovertible.

This argument has some merit, provided obviously that one agrees that the courtroom, albeit an international one, is not the appropriate forum in which to evolve controversial norms of international law relating to the use of force. However, one should be careful with the conclusion that the 'manifest violation' threshold will definitely keep the ICC into the ambit of customary law in the field, and as a result, that there will be successful aggression proceedings before the ICC only when the conduct in question constitutes an incontrovertibly illegal use of force. McDougall is right when she poses the question of whether the 'manifest threshold' will indeed restrain the ICC's jurisdiction to the most serious crimes of

[35] McDougall 2013, p. 127. This rejection is attributed by McDougall not to any disagreement on the context of this definition *per se* but possibly to the connection of the proposed Understanding to the US's proposal to exempt humanitarian interventions from the scope of the definition.

[36] 'Clear or obvious to the eye' are two of the synonym words and phrases that the Oxford English Dictionary gives for the term 'manifest' in Oxford Living Dictionaries 2017.

[37] McDougall 2013, p. 128; Kress and Holtzendorf 2010, p. 1193; Potter 2008, p. 165.

[38] Kress 2010, p. 1139.

[39] Ibid., p. 1142.

concern.[40] Specifically, her concerns relate to the extent to which some of the acts listed in Article 3 of Resolution 3314, such as those in sub-paragraphs (e) and (f),[41] could ever meet the threshold requirement and form the basis of the State conduct element of the crime of aggression. Admittedly, these acts seem to put the threshold low, maybe too low, given the general spirit of the Rome Statute to limit the ICC's jurisdiction to the most serious crimes of concern and the intention of the drafters of the definition to exclude from the ICC's jurisdiction any cases of aggression of lesser gravity and disputable illegality. In this respect, it seems that the ICC does not have enough guidance of whether it should follow a strict interpretation approach and thus lower the manifest threshold so as to cover all the acts of Article 3 or should refrain from a strict reading of the said article and put the manifest threshold so high that even some of the illustrative acts of aggression could never reach it. As a result, it remains to be seen how the ICC will interpret the 'manifest violation' threshold, either allowing a more flexible and inclusive reading of it—and as such, adopting a pro-cosmopolitan approach which would permit the development of international law in a judicial environment—or following a more politically-safe approach by admitting aggression cases only when there is consensus on their indisputably illegal status.

Should the ICC follow the second approach, the Kampala definition will most probably not apply to 'hard cases' of international law,[42] and thus developments of international law relating to its grey areas will not take place, at least not with the contribution of the ICC's practice. Moreover, the same approach somewhat conflicts with the dynamic approach followed by the ICC with respect to the other Article 5 crimes to date. It was discussed in Chap. 2 that the ICC has shown a, warranted or not, dynamic and interventionist approach in some cases, which is not clearly envisioned by the Rome Statute. While this interventionist attitude is more in line with a cosmopolitan model of international law, in which international justice should function independently and sometimes despite States' concerns, the regime of the Rome Statute was regulated by States and the final text adopted reflect State views. To what extent the ICC can or even should circumvent the intentions of the drafters of the Rome Statute in order to promote international criminal justice interests is a challenging question and will be more so, if or when the ICC is faced with an aggression case. Ultimately, it will be in the ICC's discretion whether it will establish itself as a pro-cosmopolitan court when adjudicating on aggression cases or follow a more State-centred approach by remaining within the contours of generally accepted norms of international law that pertain to the use of force.

---

[40] McDougall 2013, p. 136.

[41] UNGA 1974, Article 3(e): 'The use of armed forces of one State which are within the territory of another State with the agreement of the receiving State, in contravention of the conditions provided for in the agreement or any extension of their presence in such territory beyond the termination of the agreement'; (f): 'The action of a State in allowing its territory, which it has placed at the disposal of another State, to be used by that other State for perpetrating an act of aggression against a third State'.

[42] Paulus 2009, p. 1124; Kress 2010, p. 1142.

4.4 Sovereignty Versus Cosmopolitan Dynamics in the Context of the ICC's Jurisdiction Over the Crime of Aggression

4.4.1 The Issue of Consistency with the UN Charter and the Role of the Security Council

Apart from the complicated issue of finding a well-construed definition for the crime of aggression, the biggest thorn in the effort to make aggression a punishable crime under the ICC's jurisdiction was to ensure that the ICC, while exercising its competences, will not interfere with the powers of the Security Council as enshrined in the UN Charter. According to the 1994 ILC Draft Statute for an International Criminal Court, jurisdiction over the crime of aggression was provided by Article 20b.[43] However, Article 23(2) provided that a complaint related to aggression could not even reach the ICC before the Security Council had made a positive determination for the commission of an act of aggression,[44] safeguarding thus the prerogative of the Security Council under Article 39.

The suggestion of the ILC Draft Statute was supported by some delegations during the Rome negotiations, including Russia, Germany and Cameroon.[45] Nevertheless, Article 23(2) was not incorporated into the Rome Statute. Instead, Article 5(2) requires that the conditions of the exercise of the ICC's jurisdiction must be 'consistent with the relevant provisions of the Charter of the United Nations.'[46] This condition of consistency was interpreted by the British representative as making the Security Council's prior determination of the existence of aggression a prerequisite before the ICC can exercise its own jurisdiction.[47] Any amendment that would allow the ICC to exercise its jurisdiction without a prior determination of the existence of aggression would presumably endanger the system of collective security as established by the Charter[48] and would undermine the 'primary responsibility' of the Security Council 'for the maintenance of international peace and security.'[49] The crime of aggression presupposes that an act of aggression has occurred and thus, it seems that a positive determination from the Security Council is required for ICC prosecutions on the crime of aggression.

However, allowing the ICC to proceed with cases of aggression only after Security Council's determination would have implications for the independent

---

[43] ILC 1994, p. 38. See also Gaja 2002, p. 430.

[44] ILC 1994, pp. 33–34.

[45] Ibid.

[46] Rome Statute, above n. 25, Article 5(2).

[47] Schabas 2009, p. 136.

[48] Zimmerman 2016, p. 140.

[49] Charter of the United Nations, opened for signature 26 June 1945, 1 UNTS XVI (entered into force 24 October 1945) (UN Charter), Article 24(1).

effectiveness of the ICC itself, due to legal, judicial and political reasons. In the first place, the Security Council's powers provided by the UN Charter cannot be considered as exclusive. According to Article 24(1) of the UN Charter, the Security Council has primary responsibility in international security issues, however other organs may contribute to that end. This is not inconsistent with other provisions of the UN Charter,[50] which allow the General Assembly to play its role for the maintenance of international peace and security, by discussing matters that fall into the scope of the Charter and making recommendations to the Security Council (Article 10) as well as discussing questions relating to the maintenance of international peace and security (Article 11) and making recommendations on 'measures for the peaceful adjustment of any situation' (Article 14). In fact, the General Assembly has made use of its recommendatory powers several times, issuing resolutions that characterise uses of force as acts of aggression, including cases where the Security Council failed to act.[51] Furthermore and concerning Article 39, the power of determination of acts of aggression is given to the Security Council for the purpose of imposing sanctions on the aggressor State and is not carried out on the basis of judicial evidence nor for judicial purposes. Should a Security Council's determination constitute a part of the judgment against the individual accused, fair trial concerns will eventually arise.[52] Besides, if the ICC was able to act only after the Security Council's positive determination, then (i) it would not be able to find aggression in case the Security Council had not and (ii) an exercise of the veto right would very likely preclude any prosecutions relating to the five Security Council permanent members.[53]

Moreover, the Security Council, as mentioned in the previous chapter, has not shown so far any consistency and objectivity in determining acts of aggression[54]

[50] In two occasions, the ICJ has affirmed that the General Assembly can simultaneously with the Security Council deal with a matter concerning international peace and security and that the responsibility of the latter to maintain international peace and security is primary but not exclusive. See ICJ, *Legal Consequences of the Construction of a Wall in the Occupied Palestinian Territory*, Advisory Opinion, 9 July 2004, ICJ Rep 136, para 27 and ICJ, *Certain Expenses of the United Nations*, Advisory Opinion, 20 July 1962, ICJ Rep 151, para 163.

[51] See e.g., UNGA 1963 (South Africa); UNGA 1969 (Southern Rhodesia); UNGA 1981 and UNGA 1982 (Israel against Iraq). Cases of Security Council's inaction include UNGA 1951 (China against Korea). Besides, the UNGA 1950 ('Uniting for Peace Resolution') confirms the power of the General Assembly to make recommendations to Member States for collective measures in cases of breaches of the peace or acts of aggression.

[52] Wilmshurst 2007, p. 278.

[53] Ibid., p. 277.

[54] As Van Schaack argues, there are arguments in favour of giving the Security Council the role of gatekeeper for aggression cases before the ICC which have some merit. A prior Security Council determination for aggression cases would insulate from prosecution uses of force which might include acts of aggression but which are otherwise legitimate or desirable (such as defence of nationals, hostage rescues, humanitarian interventions etc.) (Van Schaack 2010, p. 565). However, as Van Schaack also acknowledges, while there are a few cases where the Security Council has made determinations of aggression, or at least has been referred to aggression in Security Council Resolutions, the cases that it didn't (and possibly should have) are more. Moreover, and relating to

and, given its past practice, it could not be trusted to make unbiased determinations of aggression in the future. This hesitancy of the Security Council to actually name States' acts as aggression would obviously block the ICC's jurisdiction over such cases,[55] rendering any provisions for aggression practically useless. What is more, when the Security Council downgrades an act of aggression to a breach or threat to the peace,[56] it does not necessarily indicate that aggression has not taken place. The characterisation of a State's act as a threat or breach to the peace might be due to political reasons or even the difficulty to reach the required majority for the adoption of a resolution that would condemn the act as aggression. Thus, the absence of a Security Council determination of the commission of an act of aggression does not signify that a conflict will definitely arise between the Security Council and the ICC's own findings.[57]

There were several proposals that tried to address the issue of consistency as posed by Article 5(2). A proposal by Greece and Portugal[58] suggested that the ICC shall first ascertain that the Security Council has made a positive determination and if not, it shall request it to proceed with a determination. In case of Security Council's inaction within a specific time-frame, the ICC would be able to proceed with the case in question. Other States[59] suggested that, instead of the Security Council, a different organ might act as a 'filter' before the ICC will be able to proceed with a case of aggression. This role could be played either by the General Assembly or the International Court of Justice (ICJ). In this way, in the absence of a Security Council's determination, the General Assembly could be asked to make a recommendation within a specific time-frame[60] and again, in case of inaction, the ICC would be able to proceed. A third option would allow the ICC to request the General Assembly to seek the advisory opinion of the ICJ on the existence of an act of aggression. However, while there is some logic in requesting the advisory opinion of a judicial organ as a filter for the exercise of the ICC's jurisdiction, the involvement of the ICJ could be problematic from the perspective of the individual accused. The alleged perpetrator would not be able to appear before the ICJ and bring evidence[61] and if the ICJ's ruling is binding for the ICC, then the rights of the

(Footnote 54 continued)

the discussion on the 'manifest violation' threshold in the previous section, if 'manifest' is read by the ICC as indisputably illegal, it is very likely that 'legitimate or desirable' uses of force will not fall into the ambit of the definition anyway.

55 Cryer et al. 2010, p. 330.

56 As examples, UNSC 1990 can be mentioned which defined Iraq's invasion of Kuwait as a 'breach of the peace' or UNSC 1977 and UNSC 1982 which characterised South Africa's aggressive acts against its neighbouring States and Namibia as a 'threat to the peace'. See Gaja (n. 43) 434.

57 Gaja 2002, p. 434.

58 Working Group on the Crime of Aggression 1999a.

59 See Working Group on the Crime of Aggression 2001.

60 See Working Group on the Crime of Aggression 1999b.

61 Cryer et al. 2010, p. 331.

accused are severely infringed. Moreover, a proposal of having the ICJ determine the existence of an act of aggression was also discarded for both legal and practical reasons.[62] A serious stumbling block for the ICJ to play such a role would be the requirement for the involved States' consent.[63] It was also suggested during the negotiations that the link between ICJ's jurisdiction and State consent, if it exists, does not presuppose that the said State has also consented to the ICJ's jurisdiction over the crime of aggression.[64] In more practical terms, proceedings before the ICJ can take a long time,[65] something that would risk infringement of the right of the accused for a speedy trial as provided by Article 67(1c) of the Rome Statute.[66]

*4.4.2 Article 15*bis*: A Fair Compromise?*

The compromise reached by the Kampala Resolution in this respect is regulated by Article 15*bis*, paras (6) to (8) where the role attributed to the Security Council is that of the primary but not exclusive filter of whether an act of aggression has occurred. Article 15*bis*(6) provides that the Prosecutor, before proceeding with an investigation relating to the crime of aggression, 'shall first ascertain whether the Security Council has made a determination of an act of aggression committed by the State concerned' and 'shall notify the Secretary-General of the United Nations of the situation before the Court'. In case of a Security Council determination, the Prosecutor may proceed with the investigation of the situation (Article 15*bis*(7))[67] but in the opposite case and after a six-month time lapse from the date of notification, 'the Prosecutor may proceed with the investigation in respect of a crime of aggression, provided that the Pre-Trial Division has authorized the commencement of [this] investigation…and the Security Council has not decided otherwise in accordance with Article 16' (Article 15*bis*(8)). Thus, the compromise reached in this respect is that on the one hand, the Security Council's role in international

[62] See SWGCA 2009, paras 42–43.

[63] Statute of the International Court of Justice, opended for signature 26 June 1945, Annex to UN Charter (entered into force 24 October 1945), Article 36. See also ICJ, *Case of the Monetary Gold Removed from Rome in 1943* (*Italy v United States, United Kingdom & France*), Judgment, 15 June 1954, ICJ Rep 19. The *Monetary Gold* principle required that all States involved in an act of aggression should have accepted the Court's jurisdiction before it can go forward with a case.

[64] SWGCA 2009, para 43.

[65] '… [I]n the context of the advisory opinion on the *Legality of the Threat or Use of Nuclear Weapons*, it took the Court more than three years to respond to a request from the World Health Organisation and a year and a half to act in response to the demand by the General Assembly in the same matter' in Schuster 2003, pp. 48–49.

[66] Rome Statute, above n. 25, Article 67(1c): '1. In the determination of any charge, the accused shall be entitled to…: (c) To be tried without undue delay'.

[67] Kampala Resolution, above n. 1, Article 15*bis*(7): 'Where the Security Council has made such a determination, the Prosecutor may proceed with the investigation in respect of a crime of aggression'.

peace and security matters has been acknowledged and given primacy in the proceedings before the ICC but on the other hand, in case of the Security Council's inaction, there is the safety valve of the authorisation of the Pre-Trial Division for the initiation of aggression investigations.

While the balance achieved in the regulation of competences between the Security Council and the ICC is definitely noteworthy, in that it manages to accommodate both the Security Council powers under the UN Charter and a certain degree of autonomy for the ICC aggression proceedings, several comments can be made in the context of the 'State sovereignty versus cosmopolitanism' debate. The primacy given to the Security Council as the first organ to determine the existence of an act of aggression, a power already established under Article 39 of the UN Charter and reiterated by the Kampala Resolution for criminal law purposes, reinforces the sovereign prerogatives of the Security Council Member States in international peace and security matters. History however has shown that the Security Council has been very cautious in the use of the term 'aggression' in its resolutions under Chapter VII of the UN Charter and it is unlikely that it will act differently after the coming into force of the Kampala Resolution for the purposes of the Rome Statute.[68] As was stated earlier, even when the Security Council uses the term 'aggression' or 'aggressive acts' in its resolutions, it is still unclear whether the mere reference of the term equals to a determination that an act of aggression has occurred, and consequently, whether this reference will be sufficient for the Prosecutor to proceed with an aggression case.[69] It is possible that, for the purposes of the Rome Statute, more than a mere reference to the term 'aggression' will be needed, since Article 15*bis*(6) clearly requires 'a determination of an act of aggression committed by the State concerned'. Given the practice so far of the Security Council, one would either expect the Prosecutor to make interpretations of relevant Security Council resolutions as to whether they implicitly or explicitly determine the existence of an act of aggression or expect that the Security Council will use the term 'aggression' in its resolutions, only when it clearly intends to trigger the Prosecutor's ability to initiate an aggression investigation.[70]

In an effort to counterbalance the effect that the absence of a Security Council determination would have on the independent function of the ICC, Article 15*bis*(8) introduces the Pre-Trial Division filter. This filter, and rightly so, is meant to work as an offset against a Security Council which would appear too reluctant to provide

[68] Arguably, one cannot help but consider the possibility that the Security Council, being mostly driven by political considerations and not international criminal justice purposes, might characterise incidents as aggression as a means to pressure the ICC to conduct aggression proceedings. Though this possibility might seem unlikely, it does illustrate that the need for balance between Security Council's powers and ICC's autonomy is manifested not only in situations where the former fails to determine aggression whereas the latter thinks that aggression has taken place, but also in situations where the Security Council might attempt to 'guide' the ICC as to which situations require investigation.

[69] McDougall 2013, p. 269.

[70] Ibid.

a 'green light' to the ICC to prosecute aggression cases. While it seems that Article 15*bis*(8) is a fair effort of the drafters to open the way for the promotion of cosmopolitan purposes, in the form of international criminal justice, possibly despite any contrary opinion of the Security Council Members, the final phrase of the Article reiterates the power given to the Security Council by Article 16 of the Rome Statute,[71] to block proceedings before the ICC.[72] This addition can be interpreted as a further emphasis to the interrelationship between the competence of the ICC to prosecute the crime of aggression and the role of the Security Council to maintain international peace and security. Besides, there is no reason why Article 16 should not apply to the crime of aggression since it applies to the other Article 5 crimes. Article 16 can be invoked in cases where the Security Council would assess that the interests of peace should be prioritised against the interests of international criminal justice, and as such, prosecutions should be delayed or even denied.[73] In this respect, it seems that the power given to the Security Council by Article 16, coupled with the provisions related to the exercise of the ICC's jurisdiction over aggression cases, provides substantial discretion to the former as to when an aggression case should reach the latter, regardless of whether there is a determination of the existence of an act of aggression. Ultimately, and despite the notable effort of Article 15*bis* to balance the powers of the Security Council in international peace and security matters with the independent competence of the ICC to prosecute the crime of aggression, Article 16 of the Rome Statute will always ensure that the ICC will be able to proceed with a case concerning any Article 5 crime (aggression included), only when the Security Council wishes the same.

4.5 Lessons Learnt from the Paradigm of Aggression

So far, it has been argued that (i) the leadership requirement clause contained in the Kampala definition acknowledges that individuals who commit crimes against States should be prosecuted and punished before the ICC, (ii) that the ambiguous drafting (of the provisions regarding the 'manifest violation' threshold) and the use of politically compromised texts of doubtful legal value as substantive parts of the definition (such as the list of acts of aggression in Resolution 3314) result in the

[71] Rome Statute, above n. 25, Article 16: 'No investigation or prosecution may be commenced or proceeded with under this Statute for a period of 12 months after the Security Council, in a resolution adopted under Chapter VII of the Charter of the United Nations, has requested the Court to that effect; that request may be renewed by the Council under the same conditions.'

[72] In fact, the Security Council has already made use of this Article in requesting the ICC to defer for 12 months any investigation or prosecution of cases with respect to acts committed by non-State Party troops of peacekeeping missions. See UNSC 2002, 2003. These resolutions have been characterised as Security Council legislation and it has been questioned whether Article 16 indeed allows for such general requests. See Talmon 2005, p. 178.

[73] McDougall 2013, p. 275.

creation of vagueness for the ICC to assess whether a case constitutes a manifest violation or not, and (iii) that Article 15*bis* of the Kampala Resolution, although being a decent effort to balance the Security Council's powers and the ICC competences in aggression cases, finally leans more towards preserving Security Council political interests than promoting cosmopolitan ideas. This section therefore, is going to discuss these three 'lessons to be learnt' from the Kampala process, focusing on how similar issues should be addressed in the context of terrorism under the light of the required balance to be achieved between State-centric and cosmopolitan considerations.

It is the author's view that these lessons are going to contribute to the overall argument of this study, which supports that the need to formulate a definition for, and criminalise, terrorism for the purposes of international criminal justice will not be effectively addressed, unless both State sovereignty and cosmopolitan concerns are given due weight. The definition of aggression has demonstrated that, among its aspects that pertain to the 'State sovereignty versus cosmopolitanism' debate, there are aspects that can potentially achieve this balance, aspects that rely, maybe too much, on the ICC's discretion and ability to achieve this balance, and aspects that make this balance nearly impossible.

4.5.1 How the 'Leadership Requirement' Clause of the Definition of Aggression Serves Cosmopolitan Purposes in the Context of Criminalising Terrorism

Attempting an overall assessment of the balance achieved by the Kampala Resolution in the light of the State-centric and cosmopolitan theories, one will be firstly confronted with the conclusion that the 'State sovereignty versus cosmopolitanism' debate is relevant to both the formulation of the definition for the crime of aggression and the conditions of the exercise of jurisdiction for its commission. Regarding the definition itself, in the case of aggression, cosmopolitanism is manifested by the 'leadership requirement' clause, in that, apart from its incorporation being a historical necessity, it expands the protection afforded by the Rome Statute to cover State rights as well. This manifestation of cosmopolitanism should not go unnoticed since it constitutes an acknowledgement that States' fundamental rights can be threatened by individuals occupying leadership positions in their respective States and that these individuals should be prosecuted and punished at an international level. The acknowledgment (i) that some individuals can be found in a position to target and victimise States and (ii) that despite the 'State' factor, the same individuals should be prosecuted by an international court, enhances the argument that crimes committed by individuals and which target States can, and possibly should, be prosecuted under international criminal law, regardless of any other sanction that the attacking State will face under public international law or the law on State responsibility. The complicated nature of the crime of aggression as a

'State crime' committed by individuals does not necessarily dictate that the repression or punishment of this crime should always be regulated by one organ, either a political or a judicial one (in this case either the Security Council or the ICC), excluding *a priori* any action to be taken by the other. The efficient and effective promotion of international criminal justice in the case of such complicated crimes will only be achieved by the attribution of complementary and not mutually exclusive competences to the international organs that are in a position to deal with either the State or the individual aspects of the crime in question.

Having acknowledged that, in the case of aggression, there are separate but interlinked individual and State aspects implicated in the commission of the crime, it is the author's view that this model should be followed in the case of criminalising international terrorism. Since international law acknowledges that State rights can be threatened by individuals, and since these individuals can be prosecuted and punished in an international criminal law context, then international criminal law can be an appropriate context where the individual conduct elements of international terrorism could be addressed. Apparently, this is not to argue that the suppression of terrorism should be regulated only by international criminal justice, excluding any other measure or sanction being taken against any involved State; to the contrary, it is only the individual aspects of an act of international terrorism that should be regulated in this context. Any State aspects, if they exist, should be addressed, by the law on State responsibility or the use of force.

In practice, concurrent responsibility both for aggression and terrorism has been implemented in international law history. For example, after WWII, together with the war crimes trials against high-ranking German officials charged with crimes against peace, there was concurrent State responsibility for Germany for the same conduct, which was held liable to pay heavy war damages to the victim States. In this case, State responsibility was not replaced by individual responsibility attributed to German leaders, but was addressed separately and concurrently, signifying that the attribution of one type of responsibility did not exclude the other.[74] Similarly, in the Lockerbie affair, apart from the conduct of judicial proceedings against the two accused before a Scottish court sitting in the Hague, Libya accepted civil responsibility and agreed to pay compensations to the families of the victims.[75] However, in this case, Libya's acceptance of civil responsibility did not mean that Libya admitted that the accused, who were also its officials, had indeed carried out the bombing or did so after following orders.[76] It seemed that, in the absence of any objective authority with the ability to ascertain the existence of State responsibility for Libya, the Scottish court proceedings, which convicted one of the accused,

---

[74] Trapp 2011, p. 230.

[75] Chargé D' Affaires of the Permanent Mission of the Libyan Arab Jamahiriya 2003.

[76] 'Yes, we wrote a letter to the Security Council saying we are responsible for the acts of our employees [...], but it doesn't mean that we did it in fact [....]. I admit that we played with words—we had to [...]. What can you do? Without writing that letter we would not be able to get rid of sanctions'. Colonel Gaddafi's son at BBC 2008.

functioned as a means of pressure for Libya to accept even this light form of State responsibility.

Having said that, the scheme of attributing concurrent responsibility to States and individuals for the commission of acts of aggression and terrorism is not something new. What should be noted however is that this distinction between the State and the individual aspects of terrorism, as was already done with the crime of aggression under its Kampala definition, will not only constitute a cosmopolitan response to the individual aspect of the crime but may also enhance State or UN action to be taken against the wrongdoing State.[77] Parallel competences between the political organs responsible for maintaining international peace and security and the judicial organs responsible for addressing the individual aspects of terrorism is a workable way to achieve a degree of balance between cosmopolitanism and State sovereignty considerations in the context of terrorism. The Kampala definition has shown that the ICC is considered as competent enough to prosecute and punish individuals that are in a position to target and Why the 'Manifestvictimise States in an aggression context and this can constitute a paradigm of how the individual aspects of international terrorism should be equally addressed.

4.5.2 Why the 'Manifest Violation' Threshold in the Definition of Aggression Does Not Effectively Address the Issue of Balancing State-Centric and Cosmopolitan Concerns and Should Be Abandoned in the Context of Criminalising Terrorism

Secondly, the discussion over the 'manifest violation' clause indicated that ultimately, the intention of the drafters to limit the ICC's jurisdiction only to indisputably illegal uses of force is not clearly established by the said clause. Despite the intention of the drafters, what the ICC has as guidance for assessing the 'manifestness' of an act in terms of its illegality, is the awkward criterion of 'character' and the dubious usefulness of the illustrative list of acts in Article 3 of Resolution 3314. The unclear meaning of the former and the questionable usefulness of the latter will prove of little help for the ICC, which will be left with barely any guidance as to the legality of a particular use of force, should it ever rule on the admissibility of an aggression case. Consequently, the ICC will have a certain degree of discretion in clarifying the manifest threshold itself and thus, either put it (too) low so as to cover all the possible acts of aggression indicated in Article 3 or (too) high, dismissing Article 3's utility for the purposes of the Rome Statute and refraining from adjudicating over 'hard cases' that pertain to the use of force.

---

[77] Trapp 2011, pp. 234–36.

The purpose of this study is not to suggest any workable way for the ICC to avoid the implications of the 'manifest violation' threshold described above, but rather to argue why this threshold is problematic and thus, should be abandoned in the context of criminalising terrorism. The 'manifest violation' threshold creates confusion as a constituent of the definition of the State conduct element of the crime of aggression because (i) the definition itself is based on a text (Resolution 3314) which was never meant to be used for international criminal law purposes and thus, it did not substantially contribute to the development of international law in the field and (ii) the term 'manifest' is by itself unclear in a criminal law context and its criterion of 'character' does not make it much clearer. Consequently, there are two approaches the ICC will be able to follow: either it will keep itself into a strict reading and interpretation of the definition, taking into account the relevant Articles of Resolution 3314 and especially the list of acts of aggression of Article 3 or it will dismiss the usefulness of Resolution 3314 and 'stick' only to those cases which clearly constitute violations of the prohibition on the use of force under customary law. Since the acts listed in Article 3 go far beyond the scope of customary law on aggression,[78] the ICC will either have to respect Resolution 3314 provisions and lower the 'manifest' threshold in order to include the illustrative acts of aggression or focus on the 'character' criterion of 'manifestness' and raise the threshold so high, making the list of Article 3 irrelevant for the purposes of determining the State conduct element of the definition.

Turning now to the question of whether the 'manifest threshold' can contribute to the balance between State-centric and cosmopolitan concerns in the context of the Kampala definition, the answer is that it cannot. If the ICC is to follow a 'low threshold' approach—meaning that the ICC is willing to follow a strict interpretation of the definition, taking into account the list of acts of aggression under Article 3 and thus lower the threshold of 'manifestness' in order to include all of them—there is a risk that the ICC might turn out to be overly pro-cosmopolitan and declare as admissible, cases where the use of force is of lesser gravity (such as those illustrated in Article 3(e) and (f)) or where the prohibition of the commission of a certain act is not within the ambit of customary law. In this respect, the ICC might be found in the awkward position of adjudicating over controversial cases relating to the use of force or even of evolving international law norms pertaining to this field. Of course, should the ICC show a preference towards a 'low threshold' approach in assessing the 'manifestness' of an act of aggression, States might not be

[78] ICJ, *Case Concerning Armed Activities on the Territory of the Congo (Democratic Republic of Congo v Uganda)*, Separate Opinion of Judge Kooijmans, 19 December 2005, ICJ Rep 168, para 63. McDougall argues that even the fact that Article 3(g) of UNGA 1974 ('the sending…of armed bands, groups, irregulars or mercenaries, which carry out acts of armed force against another State…') which, according to the ICJ in the *Nicaragua* case, '…may be taken to reflect customary law', does not signify that the said Article constitutes a customary definition of aggression but that the rule articulated therein (the prohibition of sending armed bands) is part of customary law. See McDougall 2013, pp. 90–1; ICJ, *Case Concerning Military and Paramilitary Activities in and against Nicaragua (Nicaragua v USA)*, Merits, 27 June 1986, ICJ Rep 14, para 195.

particularly enthusiastic with the idea of extending the ICC's jurisdiction to international terrorism (or equally to other international offences), for fear of having an over-intrusive court adjudicating over terrorist cases beyond their immediate control.

On the other hand, a 'high threshold' approach—namely a flexible interpretation of the definition where the 'manifestness' of an act of aggression will be mainly assessed by its indisputable illegality—might have the opposite effect: an ICC which will not be able to use all of its interpretative tools provided by the Kampala definition (such as the Article 3 list) and to form its own findings regarding the State conduct element of the crime of aggression in cases where the illegality of an act is not indisputable. As such, the ICC will have to limit its jurisdictional competence only to cases where there is wide State consensus (and Security Council explicit or implicit acknowledgment) that a particular use of force is indisputably illegal and will have to remain silent in the majority of the cases that pertain to the use of force whose illegality cannot be unequivocally established.

What remains true for now however is that it will be the ICC itself to decide in the end which approach it should follow. However, it seems that neither approach will contribute to a desired balance between State-centric and cosmopolitan concerns. The achievement of this balance will be highly dependent upon the ICC's decision on what the proper threshold of 'manifestness' is on a case-by-case basis, with the risk of either putting it too low (and thus, becoming too pro-cosmopolitan) or too high (becoming over reliant upon State-centric considerations). In this respect, the paradigm of the Kampala definition, through its manifest threshold, shows that the use of a text of low legal value as a basis of definition and of ambiguous language in the formulation of the threshold should be avoided in the drafting of international criminal law definitions and in the drafting of an international definition for terrorism.

4.5.3 How Article 15bis is a Manifestation of Some Pragmatic Limitations to Cosmopolitan Aspirations in the Context of the ICC's Exercise of Jurisdiction

Finally, the discussions around the balance of competences between the ICC and the Security Council showed that regulating the conditions of the exercise of jurisdiction was just as complex as the issue of finding an agreed definition. Article 15*bis* seems to be a fair effort in balancing the Security Council's primary responsibility to maintain international peace and security with the ICC's autonomy to conduct aggression proceedings. However, from a cosmopolitan perspective, the overall impact of the provisions of Article 15*bis* tends to reflect a somewhat conservative approach. While Article 15*bis*(8) introduces the Pre-Trial Division filter as an offset in case of Security Council's inaction, the overall effect of Article 15*bis* provisions is that the only aggression cases that will ever reach the ICC, will be the ones the Security Council wishes to see before the ICC. This likelihood is manifested in two ways: firstly, any reference to 'aggression' in Security Council resolutions, already being a scarce practice, may deliberately be avoided in the future for fear of providing the 'green light' to the ICC Prosecutor to initiate aggression proceedings. This scenario will possibly result in the use of 'aggression' exclusively for situations that the Security Council wishes to be investigated. Secondly, even when the Pre-Trial Division has authorised the commencement of an investigation in the absence of a Security Council determination, or even before the Prosecutor even notifies either the Security Council or the Pre-Trial Division for the existence of a situation deserving investigation, the Security Council can always, and with respect to all Article 5 crimes, invoke Article 16 of the Rome Statute, and block proceedings altogether. This latitude of Security Council powers under the Rome Statute ultimately does not create a very different impact to that of the initial proposal of some States referred to earlier in the chapter, to make a Security Council determination compulsory for the Prosecutor in order to initiate aggression proceedings.[79] The effect would still be the same, namely that the Security Council, a political organ whose practice has shown that its decisions are mostly, or even exclusively, driven by political expediency, has the last word in matters of international criminal justice and especially in the adjudication of aggression cases. This argument is obviously true for all Article 5 crimes but it becomes even more relevant especially in cases of international crimes that lie close to international security issues, such as aggression and possibly, terrorism.

The delicate compromise achieved by Article 15*bis* reflects in a straightforward manner that cosmopolitan steps with respect to the adjudication of aggression cases can only be taken in a rather conservative way. The mere fact that the Kampala Resolution safeguards a role for the Security Council for the purpose of the ICC's conducting aggression proceedings manifests the limitations posed by realpolitik to an independent and autonomous operation of the international criminal justice system.[80] While it is not the author's intention to argue for a total dismissal of the Security Council's role in the adjudication of aggression cases, preserving a special role for the determinations of a political organ with diametrically different priorities from the ICC will weigh heavily in favour of a State-centric approach in the adjudication of aggression rather than a cosmopolitan one. This state of affairs is manifested in both the circumstances where the Security Council is given a role in the adjudication of an aggression case: (i) under Article 15*bis*(6) where the Prosecutor shall ascertain whether the Security Council has made a determination as of the existence of an act of aggression and (ii) under Article 16 where the Security Council can defer investigations and prosecutions from the ICC (with respect to all Article 5 crimes).

[79] Unless a Security Council member vetoes a blocking resolution.

[80] See also Schabas 2013, p. 550 where he argues that '[t]here is no room for deference to the Security Council in a holistic, coherent and principled package of international justice'; Tiemessen 2014, p. 454.

With respect to Article 15*bis*(6), and setting aside for the moment Article 15*bis* (8) which provides for the Pre-Trial Division filter in case of Security Council's inaction, determinations of acts of aggression by the Security Council are dictated mostly—if not exclusively—by the realities of international politics and not by international law.[81] This is not to argue that the Security Council should be obliged by international law to follow certain standards when acting under Article 39 of the UN Charter. However, any determinations made by the Security Council for the purposes of this Article, if used in an international criminal law context, are bound to have severe implications in the administration of international criminal justice. It has been already mentioned that the Security Council has not shown any consistency with respect to determinations of acts of aggression, and while it can be argued that consistency is not strictly speaking required by a political organ, it is definitely required by a judicial one. In this respect, since the Security Council's practice in determining acts of aggression can be characterised as selective, then there is the risk that the ICC might end up administering selective justice.[82] As a result, any State-centric considerations upheld by Security Council Members regarding an aggression case, such as shielding from justice specific political or military leaders or protecting their own sovereign prerogatives, will interfere with the ICC's proceedings and conflict with the cosmopolitan ethos upon which the latter is meant to function.

Admittedly, Article 15*bis*(8) can provide some autonomy to the Prosecutor to investigate situations concerning the commission of the crime of aggression, in the absence of any Security Council determination. And this is as far as cosmopolitan theory can go, at least until now, with respect to the adjudication of aggression cases *without* explicit Security Council support. Without undermining the significance of Article 15*bis*(8), if the absence of a Security Council determination equals a lack of support and assistance in practical matters, such as evidence gathering, arrest and surrender of the accused, then the ICC may appear to be poorly equipped to make the most of its autonomy, and apparently, to promote any cosmopolitan aspirations concerning the administration of international justice at the expense of any opposite State sovereign prerogatives.[83]

This pragmatic limitation of cosmopolitan theory is more directly manifested in the power of the Security Council to block any investigation and prosecution before the ICC with respect to all Article 5 crimes. Although there are legitimate reasons that justify the existence of Article 16, namely that sometimes the interests of peace would dictate that prosecutions should not take place, it will be ultimately the Security Council that will assess what these interests are and which are the

---

[81] McDougall 2007, p. 307.

[82] Ibid., pp. 310–13.

[83] This holds true for all Article 5 crimes as is manifested by the Security Council referral of the situation in Sudan to the ICC. The Prosecutor's investigators have not been allowed to enter Darfur and since the initial referral, the Security Council has not exercised any pressure to Sudan to cooperate with the ICC (in Tiemessen 2014, p. 455).

appropriate means to pursue them.[84] Be that as it may, it still remains to be seen if Article 16 can possibly empower the Security Council to block investigations and prosecutions of a situation relating to the crime of aggression but otherwise allow the Prosecutor to proceed with respect to the commission of other Article 5 crimes for the same situation.[85] This interpretation will certainly further enhance the argument made above that the Security Council will be able to substantially control aggression prosecutions.

Eventually, the primary role of the Security Council in matters of international peace and security and especially that of its five permanent members as key international players cannot be overlooked and definitely not limited by the need of the current international criminal justice system to promote its cosmopolitan aspirations. This is true for any crime that falls, or will fall, into the ICC's jurisdiction, including international terrorism. While this book is obviously in favour of the international criminalisation and definition of terrorism, the author acknowledges that any effort to this direction will only partially address cosmopolitan needs. This pragmatic limitation cannot be ignored in a book whose purpose is to underline the need for balance between State sovereignty concerns and cosmopolitan theory in the process of defining international crimes but it cannot be overstated either.

4.6 Conclusion

This chapter focused on the aspects of the Kampala definition that pertain to the 'State sovereignty versus cosmopolitanism' debate. Particularly, it has been shown that the 'leadership requirement' element of the definition enforces cosmopolitanism in international criminal law by providing space for the protection of States' rights against powerful individuals that are in a position to threaten them. Secondly, the discussion on the 'manifest violation' threshold demonstrated the difficulties that the ICC will face when it has to assess whether a particular use of force can reach the required threshold or not. The guidance provided for this purpose by the Kampala definition is limited and in reality the ICC is left with substantial discretion as to where to put this threshold of 'manifestness'. Finally, the discussion shifted to the concerns that framed the issue of the conditions under which the ICC can exercise its jurisdiction and to Article 15*bis* of the Kampala Resolution which regulates these conditions. It has been argued that the issue of balancing the powers of the Security Council with the competences of the ICC goes to the heart of the 'State sovereignty versus cosmopolitanism' debate, in that it reflects in a straightforward manner the competing nature of these two dynamics. While Article 15*bis*

[84] It has been argued that, with respect to the regime of Article 39 of the UN Charter, the '… structural bias in favour of the major powers is a clear indication that decisions in the interest of peace and security will be based exclusively on (national) political considerations' (de Wet 2004, pp. 134–135, cited in McDougall 2007, p. 283).

[85] Van Schaack 2010, p. 577.

does a fair effort to achieve this sensitive balance, the critical effect of the sum of the Rome Statute provisions related to the powers of the Security Council is that of the Security Council acting as a gatekeeper of whether an aggression case will ever reach the ICC.

Ultimately, it will be the ICC itself that will determine whether the adjudication of aggression cases will follow a more cosmopolitan or a more State-centred rationale, given of course the limitations imposed by the Rome Statute. What is of relevance next is to examine whether and to what extent the 'State sovereignty versus cosmopolitanism' debate applies to international terrorism. To this end, the following chapter will attempt an analogous analysis, focusing on how the efforts of defining and/or criminalising international terrorism to date pertain to this debate. The influence of these two poles, State sovereignty and cosmopolitanism, on the formulation of a definition for terrorism and on the regulation of its criminalisation is fundamental in order to understand how an international definition for terrorism should be approached for the purposes of international criminal justice in light of these two dynamics and the lessons learnt from the paradigm of aggression.

References

Ambos K (2010) The Crime of Aggression after Kampala. German Yrbk of Int'l L 53:463–509

Barriga S (2012) Negotiating the amendments on the crime of aggression. In: Barriga S, Kress C (eds) The travaux préparatoires of the crime of aggression. Cambridge University Press, Cambridge pp 3–57

BBC (2008) Lockerbie Evidence not Disclosed. http://news.bbc.co.uk/1/hi/scotland/south_of_scotland/7573244.stm. Accessed 13 February 2017

Chargé D' Affaires of the Permanent Mission of the Libyan Arab Jamahiriya (2003) Letter to the United Nations addressed to the President of the Security Council. UN Doc. S/2003/818

Coalition for the International Criminal Court (2006) Informal inter-sessional meeting at the Liechtenstein Institute on Self-Determination, Woodrow Wilson School, Princeton University, United States, Report of the Coalition for the International Criminal Court Team on the Crime of Aggression.

Cryer R, Friman H, Robinson D, Wilmshurst E (2010) An Introduction to International Criminal Law and Procedure, 2nd edn. Cambridge University Press, Cambridge

de Wet E (2004) The Chapter VII Powers of the United Nations Security Council. Hart Publishing, Oregon

Gaja G (2002) The Long Journey towards Repressing Aggression. In: Cassese A and ors (eds) The Rome Statute of the International Criminal Court, A Commentary, vol 1. Oxford University Press, Oxford, pp 427–442

Glennon MJ (2010) The Blank-Prose Crime of Aggression. Yale J Int'l L 35: 71–114

Heinsch R (2010) The Crime of Aggression After Kampala: Success or Burden for the Future? Goettingen J of Int'l L 713–743

Heller KJ (2007) Retreat from Nuremberg: The Leadership Requirement in the Crime of Aggression. EJIL 18(3): 477–497

ILC (1994) Draft Statute for an International Criminal Court. Yrbk of the International Law Commission, Vol II, Part Two

Kress C (2010) Time for Decision: Some Thoughts on the Immediate Future of the Crime of Aggression: A Reply to Andreas Paulus. EJIL 20(4): 1129–1146

Kress C, von Holtzendorf L (2010) The Kampala Compromise on the Crime of Aggression. JICJ 8: 1179–1217
McDougall C (2007) When Law and Reality Clash - The Imperative of Compromise in the Context of the Accumulated Evil of the Whole: Conditions for the Exercise of the International Criminal Court's Jurisdiction over the Crime of Aggression. ICLR 7: 277–333
McDougall C (2013) The Crime of Aggression under the Rome Statute of the International Criminal Court. Cambridge University Press, Cambridge
Oxford Living Dictionaries. https://en.oxforddictionaries.com/definition/manifest. Accessed 13 February 2017
Paulus A (2009) Second Thoughts on the Crime of Aggression. EIJL 20(4): 1117–1128
Potter J (2008) The Threshold in the Proposed Definition of the Crime of Aggression. New Zealand Yrbk of Int'l L 6: 155–168
Preparatory Commission for the International Criminal Court (1999) Compilation of Proposals on the Crime of Aggression submitted at the Preparatory Committee on the Establishment of an International Criminal Court (1996–1998), the United Nations Diplomatic Conference of Plenipotentiaries on the Establishment of an International Criminal Court (1998) and the Preparatory Commission for the International Criminal Court (1999). UN Doc. PCNICC/1999/INF/2
Sayapin S (2014) The Crime of Aggression in International Criminal Law. TMC Asser Press, the Hague
Schabas W (2009) An Introduction to the International Criminal Court, 3rd edn. Cambridge University Press, Cambridge
Schabas W (2013) The Banality of International Justice. JICJ 11: 545–551
Schuster M (2003) The Rome Statute and the Crime of Aggression: A Gordian Knot in Search of a Sword. Crim L F 14(1): 1–57
SWGCA (2005) Discussion Paper 3: Definition of Aggression in the Context of the Statute of the ICC. UN Doc. ICC-ASP/4/32, Annex II.D
SWGCA (2008) Report of the Special Working Group on the Crime of Aggression. UN Doc. ICC-ASP/6/20/Add.1 Annex II
SWGCA (2009) Informal Inter-Sessional Meeting of the Special Working Group on the Crime of Aggression, held at the Liechtenstein Institute on Self-Determination, Woodrow Wilson School, Princeton University, United States, 8th Session, UN Doc. ICC-ASP/8/INF.2
Talmon S (2005) The Security Council as World Legislature. AJIL 99: 175–193
Tiemessen A (2014) The International Criminal Court and the Politics of Prosecution. 18 (4–5) The Int'l J Hum Rts 18(4–5): 444
Trapp K (2011) State Responsibility for International Terrorism. Oxford University Press, Oxford
UNGA (1950) Resolution 377 (V) UN Doc. A/RES/377
UNGA (1951) Resolution 498 (V) UN Doc. A/RES/498
UNGA (1963) Resolution 1899 (XVII) UN Doc. A/RES/1899
UNGA (1969) Resolution 2508 (XXIV) UN Doc. A/RES/2508
UNGA (1974) Resolution 3314 (XXIX) UN Doc. A/RES/3314
UNGA (1981) Resolution 36/27 UN Doc. A/RES/36/27
UNGA (1982) Resolution 37/18 UN Doc. A/RES/37/18
UNGA (1996) The ILC's Draft Code of Crimes Against the Peace and Security of Mankind. UN Doc. Supp No 10 (A/51/10) 83
UNSC (2002) Resolution 1422, UN Doc. S/RES/1422
UNSC (2003) Resolution 1487, UN Doc. S/RES/1487
van Schaack B (2010) Negotiating at the Interface of Power & Law: The Crime of Aggression. Colum J Transnat'l L 49: 505–600
van der Vyver J (2010–2011) Prosecuting the Crime of Aggression in the International Criminal Court. University of Miami National Security & Armed Conflict L Rev 1: 1–52
Weisbord N (2011) Judging Aggression. Colum J Transnat'l L 50(1): 82–168

Wilmshurst E (2007) Aggression. In: Cryer R, Friman H, Robinson D, Wilmshurst E (eds) An Introduction to International Criminal Law and Procedure. Cambridge University Press, Cambridge, pp 262–280

Working Group on the Crime of Aggression (1999) Discussion paper proposed by the Coordinator: Consolidated text of proposals on the crime of aggression, UN doc. PCNICC/1999/WGCA/RT.1

Working Group on the Crime of Aggression (1999) Proposal submitted by Greece and Portugal, UN Doc. PCNICC/1999/WGCA/DP.1

Working Group on the Crime of Aggression (2001) Proposal submitted by Bosnia and Herzegovina, New Zealand and Romania, UN doc. PCNICC/2001/WGCA/DP.2/Add.1.

Zimmerman A (2016) Article 5. Crimes within the jurisdiction of the Court. In: Triffterer O, Ambos K (eds) The Rome Statute of the International Criminal Court. A Commentary, 3rd edn. C H Beck, Munich, pp 111–127

Chapter 5
The Paradigm of Terrorism: State-Centric and Cosmopolitan Approaches in Some Current Efforts Towards Its Criminalisation

Abstract Just as it was shown with the crime of aggression, defining terrorism for the purposes of international criminal justice raises concerns that closely relate to the 'State sovereignty v cosmopolitanism' debate. These concerns are not only limited to strictly definitional questions but also extend to the modalities of prosecution. Construing a definition for the crime of international terrorism would mean that there has to be a proper forum for its prosecution. A suggestion that the ICC could constitute such a forum is being made in this chapter, on both a legal and pragmatic basis. However, current efforts to criminalise terrorism or terrorism-related conduct have been affected at times by both of the international law theories under examination: Security Council anti-terrorist Resolutions placed their emphasis on how to entrench and protect the sovereign interests of the US that suffered the attack of 9/11, prioritising thus State sovereignty interests over cosmopolitan purposes, whereas the Special Tribunal of Lebanon (STL) issued a quite bold pro-cosmopolitan decision that a customary law definition for terrorism exists, at least in time of peace. The General Assembly (GA) effort to draft a universal definition for terrorism seems to be so far the only example that, despite its being pro-cosmopolitan, takes into account State concerns regarding the issue of defining terrorism in a quite balanced way with its cosmopolitan aspirations. Though it still remains to be seen whether the GA negotiations will come to fruition, it seems that the most workable way to substantially develop international law in the field of terrorism, is to attempt a balance between State concerns and cosmopolitan ideas in the process of its criminalisation and definition to the maximum extent possible.

Keywords International Anti-terrorist Conventions · Treaty Crimes · Extradition · UNSC Resolution 1368 · UNSC Resolution 1373 · Special Tribunal for Lebanon · Draft Comprehensive Convention on International Terrorism

S. Margariti, *Defining International Terrorism*, International Criminal Justice Series 15, DOI 10.1007/978-94-6265-204-0_5

Contents

5.1 Introduction

In the previous chapters, it was demonstrated that the two main theories in international law, the State-centric and the cosmopolitan theory, played a defining role firstly in the condemnation, then the criminalisation and finally the definition of the crime of aggression[1] for the purposes of the Rome Statute.[2] The interplay between these two theories was what transformed aggression from an abstract and contentious concept to an international crime with its own definition and international court with jurisdiction over it. Without disregarding the flaws and weaknesses of this process, the history of the criminalisation of aggression gives an insight on how to pursue the goals of international criminal justice with due regard to State sovereignty. The historical account of the attempts to criminalise aggression and the critical analysis of the definition of the crime demonstrated that State sovereignty and cosmopolitan considerations should be reflected in both the definitions of international crimes and in the exercise of Security Council powers and ICC competences in a balanced way. Only by striking this balance will international law gain validity among States and improve its effectiveness in the fight against impunity.

[1] Resolution RC/Res.6, Annex I, Amendments to the Rome Statute of the International Criminal Court on the Crime of Aggression (11 June 2010) (Kampala Resolution) Article 8*bis*.

[2] Rome Statute of the International Criminal Court, opened for signature 17 July 1998, 2187 UNTS 90 (entered into force 1 July 2002) UN Doc. A/CONF.183/9 (Rome Statute).

Turning now to the question of criminalising and defining international terrorism, this chapter will first focus on the reasons why international terrorism should be included in Article 5 of the Rome Statute, along with the core crimes. Presenting first a brief historical account of the main efforts to define and criminalise terrorism internationally, it will be argued that the inclusion of international terrorism into the jurisdiction of the ICC may contribute to a more effective response to terrorism, as the ICC could function as a neutral forum of prosecution and thus, potentially minimise the role of politics in extradition decision-making. However, the question of whether there are also legal grounds in favour of the inclusion of an international crime of terrorism into the Rome Statute should also be examined. Terrorism differs from the Article 5 crimes in that it is prosecuted and punished at the national rather than the international level. A terrorist conduct can raise international concern to the extent that it is covered by one of the anti-terrorist conventions.[3] De Londras argues that 'while the offences created thereunder are not *international* in strict terms, they nevertheless reflect at their core the elements of terroristic activity that are to be deemed "criminal" or deserving of criminal sanctions within the international *milieu* from which they emerged'.[4] However, the anti-terrorist conventions create obligations for States to criminalise particular terrorist conducts without being directly binding on individuals. Therefore, the first section will conclude with an analysis of why a so-called 'treaty-based'[5] crime may merit inclusion into the Rome

[3] Convention for the Suppression of Unlawful Seizure of Aircraft, opened for signature 16 December 1970, 860 UNTS 105 (entered into force 14 October 1971); Convention for the Suppression of Unlawful Acts against the Safety of Civil Aviation, opened for signature 23 September 1971, 974 UNTS 177 (entered into force 26 January 1973); Convention on the Prevention and Punishment of Crimes Against Internationally Protected Persons, opened for signature 14 December 1973, 1035 UNTS 167 (entered into force 20 February 1977); International Convention Against the Taking of Hostages, opened for signature 17 November 1979, 1316 UNTS 205 (entered into force 3 June 1983); Convention on the Physical Protection of Nuclear Material, opened for signature 26 October 1979, 1456 UNTS 246 (entered into force 8 February 1987); Protocol for the Suppression of Unlawful Acts of Violence at Airports Serving International Civil Aviation, Supplementary to the Convention for the Suppression of Unlawful Acts Against the Safety of Civil Aviation, opened for signature 24 February 1988, 1589 UNTS 474 (entered into force 6 August 1989); Convention for the Suppression of Unlawful Acts against the Safety of Maritime Navigation, opened for signature 10 March 1988, 1678 UNTS 201 (entered into force 1 March 1992); Protocol for the Suppression of Unlawful Acts against the Safety of Fixed Platforms located on the Continental Shelf, opened for signature 10 March 1988, 1678 UNTS 304 (entered into force 1 March 1992); International Convention for the Suppression of the Financing of Terrorism, opened for signature 9 December 1999, 2178 UNTS 197 (entered into force 10 April 2002) (Financing of Terrorism Convention); International Convention for the Suppression of Terrorist Bombings, opened for signature 15 December 1997, 2149 UNTS 256 (entered into force 23 March 2001) (Terrorist Bombings Convention); International Convention for the Suppression of Acts of Nuclear Terrorism, opened for signature 15 April 2005, UN Doc. A/RES/59/290 (entered into force 7 July 2007).

[4] Londras 2010, p. 177.

[5] For the distinction between international crimes *stricto sensu* and treaty-based crimes see Introduction, text to note 33.

Statute despite the existence of the system of State cooperation established by these conventions.

Subsequently, the second and third sections will explore the extent to which current attempts to criminalise terrorism are influenced by either State-centric or cosmopolitan concerns. It will be demonstrated that, by laying too much emphasis on one theory over the other, the effectiveness and functioning of international law in this field will be problematic. Unless both State sovereignty and cosmopolitan considerations are given due weight, international criminal law runs the risk of either developing only in theory without the support of the community of States in the pursuit of cosmopolitan goals or not developing at all, due to too much emphasis on national sovereign interests. To this end, the second section will focus on some post 9/11 Security Council Resolutions, which treated the issue of combatting terrorism in a way that shielded State sovereignty interests at the expense of the promotion of international justice purposes. On the other hand, the third section will analyse the Appeals Chamber's Decision of the UN Special Tribunal for Lebanon (STL Decision),[6] which, being more pro-cosmopolitan, identified a customary international crime of transnational terrorism, raising thus a lot of discussion as to whether a customary definition of international terrorism actually exists. Finally, the UN negotiations on a Draft Comprehensive Convention on International Terrorism[7] will complement this analysis, as an example of an effort led by the General Assembly to promote international law in the field of terrorism by taking due consideration of the differing views of States as to how terrorism shall be defined. While it is true that the General Assembly's negotiations might be more time-consuming than expected, this effort is noteworthy for the balance it tries to achieve between the two opposing dynamics of State sovereignty and cosmopolitan purposes.

5.2 Why Terrorism Should Be Introduced into the Article 5 Crimes of the Rome Statute

5.2.1 A Brief Historical Account of the Efforts to Criminalise Terrorism

Ironically, terrorism was the reason for the first efforts to establish a permanent international criminal court in 1937.[8] The 1937 Convention on the Creation for an

[6] STL, *Interlocutory Decision on the Applicable Law: Terrorism, Conspiracy, Homicide, Perpetration, Cumulative Charging*, 16 February 2011, Case No. STL-11-01/1 (STL Decision).

[7] The first draft on a Comprehensive Convention was presented by India. See UNGA Sixth Committee 2000, Annex II (Indian proposal).

[8] Boister 2009, p. 360.

International Criminal Court[9] provided for the establishment of a international court that would serve as a judicial forum to punish terrorism as was to be defined in the corresponding 1937 Convention for the Punishment and Prevention of Terrorism.[10] Although the latter never came into force and there were no ratifications of the Convention on the Creation for an International Criminal Court,[11] it is worth noting that this preliminary effort constituted the first acknowledgment by the international community that terrorism merits international concern.[12] The 1937 Convention for the Punishment and Prevention of Terrorism was the first comprehensive convention on terrorism that included the first definition of what constitutes 'acts of terrorism': 'criminal acts directed against a State or intended to create a state of terror in the minds of particular persons, or a group of persons, or the general public'.[13] However, World War II and the subsequent demise of the League of Nations diverted attention from the Convention and thus, it never came into force.[14]

From then on, there were several times when the UN addressed concerns regarding terrorism with Declarations, Conventions and Security Council Resolutions.[15] UNGA 42/159 of December 7, 1987[16] actually stated that agreement on a universal definition of terrorism would enhance 'the effectiveness of the struggle against terrorism'. Also, the International Convention for the Suppression of the Financing of Terrorism (Financing of Terrorism Convention) provides a two-tier type of definition for terrorist offences: Article 2(1a) prohibits acts that constitute offences under nine anti-terrorist treaties and Article 2(1b) gives an all-inclusive formula of acts whose funding is prohibited by making reference to

> any other act intended to cause death or serious bodily injury to a civilian, or to any other person not taking an active part in the hostilities in a situation of armed conflict, when the purpose of such act, by its nature or context, is to intimidate a population, or to compel a government or an international organization to do or to abstain from doing any act.[17]

At a State level, in 1989, a coalition of Caribbean States proposed that transnational crimes should be prosecuted by an international criminal court.[18]

---

[9] Convention for the Creation of an International Criminal Court, opened for signature 16 November 1937, League of Nations Official Journal Special Supplement No. 156.

[10] Convention for the Prevention and Punishment of Terrorism, opened for signature 16 November 1937, 19 League of Nations Official Journal 23.

[11] Maogoto 2009, p. 22.

[12] Sailer 1999, p. 325.

[13] Convention for the Punishment and Prevention of Terrorism, above n. 10, Article 1(1).

[14] Saul 2006, p. 82.

[15] UNGA 1987; UNGA 1994; Terrorist Bombings Convention, above n. 3; Financing of Terrorism Convention, above n. 3; UNSC 1999 ('on the responsibility of the Security Council in the maintenance of international peace and security'); UNSC 2001a ('Threats to international peace and security caused by terrorist acts'); UNSC 2001b ('Threats to international peace and security caused by terrorist acts').

[16] UNGA 1987.

[17] Financing of Terrorism Convention, above n. 3, Articles 2(1a) and 2(1b).

[18] Schabas 2011, p. 10.

Although they emphasised the prosecution of drug-related crimes, their motivation was largely based on the fact that they found themselves unable to cope with this type of criminal activity due to the influence that the organised crime exerted to the political power and national judicial authorities.[19] It was after a call from those States that the General Assembly adopted a resolution for the creation of an ICC with jurisdiction over transnational drug-trafficking 'and other recognized criminal activities which endanger the constitutional order of states and violate basic human rights.'[20] Although terrorism was not explicitly mentioned in the Resolution, it is undeniable that it falls into the category of criminal activity that threatens the internal sovereignty of a State and violates the fundamental rights of its citizens.

During the Rome negotiations and despite the support of some delegations for the inclusion of transnational crimes into the ICC's jurisdiction, transnational crimes were ultimately omitted entirely, for reasons that will be discussed below. In brief, the reasons for their omission from the Rome Statute revolve partly around the fact that treaty-based crimes were not defined, or clearly defined, in their respective treaties in order to meet the *nullum crimen sine lege* requirements for the purpose of conducting a criminal trial.[21] As Rubin argues with respect to terrorism, the anti-terrorist conventions 'leav[e] it to [their] States-Parties to define with particularity the crimes set forth only broadly within [the conventions]'.[22] Unlike the core crimes which have attained customary law status, treaties that oblige States to criminalise a particular conduct create obligations only for the States Parties to them.[23] While international crimes establish individual responsibility and are directly binding on individuals, the implementation of treaty-based crimes is dependent upon State compliance, meaning that non-compliance entails only State responsibility for the violation of an obligation.[24] Be that as it may, before arguing that treaty-based crimes might also merit inclusion in the ICC's jurisdiction, this section is firstly going to focus on the primary reason why terrorism should be included into the Rome Statute and thus, have an international definition for criminal law purposes: it will complement the current extradition system and possibly constitute a more effective response to terrorist conduct. It should be noted, however, that it will not be argued that national efforts to combat terrorism should be rendered redundant; rather an international authority could be used as an alternative forum (or perhaps an incentive) of adjudication of terrorist cases when the

---

[19] Boister 2009, p. 343.

[20] UNGA 1989.

[21] Boister 2009, p. 345.

[22] Rubin 2002, pp. 66–67.

[23] Boister 2009, p. 348. However, the treaty-based nature does not always distinguish an international crime *stricto sensu* from a transnational offence, such as is the case of the crime of genocide which was regulated firstly by the Convention on the Prevention and Punishment of the Crime of Genocide, opened for signature 9 December 1948, 78 UNTS 277 (entered into force 12 January 1951).

[24] Ambos and Timmermann 2014, p. 24.

current extradition system is insufficient to respond to the needs of international accountability for terrorist offenders.

5.2.2 International Jurisdiction Over Terrorism as a More Effective Response to Terrorist Acts

In 1995, during the first sessions of the Ad Hoc Committee on a Permanent International Criminal Court, the United States presented a strong line of arguments against the inclusion of drug-related crimes and terrorism into the subject-matter jurisdiction of the ICC.[25] Among the arguments presented, it was argued that the international anti-terrorist conventions 'aim at the development of strong national investigative capabilities within effective law enforcement agencies working in an increasingly cooperative manner with their counterparts in other countries', emphasised that national criminal justice systems have made 'considerable ongoing permanent efforts to detect and prevent terrorist activity, utilizing diplomatic, intelligence, and law-enforcement resources' and argued that an ICC Prosecutor would be less competent to deal with complex terrorist cases than national authorities.[26] In other words, the US argumentation was based on some pro-State sovereignty considerations, namely the national ability to deal with terrorist offences, the conviction that international conventions are successful in the prevention and suppression of terrorism based on State cooperation and the belief that an international Prosecutor will not do the job as competently as national governments in terms of investigation and collection of evidence.

The US argumentation could have been sound if the ICC was to function on the basis of primary jurisdiction over national courts and not under the complementarity principle as enshrined into the Rome Statute. Firstly, and as the Rome Statute was to be shaped three years after the US comments, the complementarity regime of the ICC gives absolute priority to States to make the investigation and prosecution of all the crimes listed in Article 5 of the Rome Statute, and thus it would not undermine national capabilities in dealing with terrorist offences should terrorism be included in Article 5. Besides, the Rome Statute includes provisions concerning international cooperation and judicial assistance and thus it cannot be said that the goals of the international anti-terrorist conventions and those of the Rome Statute conflict in terms of State cooperation in the fight against terrorism.[27] The subsidiary jurisdiction of the ICC is only to be triggered in cases of State unwillingness or inability to conduct investigation or prosecution and a State with developed 'national investigative capabilities within effective law enforcement agencies'[28] that

[25] UNGA 1995a, b.

[26] Ibid., paras 38 and 41.

[27] Rome Statute, above n. 2, Articles 86–102.

[28] UNGA 1995a, b.

makes efforts for the prevention and suppression of terrorism using its resources cannot be considered either as unwilling or as unable in the context of the Rome Statute.[29]

5.2.2.1 Why States Prefer to Address Terrorism Under a State-Centric Approach

Before examining the contribution of the ICC to the improvement of the current system of State cooperation and extradition, it is worth looking at the two main reasons why States prefer to keep terrorism under their exclusive jurisdiction without the option of an international court adjudicating over such cases. As was pointed out in Chap. 1, the definition and inclusion of a crime of terrorism into the ICC's jurisdiction was obstructed mainly for the following reasons: (i) the lack of a universally accepted definition, (ii) the conviction that not all acts of terrorism can meet the threshold of sufficient gravity of Article 5(1) of the Rome Statute, (iii) the assertion that national authorities can respond more effectively to the prosecution and punishment of terrorism than an international court and (iv) the risk of politicising the ICC if it is called upon to adjudicate over terrorism cases. It was further argued that the lack of a universally accepted definition cannot constitute per se a sufficient reason for its non-inclusion into the Rome Statute, as the paradigm of aggression has shown that negotiations conducted by States Parties and non-governmental actors can be fruitful and succeed in formulating definitions for international crimes. Concerning the threshold of sufficient gravity, just as not all war crimes or crimes against humanity can be adjudicated by the ICC on grounds of not being of sufficient gravity, similarly not all terrorist acts would be prosecuted and punished by the ICC if the same threshold is not reached. However, the remaining reasons demonstrate the particular sensitivity of States towards issues that pertain to national security and the protection of their own sovereignty interests. Firstly, terrorist crimes are thought to be better prosecuted by national courts[30] because terrorism is mostly seen as a national, or at best, a transnational crime (namely of concern only for the States involved) and not an international one (raising international concern). Creegan suggests that, since most terrorist crimes are directed against a single State, then they should be tried nationally.[31] However, he also admits that terrorism may constitute a threat to international peace and security and that there have been instances of truly international terrorism where their referral to an international court would have been appropriate, such as the 1998 embassy bombings in Nairobi, Kenya and Dar es Salaam, Tanzania and the

[29] For a thorough discussion on the deliberations of the terms 'unwillingness' and 'inability' for the purposes of the Rome Statute see Holmes 1999.

[30] Creegan 2010–2011, pp. 262–266.

[31] Ibid., p. 266.

11 September 2001 terrorist attack in the United States.[32] When an act of terrorism reaches the threshold of being a threat to international peace and security and presents the characteristics of transnational consequences and egregious violence, coupled with the jurisdictional States' unwillingness or inability to prosecute, then the existence of an international court with jurisdiction will not only be helpful but also be imperative in order to promote international accountability. Therefore, it is safer, from an international criminal justice perspective, to view terrorism as a non-international crime, only when the threshold of threat to international peace and security has not been met.

Secondly, and perhaps more convincingly, States are opposed to the idea of an international court for terrorism for fear of losing their own control over national prosecutions.[33] It is unlikely that States with developed anti-terrorist laws and enforcement measures would want to see terrorists that have targeted them tried by an international court.[34] Those States that are often the targets of terrorist activities are wary of relinquishing jurisdiction to an international authority which might have different priorities in the application and different views on the interpretation of the law in the field,[35] and which may not protect the national interests of the affected State to the same extent as the State itself. For example, the US and India have the right under their domestic laws to impose preventative detention of suspected terrorists without trial.[36] While domestic due process considerations are not explicitly a ground of admissibility before the ICC, there might be instances where lack of substantial due process might be deliberate for the purpose of conducting a show trial, with the intention of shielding the accused and avoiding a genuine prosecution,[37] or of indefinitely detaining the accused for purposes different from conducting a trial (such as extracting information). The original interpretation of 'unwillingness' under Article 17(2) means that a State is unwilling to try an accused for the purposes of shielding him or her from justice,[38] and obviously a State that keeps an accused detained without trial for purposes such as extracting information, does not show an intention to shield him or her, but exactly the opposite. However, given that the ICC is first and foremost an anti-impunity mechanism,[39] the outcome

[32] Note 2002, pp. 1220–21.

[33] Creegan 2010–2011, p. 264.

[34] Ibid.

[35] Morris 2004, p. 478.

[36] Creegan 2010–2011, p. 265.

[37] Mégret and Samson 2013, p. 587 giving the example of the Pol Pot trial where the violations of due process rights were such so as to signify that there was no genuine intention to really prosecute him.

[38] Rome Statute, above n. 2, Article 17(2a).

[39] Mégret and Samson 2013, p. 573.

it seeks is the conduct of judicial proceedings, the lack of which might be considered as ground of admissibility.[40]

So far, one can discern two interrelated arguments which favour the non-inclusion of terrorism into the jurisdiction of the ICC: on the one hand, terrorism is mostly seen as a domestic or transnational crime and as such, States prefer to deal with it at a national level. On the other hand, even when a terrorist crime amounts to a threat to international peace and security, States still prefer that it remains a national issue, for fear of losing control over the prosecution and punishment of the offenders. Consequently, one cannot help but ask whether the real argument for the exclusion of terrorism from the jurisdiction of the ICC is not its domestic nature *per se* but mainly the fact that States consider it as too important an issue to be handled by an international authority which will function beyond the immediate control of the affected State. Precisely because terrorism can have political and foreign relations dimensions and can constitute a threat to international peace and security,[41] States do not trust that an international authority would act in their interest.[42] As Boister illustrates, the uneasy relationship between the US and the ICJ is an indication of the reluctance with which the US views international tribunals due to their 'non-compliant' nature.[43] Unlike smaller States which appear willing to relinquish their jurisdiction to the ICC,[44] powerful States are less willing to do the same and seem to favour the current 'extradite or prosecute' approach adopted by the majority of anti-terrorist conventions than the surrender of jurisdiction over terrorist offences to a neutral, international authority.[45]

[40] Rome Statute, above n. 2, Article 17(1a). Outside a terrorism context, the case of ICC, *Prosecutor v Saif Al-Islam Gaddafi*, Case No. ICC-01/11-01/11 gave rise to a debate on whether domestic due process violations, especially against an accused for whom the ICC has issued an arrest warrant, should constitute a ground of admissibility (Mégret and Samson 2013, p. 572). The case was admitted before the ICC but the Decision on the Admissibility of the Case Against Saif Al-Islam Gaddafi, Case No. ICC-01/11-01 Pre-Trial Chamber I, 31 May 2013, paras 206–208, does not make any reference to human rights considerations, although it holds that the admissibility was based in part on issues relating to Libya's failure to take custody of the accused. While there is a strong line of arguments against this 'due process thesis' (Heller 2006, p. 255), Mégret argues that in such cases, the ICC's role is not to assess whether human rights violations have occurred but whether 'something that can recognizably be described as trial' has occurred (Mégret and Samson 2013, p. 586). More generally about Rome Statute's safeguards concerning due process protection see Fry 2012, p. 35.

[41] Morris 2004, p. 478.

[42] Boister 1998, p. 38.

[43] Ibid.

[44] 'Trinidad and Tobago and Colombia both indicated that an ICC would present an attractive third alternative to extradition or prosecution' (Ibid.).

[45] Ibid. This tendency is illustrated in the Lockerbie case, where the US insisted the suspects be extradited either to the US or the UK and refused Libya's offer for the establishment of an international tribunal to try them. See Dugard 1997, p. 334.

5.2.2.2 How the 'Extradite or Prosecute' Principle May Serve the State-Centric Approach at the Expense of International Criminal Justice

The 'extradite or prosecute' principle, provided for by many existing anti-terrorist conventions,[46] is designed to bring transnational criminals to justice by requiring a State 'which has hold of someone who has committed a crime of international concern either to extradite the offender to another state which is prepared to try him or else to take steps to have him prosecuted before its own courts'.[47] However, this State-based system of dealing with transnational crimes is not always unaffected by the sovereignty interests of the involved States. There is the possibility that States, despite the presence of an extradition treaty, refuse to extradite their own nationals to the requesting State due to, among others, political or diplomatic reasons.[48] Political expediency plays a significant role in the decision of a State to extradite or prosecute an offender.[49] The risk of having its foreign relations disturbed if a State does extradite an offender or even appear weak if it gives into an extradition request might determine whether eventually an offender will escape justice by being prosecuted with unwarranted leniency or not being prosecuted at all.[50] An illustrative example of this state of affairs is the Turkish refusal to extradite Osama Bin Laden's son-in-law, Suleiman Abu Ghaith, to the US. Ghaith, after his capture in a detention camp in Iran, allegedly escaped and entered Turkey on a forged passport. Turkish authorities claimed that they were obliged to return him to Iran despite US requests for extradition. Turkey has repeatedly denied assistance to the US counter-terrorism agencies for political and foreign relations reasons, such as the US's 'alleged favourable treatment of Kurdish interests in Northern Iraq and its alleged support of Israel in its ongoing dispute with Turkey'.[51] Moreover and more directly related to terrorism, there is also the scenario that the requesting State might have supported the criminal activity, as was the case with Libya in the Lockerbie affair. There were substantial indications that the offenders would be prosecuted favourably or even be acquitted if tried in Libya, while Libya insisted it would not

---

[46] Indicatively, see International Convention Against the Taking of Hostages, above n. 3, Article 10; Financing of Terrorism Convention, above n. 3, Article 9(2); Terrorist Bombings Convention, above n. 3, Article 9; International Convention for the Suppression of Acts of Nuclear Terrorism, above n. 3, Article 11(1).

[47] Bassiouni and Wise 1995, p. 3.

[48] Sailer 1999, p. 326.

[49] The ICC has already faced obstacles in having alleged offenders extradited, not the least because of political interventions. An indicative example is the recent failure of South Africa, being a State Party to the Rome Statute, to extradite Omar Al Bashir to the ICC despite the South African High Court's decision that he shall not leave the country until the ICC's request for extradition has been examined. See ICC Press Release 2015. However, at least in principle, States Parties are under obligation to cooperate fully with the ICC, including the execution of arrest warrants, in order to bring international offenders to justice. (Rome Statute, above n. 2, Articles 86–102).

[50] Sailer 1999, p. 327.

[51] Fitsanakis 2013.

extradite them either to the US or to the UK, despite the continuous sanctions imposed by the Security Council. The offenders were finally tried by a Scottish court sitting in the Netherlands; however the administration of justice was blocked for over 12 years due to Libya's refusal to extradite its nationals.[52] A similar example where a refusal to extradite a terrorist suspect blocked the administration of justice for years was the case of Luis Posada Carriles, of Cuban-Venezuelan nationality, who was accused of the 1976 bombing of a Cuban airliner which resulted in 73 deaths and of involvement in a terrorist bombing in Washington DC in the same year.[53] Posada escaped from Venezuela while awaiting his trial and in 2005 was found in the US seeking asylum.[54] The US denied the extradition request made by Venezuela on grounds that the suspect might be subjected to torture if extradited to Venezuela.[55] Instead, he was prosecuted in the US on immigration charges and was finally acquitted, despite the US Patriot Act, which requires that an alien suspected of terrorism should be kept in detention.[56]

In all the above circumstances, the ICC can function as a third, alternative and neutral forum of prosecution. The Office of the Prosecutor has stated that '[g]roups bitterly divided by conflict may oppose prosecutions at each other's hands and yet agree to a prosecution by a Court perceived as neutral and impartial'.[57] Also, Articles 36(3a) and 36(8a)(ii) of the Rome Statute provide respectively that 'judges shall be chosen from among persons of high moral character, impartiality and integrity' and that their selection should be based, among other criteria, on an 'equitable geographical representation'. Moreover, the ICC can serve as a solution in cases of concurrent jurisdictions,[58] such as were seen in the competing jurisdictional claims over the offenders in the Lockerbie case.[59] Thirdly, the existence of an international, neutral forum may minimise the role of politics in extradition decisions, regardless of the existence of an extradition treaty. As was said before, States' decisions for extradition are frequently driven by political considerations and not by a sentiment of commitment to extradition treaties or to the anti-terrorist conventions to which they are parties. Admittedly, the introduction of the European

---

[52] Sailer 1999, pp. 327–329. A similar example that can be cited is the refusal of Afghanistan to extradite Osama Bin Laden before the 2001 bombing of Afghanistan and after the UNSC 1999 which set out sanctions to be imposed if Afghanistan refused Bin Laden's extradition.

[53] Norberg 2010, p. 13.

[54] Ibid., p. 14.

[55] BBC 2011. One cannot help but notice the irony on the part of the US, which denies extradition of a terrorist suspect on grounds of human rights considerations.

[56] Uniting and Strengthening America by Providing Appropriate Tools Required to Intercept and Obstruct Terrorism Act of 2001 Pub L No. 107-56, 115 Stat 271 (USA PATRIOT).

[57] ICC Office of the Prosecutor 2003, p. 5.

[58] See Schloenhardt 2004, where he argues that the ICC 'offers a neutral forum to try offenders that are not extradited because too many countries are seeking jurisdiction, or because a country remains too fearful its nationals or other alleged offenders may face biased trials in a foreign jurisdiction'.

[59] Boister 1998, pp. 33–34.

Arrest Warrant (EAW)[60] has replaced the traditional extradition scheme with judicial cooperation[61] among the European Union (EU) Member States with respect to certain offences, terrorism included. However, for those States outside the EU (and before the adoption of the EAW), it remains true that there is the risk of *ad hoc* political intervention without any judicial oversight.[62] In the current state of affairs, terrorists can escape punishment if they flee to a State that would deny their extradition or prosecution on grounds irrelevant to the purposes of international criminal justice, such as opposing ideology, adverse relations or distrust towards the requesting State.[63] The ICC can offer a way through jurisdictional technicalities and function as a neutral, alternative venue of prosecution, despite the existence of an international system of State cooperation based on anti-terrorist conventions and extradition.

5.2.3 The Question of the Inclusion of Treaty Crimes into the Rome Statute

So far this chapter examined the main reasons why there was disagreement on the inclusion of terrorism into the Rome Statute. The reasons related to some pragmatic aspects, such as that it can be effectively addressed by States through the system of State cooperation or extradition. However, it has been argued that this system might not be unaffected by political expediencies and therefore, the establishment of the ICC's jurisdiction over terrorism can provide a solid solution in such cases as a neutral forum of prosecution. Nonetheless, from a legal perspective, the main argument against the inclusion of terrorism into the Rome Statute has to do with terrorism's own genesis in international law: terrorism, even international terrorism, is a treaty-based crime, for which universal jurisdiction has not been established[64]

---

[60] Council Framework Decision on the European arrest warrant and the surrender procedures between Member States (2002/584/JHA), opened for signature 13 June 2002, OJ L 190 (entered into force 7 August 2002) Article 1.1.

[61] See Sliedregt 2007, for a critique on the application of the EAW and its similarities with the classic extradition scheme.

[62] Fenelly 2007, p. 522.

[63] Sailer 1999, p. 338.

[64] The 'extradite or prosecute' principle, provided by many anti-terrorist conventions, allows a State with no traditional jurisdictional link over a committed crime, to assume subsidiary jurisdiction on behalf of the competent State. Although this scheme resembles to a model of universal jurisdiction, it still differs in that the 'extradite or prosecute' principle requires the presence and arrest of the alleged perpetrator in the State where prosecution shall take place (Ambos and Timmermann 2014, p. 35; Perera 2014, p. 154). Ambos also argues that the fact that the UNGA Draft Comprehensive Convention, under draft Article 21, provides for the obligation of States to respect territorial sovereignty and the principle of non-intervention, signifies that, at least at present, there is no intention to make terrorism universally prosecutable.

and which has a very questionable customary law status.[65] These features are in fact what conceptually separates the core crimes already incorporated into the Rome Statute from the crime of terrorism and consequently from any other treaty-based crime that will ever pose its candidancy for inclusion into the ICC's jurisdiction.[66] Thus, this section is going to examine to what extent the lack of universal jurisdiction could hamper terrorism's inclusion into the Rome Statute and whether individual accountability for treaty-based crimes could be equally established.

Looking back at the drafting history of the Rome Statute, in 1991 the International Law Commission (ILC)'s Draft Code of Crimes against the Peace and Security of Mankind incorporated treaty crimes into the ICC's jurisdiction.[67] Treaty crimes were continuously being included into the Draft Codes until 1995,[68] but in 1996, due to opposition from some members of the ILC,[69] offences regulated by the anti-terrorist conventions were finally excluded.[70] The persistence of the ILC in arguing for the inclusion of treaty crimes in the ICC's jurisdiction was based on the following legal reasoning, later to be confronted with more complex issues of jurisdiction and customary law status of treaty crimes: treaty-based crimes were already recognised offences under international law, their punishment was provided for by national laws, the related treaties included provisions of extra-territorial jurisdiction, extradition and mutual assistance and also the 'extradite or prosecute' principle was applicable.[71] Overall, they appeared to constitute transnational crimes that merited punishment and international concern since mechanisms of State cooperation and provisions on extra-territorial jurisdiction could be triggered as a response to their commission. It is true that no other international tribunal before had jurisdiction over treaty-based crimes; however this lack of precedent did not pose any legal problem for the ILC to suggest their inclusion into the ICC's jurisdiction.[72]

Nevertheless, the incorporation of treaty crimes into the ICC's jurisdiction was confronted with two serious legal complexities. The first concerned the fact that the relevant treaties create obligations only for the States that are Parties to them and do not extend to non-Parties. To the contrary, core crimes are prosecutable under

[65] However, the Appeals Chamber of the Special Tribunal for Lebanon, in the STL Decision, above n. 6, held, controversially, that a customary international crime of transnational terrorism in time of peace exists.

[66] For an examination of the differences between international crimes and crimes established by treaty see Ambos and Timmermann 2014. He argues however that an originally treaty-based crime can rise to a 'true' international crime by way of customary law (Ambos and Timmermann 2014, p. 25).

[67] UNGA 1991, paras 238–250.

[68] UNGA 1995a, b, paras 112–118.

[69] Boister 1998, p. 27.

[70] UNGA 1996a, b, Articles 16–20, including only aggression, genocide, crimes against humanity, crimes against UN personnel and war crimes.

[71] UNGA 1993, para 282.

[72] Boister 1998, p. 30.

general international law without any discrimination between Parties and non-Parties to the Rome Statute.[73] Secondly, the status of treaty crimes as international crimes *stricto sensu* must be established separately from the fact that they are regulated under a specific treaty. In *Prosecutor v Tadić*, the International Criminal Tribunal for the former Yugoslavia held that, for a conduct to turn into a crime under international law, three criteria must be met: (i) the prohibition of the particular act(s) must be a part of international law, (ii) the breach must affect important universal values and (iii) the breach must entail individual responsibility in its own right, regardless of its criminalisation under domestic criminal laws.[74] This third criterion requires that a prohibition of a certain conduct must 'have a direct binding effect on individuals, without state mediation, and it has to be prosecutable either by the ICC or [...] by states, independent of specific jurisdictional links'.[75] Ambos and Timmermann argue further that this requirement of 'universal prosecutability' is what ultimately makes States to 'express their serious interest in the recognition of certain conduct as a crime under [international criminal law] *stricto sensu*'.[76]

Be that as it may, there is no reason in principle why the ICC should not have jurisdiction over treaty crimes even if it has to follow a 'selective application' approach for treaty crimes as opposed to the universal application for the core crimes.[77] As Boister argues, a 'selective application' approach would mean that with respect to treaty crimes, the ICC would not exercise jurisdiction automatically but only when the State concerned is linked in a jurisdictionally acceptable way to the relevant treaty or when it consents to the ICC's jurisdiction over the conduct in question. In contrast, with respect to the core crimes, 'universal application' means that the ICC's jurisdiction is automatic due to the universality principle and the customary status the core crimes have attained. With respect to treaty crimes, there will be no legal hurdle for the ICC to have jurisdiction in cases where the State of nationality of the offender or the State in whose territory the crime has been committed, are Parties to the Rome Statute and to the relevant treaty because only under this condition would it be ensured that both States are under obligation to implement that treaty. Of course, a single regime of universal application of the Rome Statute provisions would be more preferable,[78] but on the other hand, perpetrators should not simply escape justice due to jurisdictional technicalities.[79] Moreover, and with respect to terrorism as a treaty crime, the situation is

[73] Boister 2009, p. 347. For the ICC's jurisdiction over nationals of States non-Parties see Morris 2000, p. 363; Akande 2003, p. 618.

[74] ICTY, *Prosecutor v Tadić,* Decision on the Defence Motion for Interlocutory Appeal on Jurisdiction, 2 October 1995, Case No. ICTY-94-1, para 94. The Article 5 crimes of the Rome Statute meet all the above requirements.

[75] Ambos and Timmermann 2014, p. 26.

[76] Ibid., p. 27.

[77] Boister 1998, p. 31.

[78] Boister 1998, p. 31.

[79] Sailer 1999, p. 330.

significantly ameliorated by the fact that most States Parties to the Rome Statute are Parties to the two most popular anti-terrorist treaties,[80] the Terrorist Bombings and the Financing of Terrorism Conventions. These two treaties have far more Parties than the Rome Statute at the time of writing, which means that the situation most likely to arise is that of a State being a Party to one or both treaties, but not to the Rome Statute, an occasion which rules out ICC's jurisdiction altogether.

Turning now to the customary status of the crime of terrorism, opinions are divided as to whether treaty crimes in general and terrorism in particular can constitute violations of customary law. On the one hand, it has been argued that treaty crimes cannot be considered as international crimes at all[81]; the crimes regulated by the treaties are already codified in national laws, so it is not the treaties that create the crimes, but the States that enact them.[82] Besides, these treaties do not produce any direct relation between the States Parties to them and the individual offender except the one already established under the States' national laws.[83] Thus, one can talk about national crimes for which there is a level of international concern and not for international crimes *stricto sensu*, such as the core crimes, for which individual criminal responsibility is established in customary law. On the other hand, Cassese argues that terrorist offences—at least those included in international treaties—are prohibited by customary law, and thus, can no longer be considered only as treaty crimes.[84] This affirmation has been based on the increasing number of statements and declarations of States and international organisations, as well as actions taken by States in the fight against terrorism at various levels, evincing that terrorism has become a crime under customary law.[85] This view is also supported by Wertheim and others, who further argue that both current State practice and *opinio juris*[86] attest this transition.[87] Under this approach, treaty-based crimes cannot be excluded from being developed into crimes under customary law, provided that both State practice and *opinio juris* point to that direction.

Even if terrorism, for all the above reasons, has some potential to be included into Article 5 of the Rome Statute, it still needs to be defined for the purposes of attributing individual criminal liability. In this respect, it is crucial to examine how some recent definitional frameworks for terrorism are influenced by the two main international law theories, namely the State-centric theory and cosmopolitanism. The instruments chosen for such an analysis are firstly, the most significant

[80] Up to date, the Parties to the Rome Statute are 124 whereas the number of the Parties to these two treaties is much higher: 169 Parties to the Terrorist Bombings Convention and 187 to the Financing of Terrorism Convention. See *United Nations Treaty Collection* database.

[81] Boister 2003, p. 963.

[82] Boister 2009, p. 350.

[83] Ibid.

[84] Cassese 2004, p. 218.

[85] Ibid., p. 224.

[86] STL Decision, above n. 6; Saul 2011, p. 677.

[87] Wertheim 2003, p. 5; Filippo 2008, p. 561; Much 2006, p. 125.

anti-terrorist Security Council Resolutions,[88] which, it will be argued, show a preference towards the protection of State sovereignty interests, even sometimes at the expense of cosmopolitan purposes. Secondly, the STL Decision, which dynamically concluded that there is a customary definition of international terrorism, will be analysed as an example of whether and how cosmopolitan considerations alone can push the development of international law even without due regard to State sovereignty protection. Finally, the so far unsuccessful UN negotiations on a Draft Comprehensive Convention on International Terrorism will be used as an example of the extent to which State sovereignty and cosmopolitan considerations alike can be taken into account in the effort to define and criminalise international terrorism.

5.3 How State Sovereignty Concerns Have Influenced the Process of Criminalising International Terrorism in Prominent Anti-Terrorist Security Council Resolutions

Although a significant number of international anti-terrorist legal instruments have been drafted since 1970 obliging States to criminalise different aspects of terrorist activities,[89] this section is going to focus on some post 9/11 Security Council Resolutions. The reason for this selection is that the Security Council Resolutions drafted after the 9/11 attacks reflect the more recent stance that the Security Council has adopted with respect to what it understands by 'terrorism' as well as what it regards as the best way to confront it.[90] Contrary to the several anti-terrorist conventions which cover and define specific terrorist activities, Security Council Resolutions offer a more generic approach as to how terrorism is understood, and even the fact that they lack an umbrella definition for terrorism is indicative of this understanding. Finally, these Resolutions were chosen also for the reason that they revealingly give space to States to confront terrorism unilaterally, without any outer legal boundaries of what is defined as terrorism or which the lawful means to combat it are. This latest attitude towards terrorism reveals that, despite the coordinated UN efforts for a multilateral fight against terrorism and despite the several legal frameworks provided by the anti-terrorist treaties, States have the discretion to

---

[88] UNSC 2001a, b, 2004.

[89] For a list of all international anti-terrorist instruments since 1970, see UN, International Legal Instruments, www.un.org/en/terrorism/instruments.shtml.

[90] Nuotio 2006, pp. 1002–1003.

choose unilaterally what they understand as terrorism, even if this understanding conflicts with their international obligations.[91]

First of all, it should be remembered that Security Council Resolutions do not create law and are driven mostly by political considerations.[92] However, they prescibe normative obligations for the Member States under the UN Charter.[93] They evince general principles of law and they can assist in interpreting Charter provisions.[94] In this respect, it has been argued that the actions and decisions of the Security Council have legal consequences,[95] framed by the terms used in the Resolutions, the surrounding discussions, the invoked Charter provisions and the circumstances.[96] Moreover, Security Council Resolutions acquire additional value due to their precedential effect in similar situations,[97] especially regarding issues of international peace and security, where 'the body of principles is still so fragmentary and abstract'.[98] Therefore, resolutions adopted right after the 9/11 attacks merit a detailed examination, in order to understand how the Security Council approached the issue of international terrorism by focusing mostly on the most appropriate measures to combat it.

5.3.1 'Threat to the Peace', 'Armed Attack' or Both? The Pro-State Sovereignty Ambiguousness of Resolution 1368

Security Council Resolution 1368 (Resolution 1368), drafted one day after the 9/11, revealed on the one hand the intention of the Security Council to take on the responsibility of responding to the attacks while, on the other hand, it left the door

[91] For example, the lack of a definition for terrorism in Resolution 1373 permitted Syria to adopt the definition contained in the Arab Convention for the Suppression of Terrorism (opened for signature 22 April 1998), which distinguishes between terrorism and legitimate struggle against foreign occupation (Article 2). The Financing of Terrorism Convention, above n. 3, does not make such a distinction and thus, violent acts regarded as terrorist by the Financing Convention, fell outside the scope of the Syrian definition (Talmon 2005, p. 189). Apparently, this is only one of the interpretative problems created by Security Council Resolutions due to the lack of an international definition for terrorism. For a more elaborative analysis on this issue, see Ibid., pp. 188–192.

[92] Saul 2005, p. 142.

[93] Ibid.

[94] Ibid.

[95] Brichambaut 2001, p. 268.

[96] ICJ, *Legal Consequences for States of the Continued Presence of South Africa in Namibia (South West Africa) notwithstanding Security Council Resolution 276* (1970), Advisory Opinion, 21 June 1971, ICJ Rep 41.

[97] Schachter 1964, pp. 963–964.

[98] Ibid., p. 964.

open for unilateral State response. Resolution 1368 attempted to promote international justice goals by regarding the attacks as crimes and by making reference to 'bringing the perpetrators to justice',[99] an expression that signifies that one day after the attacks, the terrorist acts were primarily seen as criminal rather than acts of war. A further indication that the Security Council had not, at least initially, ruled out the possibility of collective action, was the recognition that the attacks constituted a threat to international peace and security,[100] a characterisation which triggers Security Council's competence to take action. However, Resolution 1368 appeared to take into serious consideration the sovereign interests of the UN Member States, since it made explicit reference to the 'the inherent right of individual or collective self-defence in accordance with the Charter'[101] in connection with a terrorist act. This reference would not necessarily have created any confusion since it only repeated the words of the UN Charter. However, its connection with a terrorist act was something unprecedented for a Security Council Resolution.[102] Despite the assertion of the Security Council that it is ready to 'take all necessary steps to respond to the terrorist attacks…and to combat all forms of terrorism',[103] it did not authorise any collective military action, leaving room for unilateral State response.[104] Article 51 of the UN Charter provides for a temporary right to self-defence, which, in theory, is terminated once the Security Council takes all the necessary measures for the maintenance of international peace and security.[105] Between the conflicting ideas of collective security and self-defence,[106] the Security Council seemed to lean towards the latter as the most appropriate way to respond to a terrorist attack, even though it was not yet clarified on the day the Resolution was drafted, whether the attacks had been committed by private actors or were State-sponsored, in which case the self-defence arguments would have had a sound basis.[107]

In this respect, it seems that, according to the Security Council's understanding, a terrorist act can constitute a form of armed attack within the context of the UN Charter, since self-defence is recognised as a legitimate response. This recognition

---

[99] UNSC 2001a, para 3.

[100] Ibid., Preambular para 4.

[101] Ibid., '*Recognizing* the inherent right of individual or collective self-defence in accordance with the Charter…'.

[102] Fassbender 2004, pp. 86–87.

[103] UNSC 2001a, para 5.

[104] Saul 2005, p. 155.

[105] Gray 2010, p. 633. In practice, the Security Council usually avoids making pronouncements on the legality of the right to self-defence, with the exception of UNSC 1990, where it openly supported Kuwait's right to self-defence against Iraq.

[106] Cassese argues that the characterisation of the 9/11 attacks as a threat to the peace does not legitimise self-defence because the concept of a threat to the peace differs from that of an armed attack, for which Article 51 of the UN Charter recognises the right to self-defence (Cassese 2001, p. 996); Fassbender 2004, p. 88.

[107] Fassbender 2004, p. 88.

signifies that a terrorist act, at least of the magnitude of the 9/11 attacks, is better addressed in the context of the UN Charter (by invocation of Article 51) rather than international criminal justice. In other words, the Security Council viewed that, in that particular case, what mattered most was not to hold those responsible accountable under international criminal law, not even under national criminal law, but rather, to ensure that the US could act unilaterally in whatever way deemed appropriate. However, what is of relevance to the question of defining terrorism is that, a definition formulated for international criminal law purposes will be interpreted and used in a more cosmopolitan way than that of providing the right to use force to the victim State of a terrorist attack as a way of response. Those States wary of seeing international terrorism defined in the context of international criminal law might fear that such a definition will not leave room for the use of force as a legitimate response to a terrorist act or generally, it will not allow any other response different from the conduct of a trial either at a national or an international level. Resolution 1368 demonstrated that, precisely because there is no definition of international terrorism, its context can be broadened to an extent which overlaps with the concept of armed attack and which justifies the use of force as a legitimate response.

Therefore, the terrorist attacks of 9/11 seem to have expanded the notion of armed attack, in order to cover attacks carried out by terrorist, non-State groups.[108] Even before 9/11, the US, among other States, promoted this widened right of self-defence,[109] but the response to this position has never been clear enough.[110] The International Court of Justice (ICJ) in the *Nicaragua* case held that self-defence can constitute a response to

> the sending by or on behalf of a State of armed bands, groups, irregulars or mercenaries, which carry out acts of armed forces against another State of such gravity as to amount to (*inter alia*) an actual armed attack conducted by regular armed forces, or its substantial involvement therein.[111]

Thus, according to the ICJ's ruling, self-defence as a response to an attack committed by non-State actors can be justified only when there is a close link between a State and a non-State actor and the seriousness of the committed acts is analogous to an attack committed by a State.[112]

---

[108] Gray 2010, p. 626. See also Wilmshurst 2006, pp. 969–971, where it is widely argued that self-defence can be invoked against non-State actors when the State on whose territory they are based, is either unwilling or unable to take action against them.

[109] Byers 2002, p. 406. US Secretary of State George Shultz stated in 1986 that '[i]t is absurd to argue that international law prohibits us from capturing terrorists in international waters or airspace; from attacking them on the soil of other nations, even for the purpose of rescuing hostages; or from using force against states that support, train, and harbor terrorists or guerrillas' (in Schultz 1986, p. 206).

[110] Byers 2002, p. 407.

[111] ICJ, *Case Concerning Military and Paramilitary Activities in and against Nicaragua (Nicaragua v United States of America)*, Merits, 27 June 1986, ICJ Rep 14, para 195.

[112] Byers 2002, p. 408.

In State practice, incidents prior to 9/11 have shown that attacks by non-State actors do not *per se* justify an invocation of the right to self-defence by the victim State. When Israel attacked the Palestine Liberation Organisation Headquarters in Tunisia in 1985 claiming to be attacking terrorist targets under its right of self-defence, the Security Council condemned that action.[113] Also, following the bombings in US embassies in Kenya and Tanzania in 1998, the US, claiming its right to self-defence, launched a cruise missiles attack against Sudan and Afghanistan in an effort to target the terrorists that were allegedly in their territory.[114] Several governments expressed concerns related to the violation of these States' territorial sovereignty, as the attacks were not directed against the States themselves.[115] Moreover, even in cases where there was evidence of State implication in a terrorist act, self-defence arguments were not sufficient to justify the use of force. When the US bombed Tripoli in 1986 as a response to a terrorist bomb attack in a nightclub in Berlin that killed American soldiers, their claim to self-defence was widely rejected.[116] However, regarding a post-9/11 attack by non-State actors against Israel, the Security Council remained silent as to whether the attack could be classified as armed attack and thus, justify Israel's right to self-defence. In the case of Hezbollah's minor cross-border attack against Israeli forces from Lebanon in 2006, Israel responded in a rather disproportionate manner, launching attacks by land, sea and air, provoking destruction to Lebanese infrastructure and causing massive population displacement.[117] The Security Council avoided discussions related to the Israel's right to self-defence and focused on issues of proportionality. Most States found the Israeli response disproportionate to the initial attack, while Israel, the US and the UK argued that the continuous threat posed by Hezbollah justified the use of force in order to prevent future attacks.[118]

As was noted previously, at the time when Resolution 1368 was drafted, it was not clear whether there was a close link between the non-State actors that carried out the 9/11 attacks and a State (in this case the State of Afghanistan). Thus, the question remained whether the right to self-defence can be extended in order to cover military responses to terrorist acts carried out by non-State actors only. Therefore, while Resolution 1368 did not explicitly authorise the use of force by the US as the victim State, it was drafted and interpreted in such a way so as to implicitly encourage the US to claim its right to self-defence by taking unilateral military action.[119] The reference to the inherent right of individual or collective self-defence could not but be recognised as a legitimisation of resort to force by the

[113] UNSC 1985.

[114] Byers 2002, p. 407.

[115] Final Document of the XIIth Summit of the Non-aligned Movement, para 159.

[116] Reisman 1999, pp. 33–34. In fact, the Security Council attempted to issue a resolution stating that the US attack was a violation of the UN Charter (Ibid.).

[117] Gray 2010, p. 630.

[118] Ibid., 631.

[119] Bianchi 2004, p. 500.

victim that suffered the attack.[120] Had the Security Council authorised the use of force explicitly in Resolution 1368, it would have been likely that the Security Council would also impose a time-limited mandate on the use of force carried out in self-defence or that it would authorise force in a necessary and proportionate manner, namely for the purpose to capture Osama Bin Laden and members of Al Qaeda only.[121] Thus, the controversial interpretation of Resolution 1368 as implicitly providing an argument for the US to use force without directly authorising it, is obviously the result of the ambiguous drafting of the Resolution which, in turn, is indicative of the political divide among the main actors of international politics on how to combat terrorism. As a general remark, it can be said that this political divide, particularly among the five permanent members of the Security Council, makes the UN decision-making process even harder, with the Security Council members either exercising their right of veto or threatening to exercise it or resorting to ambiguous drafting in an effort to accommodate all their political interests.[122] For the purposes of this book, this ambuiguousness was partly due to the fact that international terrorism still remains outside the realm of international criminal justice and without a universally accepted definition. As such, until an international definition is agreed upon, the fight against international terrorism will heavily rely on individual (and the most powerful) States' understanding of what constitutes the best response, even if this response requires the use of force in a manner not clearly envisioned by the provisions of the UN Charter.

5.3.2 Resolution 1373: Security Council Legislation Without UN Definition

Turning now to Security Council Resolution 1373 (Resolution 1373), it has been argued that the Security Council adopted a more legislative role[123] in combatting international terrorism by introducing wide-ranging counter-terrorism measures. Resolution 1373 included three types of obligations imposed on States: (i) mandatory measures against terrorism financing, (ii) different types of measures against terrorism (which were also mandatory) and (iii) general counter-terrorism measures which States are just 'called upon' to adopt.[124] Moreover, the text of the Resolution reaffirmed the inherent right to self-defence and repeated the assertion that the

---

[120] Ibid.

[121] Byers 2002, p. 401.

[122] Bianchi 2002, p. 503.

[123] Ibid., p. 498; Talmon 2005; Szasz 2002, pp. 901–904.

[124] Hinojosa-Martínez 2014, pp. 626–627.

attacks constituted a threat to international peace and security.[125] However, the reference to the Security Council's readiness to 'take all necessary steps to respond…' was omitted and instead obligations were imposed on States to outlaw *inter alia* the financing of terrorist acts and to improve international cooperation. Thirdly, Resolution 1373 established the Counter-Terrorism Committee (CTC) with the mandate to monitor the implementation of the Resolution and to receive State reports on actions they take in the fight against terrorism.[126]

Resolution 1373 also stated that threats to international peace and security caused by terrorist acts should be combatted 'by all means', an expression which cleared the ground for any US military action against Afghanistan.[127] By the time Resolution 1373 was adopted, it had been made clear that the US was not going to subject its military response to the rules and procedures of the Security Council, which, as a sign of support to the US, stepped back from its responsibility for collective security under the UN Charter.[128] Thus, the US could base their military actions against those considered as their targets on self-defence arguments.[129] In this respect, the paradox created by Resolution 1373 is that, while the Security Council abstained from triggering Chapter VII provisions for the purpose of authorising force (and did not authorise force even as a continuation of the unilateral US response), it overstepped its role as an executive organ to assume an unprecedented legislative competence. The language of Resolution 1373, focusing on the inherent right to self-defence, appeared to give an almost unlimited competence to the US to use force.[130] It has been argued that, if the Security Council had not made any reference to the right of self-defence in the two Resolutions, then it would have been forced to remain silent altogether, probably due to a likely exercise of veto by the US, and thus, its role would not have been any greater.[131] However, it is still one thing for the Security Council to remain silent due to the veto power while otherwise condemning a particular course of action[132] and another thing to pass ambiguous Resolutions implying support to an act which can be seen as a violation of the UN Charter. Even if it is accepted that after the 9/11

[125] UNSC 2001b, '*Reaffirming further* that such acts, like any act of international terrorism, constitute a threat to international peace and security, *[r]eaffirming* the inherent right of individual or collective self-defence as recognized by the Charter of the United Nations as reiterated in resolution 1368 (2001) …'.

[126] Ibid., preambular para 2. For an elaborate analysis of the CTC's work and progress since the adoption of Resolution 1373 see Hinojosa-Martinez 2014.

[127] Subedi 2002, p. 160.

[128] Fassbender 2004, p. 89.

[129] Ibid. See also Byers 2002, p. 402, arguing that '[t]he point, therefore, is not that the resolution *should* (emphasis in the text) be read as authorising the use of force…but that it *could* (emphasis in the text) provide the US with an at-least-tenable argument whenever and wherever it decides, for political reasons, that force is necessary to "prevent the commission of terrorist acts"'.

[130] Byers 2002, p. 401.

[131] Fassbender 2004, p. 91.

[132] As happened with the 1986 US bombing against Libya. See text to above n. 116.

attacks, the right to self-defence has been widened in order to cover terrorist attacks carried out by non-State actors, it has been argued that a possible restriction to this 'new doctrine' of self-defence is that this right 'may exist only in cases where [it] has been asserted by the Security Council, as…in Resolutions 1368 and 1373.'[133] The US expected Security Council backing[134] and the Security Council responded with a resolution that could be interpreted according to the US's expectations.[135] These expectations, according to Byers, might include a US strategic movement of loosening international law on the use of force 'to the *ongoing* (emphasis in the text) advantage of the US', even when circumstances are not as grave.[136]

This preference of the Security Council to support an individual State's sovereign interests and not to assume its responsibility of collective security in a circumstance characterised as a threat to international peace and security reflects the tendency towards the protection of a State's own political priorities in the fight against terrorism. This tendency is also evidenced by the fact that neither the Resolution nor the CTC introduced a definition for terrorism. While, generally, the work of the CTC aims at promoting a coordinated effort in combatting terrorism, more prone to a cosmopolitan model of law implementation,[137] the lack of an agreed definition of terrorism showed that this was not possible. In the past, the absence of a definition did not create any implications since no international rights or duties were built upon the terms 'terrorism' or 'terrorist' but after the adoption of Resolution 1373 this has changed.[138] The Resolution relies greatly on these terms, creating obligations for States to criminalise financing of *terrorism*; suppress *terrorist* groups; deny refugee status to *terrorists*; prevent the movement of *terrorists*; bring *terrorists* to justice; and, vitally, establish *terrorist acts* as serious domestic crimes. The lack of a definition, though it made it easier to achieve consensus on the text of the Resolution,[139] allowed States to unilaterally define terrorist acts without having any outer international legal standards of what is terrorism or who is considered as terrorist.[140] The CTC relied on domestic terrorism laws which, it

[133] Gray 2010, p. 630.

[134] Ibid.

[135] Fassbender 2004, p. 88.

[136] Byers 2002, p. 410. Byers further argues that '[h]ad the US relied on arguments of Security Council authorisation, invitation or humanitarian intervention, it is unlikely that many States would have objected, but next time it would have been more difficult to act alone or in the absence of such additional conditions'.

[137] While the CTC's main mandate was to evaluate States' implementation of Resolution 1373, it progressively responded to States in a more detailed and stringent manner, as weaknesses in national counter-terrorism law and policy were exposed. At some point, States became uncomfortable with the revelation of their defects and differences with the CTC, and as a result, the publication of State reports was discontinued from 2007 (in Hinojosa-Martinez 2014).

[138] Saul 2008, p. 6.

[139] Ibid., p. 6.

[140] Ibid., p. 6.

advocated, should be widened in order to cover international terrorism,[141] encouraging States to ratify the anti-terrorist conventions. Leaving so much discretion on States and on their domestic legal systems to implement their own framework on terrorist cases results in divergence in the adoption of counter-terrorism measures,[142] in the lack of harmonisation of national definitions for terrorism and in an arbitrary categorisation of a variety of national security or public order offences as terrorist.[143] Moreover, the text of Resolution 1373 does not designate specific temporal or geographical limitations concerning the States' response to terrorism[144] and characterises terrorism in general as a threat to international peace and security.[145] While incidents of terrorism such as the 9/11 attacks or the 2002 and 2005 Bali bombings reach the threshold of threat to international peace and security, it is difficult to say that this holds true for any terrorist attack. This very broad scope of the Resolution's mandate and the wide discretion of States to define their own 'terrorisms', results in a widened State discretion to identify particular incidences as terrorist without any kind of criteria of reference.[146]

The definitional gap left open by Resolution 1373 as to what constitutes terrorism was partly remedied by Security Council Resolution 1566 (Resolution 1566) which, though not expressly referring to a definition for terrorism, sets a frame about which acts are unjustifiable under any circumstances:

> criminal acts, including against civilians, committed with the intent to cause death or serious bodily injury, or taking of hostages, with the purpose to provoke a state of terror in the general public or in a group of persons or particular persons, intimidate a population or compel a government or an international organization to do or to abstain from doing any act, and all other acts which constitute offences within the scope of and as defined in the international conventions and protocols relating to terrorism, are under no circumstances justifiable by considerations of a political, philosophical, ideological, racial, ethnic, religious or other similar nature…[147]

[141] CTC Chair (Ambassador Jeremy Greenstock) 2002.

[142] Saul 2005, p. 160.

[143] Saul 2008, p. 6. With respect to human rights violations in the context of countering terrorism, the main areas of concern are: '(i) the abusive application of state of emergency laws to presumed terrorists with the consequent denial of fundamental rights, (ii) the enactment of special laws for the investigation and prosecution of terrorism that allow for long preventative or military detentions, inaccessibility to secret information for the detainee's lawyers, or grave infringements of the right to privacy, and (iii) overtly broad definitions of terrorism or of incitement to terrorism in national legislation as an excuse to restrict freedom of expression, conscience and assembly, or to repress political opposition.' (Hinojosa-Martinez 2014, p. 636).

[144] Krisch 2004, p. 889.

[145] UNSC 2001b, '*Reaffirming further* that such acts, like any act of international terrorism, constitute a threat to international peace and security,…'.

[146] Brownlie 1963, p. 356.

[147] UNSC 2004, para 3.

This paragraph of Resolution 1566, seen mostly as a compromise among the States Members of the UN rather than an attempt to define the concept of terrorism,[148] reveals that it is a common acknowledgment among the Security Council that terrorism is the aggregate of the definitions already provided in international anti-terrorist instruments.[149] It is a definition limited to acts constituting sectoral offences as well as 'all other acts which constitute offences within the scope of and as defined in the international conventions and protocols relating to terrorism'. Therefore, this paragraph adds little to the development of the legal concept of terrorism.[150] Consequently, its usefulness and precedential value remains doubtful. Also, in the 3-year time lapse since the adoption of Resolution 1373, States would have already adopted domestic anti-terrorist laws which it would be very unlikely to reform in order to conform them with the text of the Resolution 1566.[151]

The above analysis reflects the Security Council's conviction that international terrorism can—and obviously should—be combatted without the adoption of a universal definition for it, since it suffices to turn to domestic anti-terrorist legislation and definitions. The Security Council, instead of defending the powers conferred on it by the UN Charter, views a decentralised response to international terrorism as a more opportune means to combat it, regardless of the cost that this response may bear to the international order it is meant to protect. On the other hand, we have recently witnessed efforts to criminalise international terrorism in a rather cosmopolitan perspective. These efforts include the STL Decision, which identified a customary international crime of transnational terrorism[152] as well as the ongoing discussions on a UN Draft Comprehensive Convention on International Terrorism, seeking to define the crime at an international level and delimit the scope of application of such a Convention. Although there is some criticism of these efforts, judicial intervention in the development of international law for the former and substantial divergence in States' attitude towards different aspects of terrorism for the latter, both these steps should be considered as noteworthy efforts in the 'cosmopolitan' fight against terrorism. Therefore, the last section of this chapter is going to examine how the cosmopolitan theory has influenced recent attempts to define and criminalise international terrorism, at times provoking reactions about bold judicial decisions but also creating hope for more concerted and less politically driven efforts towards this end.

[148] UN Press Release 2004.

[149] Young 2006, p. 45.

[150] Ibid., p. 46.

[151] Saul 2005, p. 165.

[152] STL Decision, above n. 6.

5.4 Pro-Cosmopolitan Efforts to Define and Criminalise International Terrorism

5.4.1 Judicial Activism Versus State Sovereignty: A Customary Law Definition of International Terrorism?

As opposed to the Security Council's approach in combatting terrorism, the cosmopolitan approach favours a more centralised response to international terrorism, without much room for State sovereignty concerns. Even before the STL Decision, which identified a customary international crime of transnational terrorism, Cassese argued that 'a customary rule on the objective and subjective elements of a crime of terrorism in time of peace has evolved'.[153] Di Filippo is also of the view that 'a definition of a terrorist crime is already present in the mass of international practice' and that it 'could quickly enjoy customary status'[154] and Much also contended that 'terrorist acts—at least the most severe ones—have advanced into the category of international crimes.'[155] The most recent and indicative example of this cosmopolitan approach with respect to terrorism is the Decision of the Appeals Chamber (AC) of the Special Tribunal of Lebanon (16 February 2011), which, among other things, ruled that there is a customary law definition of international terrorism[156] and that this definition should be applied in the interpretation of domestic terrorist offences under Lebanese law.[157] The STL was established after Security Council Resolution 1757 (Resolution 1757)[158] with jurisdiction over the crime of terrorism, to prosecute those responsible for the 2005 assassination of Lebanese Prime Minister Rafiq Hariri and twenty-two others.[159] After a request of the Pre-Trial judge, the AC issued a ruling concerning questions on, among other things, the substantive criminal law to be applied by the STL, and held unanimously that a customary law definition of the international crime of terrorism exists. Although this ruling may contribute to the emergence of an international crime of terrorism and to its definition,[160] there has been much controversy among scholars[161] about this type of judicial activism which, according to Saul, invented a new

[153] Cassese 2006, p. 935. This view is also shared by Londras 2010, pp. 175–176.
[154] Filippo 2008, p. 561.
[155] Much 2006, p. 125.
[156] STL Decision, above n. 6, paras 83 and 85.
[157] Ibid., paras 19–20.
[158] UNSC 2007.
[159] STL Decision, above n. 6, para 13.
[160] Ambos 2011, p. 655; Ventura 2011, p. 1041 (arguing that States that negotiate the UNGA Draft Comprehensive Convention might benefit from this ruling).
[161] Ambos 2011, p. 675; Saul 2011.

and *post facto* individual criminal liability for terrorism[162] and overruled the judicial sovereignty of Lebanon.

In particular, the points of contention were: firstly that a customary international law definition for terrorism, at least in time of peace, exists and has been crystallised by UN Resolutions, international treaties and legislative and judicial State practice,[163] and secondly that the Lebanese criminal code provisions with respect to terrorism should be construed in accordance with international treaty and customary law.[164] Regarding the first point, the AC concluded that the customary definition of terrorism has three key elements:

(i) the perpetration of a criminal act (such as murder, kidnapping, hostage-taking, arson, and so on), or threatening such an act;
(ii) the intent to spread fear among the population (which would generally entail the creation of public danger) or directly or indirectly coerce a national or international authority to take some action, or to refrain from taking it and
(iii) when the act involves a transnational element.[165]

While neither the prosecution nor the defence agreed that terrorism is a customary law crime,[166] the prosecution coincidentally asserted that the first two elements of the offence, as concluded by the AC, constituted components of a potential customary norm.[167] However, the requirement of a transnational element goes beyond purely domestic Lebanese law.[168] The AC's subject-matter jurisdiction and applicable law 'remain national in character'[169] and thus, the Lebanese criminal law provisions are the applicable law.[170] Of course, the STL, being an international or mixed tribunal, should only apply national law which is compatible with international law and 'high standards of justice'[171]; in other words, international law can serve as an interpretative aid in cases of correcting 'unreasonable' or 'manifestly unjust' national law.[172] However, the AC moved beyond this approach, favouring a teleological interpretation of the law from the start, rather than determining first the existence of a lacuna and then closing it by interpretation.[173] Namely, the AC did not find any 'unreasonable' or 'manifestly unjust' national law and try to correct it by interpretation; rather it concluded from the start that since the

[162] Saul 2011, p. 678.
[163] STL Decision, above n. 6, paras 85–89.
[164] Ibid., paras 45 and 62.
[165] Ibid., para 85.
[166] Saul 2011, p. 677.
[167] STL Decision, above n. 6, para 85.
[168] Saul 2011, p. 679.
[169] UNSC 2006, para 7.
[170] UNSC 2007, Statute of the Special Tribunal for Lebanon, Article 2.
[171] UNSC 2006, para 7.
[172] STL Decision, above n. 6, para 40.
[173] Ambos 2011, p. 658.

national applicable law should be compatible with international law, which provides a customary law definition of international terrorism, then this definition should be applicable in domestic Lebanese criminal code. This approach weighs heavily in favour of the role of cosmopolitan theory in the development of international law, by allowing the principle of teleological interpretation to overturn the principle *in dubio mitius*, which favours State sovereignty.[174] The Decision clearly states that the latter principle, according to which, 'in case of doubt, the most favourable construction [to State sovereignty] should be chosen', is indicative of an 'old international community' construed by sovereign States for sovereign States, where the role of the individual was limited or non existent.[175] Modern international courts no longer or rarely use this principle, since the 'modern international community' gives more weight to universal values and the doctrine of human rights rather than to State sovereignty interests.[176]

As Ambos argues, this line of argumentation, while totally compatible with the model of cosmopolitanism, overturns the sovereignty of Lebanon in a manner that is not justified by human rights concerns or other universal values.[177] Resolution 1757 which established the STL, makes a clear reference to 'the strict respect of the sovereignty…of Lebanon'[178] and the only issue in question did not concern human rights or universal values[179] but what the applicable law of the STL should be,[180] an issue addressed already in Article 2 of the STL Statute. As Ambos suggests, even the fact that the Security Council characterised the events in Lebanon as a threat to international peace and security cannot imply that the applicable law of the STL should be international law instead of the national applicable law.[181] This could have only been the case had the Security Council made an express reference that international law is the applicable law, a quite unlikely scenario given the fact that there is no international agreed definition of terrorism.[182]

The Decision of the STL reflected mostly the desire of the judges to push forward the development of international law in criminalising international terrorism without due regard to Lebanon's sovereignty as to the applicable law. While, from a cosmopolitan perspective, international law should develop independently from, and sometimes despite State sovereignty considerations, it should always move into certain boundaries which would ensure the legitimacy of this

[174] Ibid.

[175] STL Decision, above n. 6, para 29.

[176] Ibid.

[177] Ambos 2011, p. 659.

[178] UNSC 2007, Statute of the Special Tribunal for Lebanon, preamble para 3.

[179] For example, the STL exempted certain penalties from the applicable national law, namely the death penalty and forced labour, considering them too cruel to be applied by an international tribunal. See UNSC 2006, para 22.

[180] Ambos 2011, p. 659.

[181] Ibid.

[182] Ibid.

development. The STL Decision seems to surpass those boundaries by considering as fact something which, at best, constitutes a desirable development in international criminal law, namely the customary law definition of international terrorism. All in all, it remains to be seen whether this Decision will acquire a precedential value in the jurisprudence concerning international terrorism or will be overturned by future State practice and *opinio juris*.[183]

5.4.2 *The UNGA Draft Comprehensive Convention on International Terrorism: A Road to Balance?*

A less dynamic attempt to define international terrorism for the purpose of attributing individual criminal responsibility[184] has been made by the GA, starting in 1994, with the adoption of the Declaration on Measures to Eliminate International Terrorism, as part of the GA Resolution 49/60 of 9 December 1994.[185] This Resolution encouraged States to review existing international anti-terrorist legislation in order to ensure that all issues surrounding terrorism are covered by the existing international legal framework and in 1996, the GA established an Ad hoc Committee with the mandate to elaborate a comprehensive convention on international terrorism.[186]

However, the 9/11 attacks expedited the GA's efforts on drafting a comprehensive convention on international terrorism. Apart from the adoption of a Resolution on 12 September 2001,[187] which condemned the attacks, the GA felt pressured to respond to the events in a separate way than that of the Security Council.[188] The Ad hoc Committee submitted a report to the GA in its 56th Session in September 2001, with the points of contention that surfaced during its work regarding a draft comprehensive convention: (i) what the scope of this convention will be, (ii) how the crime of terrorism is going to be defined, (iii) whether activities of the armed forces during an armed conflict should be exempted from the convention and (iv) what the relationship between the draft convention and the sectoral anti-terrorist conventions should be.[189] Eventually, the issue of the drafting of a comprehensive convention on terrorism, along with the discussions about the

[183] In *R v Mohammed Gul*, the Court of Appeals of England and Wales issued a decision in line with the STL Decision and accepted that customary law has evolved so as to include an international crime of terrorism in times of peace. See Court of Appeals of England and Wales (Criminal Division) *R v Mohammed Gul*, Judgment, 22 February 2012, EWCA Crim 280. See also Coco 2013, p. 425.

[184] Perera 2014, p. 158.

[185] UNGA 1994.

[186] UNGA 1996a, b.

[187] UNGA 2001b.

[188] Hmoud 2006, p. 1035.

[189] UNGA 2001a.

abovementioned contentious matters, were assigned to a Working Group established for this purpose by the 6th Committee on 8 October 2001.[190]

The discussions about a comprehensive convention had as a starting point a proposal submitted by India.[191] After deliberations between States, there was substantial convergence in several of the proposed provisions, however the issues of the definition and the exemption from the convention of the activities of armed forces remained controversial.[192] In short, it could be said that the main controversy around these issues was the question of who could have the right to use force without the risk of being described as terrorist.[193] On the one hand, some States favoured the addition of a provision which would exclude from the scope of the convention any activities carried out for the purpose of a people's struggle for self-determination.[194] On the other hand, some States, the Organisation of Islamic Countries among them, sought to exclude Article 18(2) of the draft convention which provides for the non-applicability of the term 'terrorism' to the conduct of States. Both these suggestions reveal the real bone of contention with respect to defining terrorism, namely which group or individuals could have the privilege of carrying out any acts without the risk of being labelled as terrorist. The Indian proposal, with its Article 18(2), provides that '[t]he activities of armed forces during an armed conflict…' as well as 'the activities undertaken by the military forces of a state in the exercise of their official duties, (…) are not governed by this Convention',[195] leaving out of the scope of the convention any State terrorist activity. By the same token, the Malaysian proposal to exclude activities carried out for the purpose of self-determination would justify any acts carried out by private actors 'against foreign occupation, aggression, colonialism, and hegemony'.[196] While the right for self-determination is well established in international law,[197] it does not constitute an absolute right but is subjected to limitations in accordance with international humanitarian law.[198] Therefore, a struggle for self-determination is not justified if carried out by whatever means necessary but only when these means do not violate international humanitarian law provisions.

---

[190] UNGA Sixth Committee 2001, para 2.

[191] UNGA Sixth Committee 2000, Annex II.

[192] Ibid., Articles 2 and 18(2) respectively.

[193] Hmoud 2006, p. 1033.

[194] UNGA Sixth Committee 2000, Annex III, para 30 (Malaysian proposal on behalf of the Organisation of Islamic Countries [OIC] Group). The proposed provision was taken verbatim by the 1999 Convention of the Islamic Conference on Combatting International Terrorism, Article 2.

[195] UNGA 2000, Annex II, Article 18(2).

[196] UNGA Sixth Committee 2000, Annex III, Article 2.

[197] International Covenant on Civil and Political Rights, opened for signature 16 December 1966, 999 UNTS 171 (entered into force 23 March 1976) Article 1 which unequivocally provides for the right to self-determination to all people; 1977 Protocol Additional to the Geneva Conventions of 12 August 1949, and relating to the Protection of Victims of International Armed Conflicts, opened for signature 8 June 1977, 1125 UNTS 3 (entered into force 7 December 1978) Article 1(4).

[198] Subedi 2002, p. 165.

Despite the disagreements that emerged from the discussion on a draft comprehensive convention on terrorism, it should be noticed that the GA chose to follow a more long-term and systematic approach on the problem of international terrorism.[199] While definitely more time-consuming, the GA approach is commendable, in that it tries to accommodate the need to develop and push forward international law with respect to terrorism with the need to take into account State sovereignty considerations and the differing views of States in the field. Unlike the Security Council approach, which, after having assumed a role as a world legislator and imposed legal obligations to States, offered little or no development in the field of international law on terrorism, and the STL's approach, which offered a questionable one, it seems that GA's work, if ever completed, might be able to significantly develop international law in the field without giving rise to any legitimacy issues. However, the fact that the GA discussions on a comprehensive convention on terrorism have currently ceased, is indicative of the complexity of the issue and of the dubious willingness of States to finally evolve international law on terrorism.

5.5 Conclusion

The aim of this chapter was to demonstrate how the pro-sovereignty and pro-cosmopolitan theories are present at and substantially affect the development of international law in the field of terrorism. After the 9/11 attacks which initially triggered what has been known as 'the war on terror', the Security Council has urged States to combat terrorism by any means and has allowed unilateral State response against a terrorist act that, according to the text of the relevant Resolutions, amounted to a threat to international peace and security. Although by this determination one should have expected the Security Council to assume collective security measures, it seemed that the sovereign interests of the US, the victim State of the attack, superimposed unilateral US action over collective UN response. Before the 9/11 events, attacks by non-State actors did not amount to an armed attack[200] and thus invocation of the right of self-defence by the victim State was often rejected. At the other end of spectrum, the STL held that the international law on terrorism has been developed to such an extent that a customary law definition of terrorism has been indeed crystallised and can therefore be applied in a terrorist case which would otherwise fall under the jurisdiction of Lebanon (and its national law provisions). Both these efforts of criminalising and defining terrorism reveal the weaknesses that each of the two theories bring along, weaknesses that are reflected in the very development of international law that these efforts mean to promote. As

---

[199] Ibid., p. 161.

[200] Wood 2014, p. 197. After 9/11 however, self-defence can be invoked against non-State actors if the State where the perpetrators are based is either unwilling or unable to take action against them. See Wilmshurst 2006, pp. 969–971.

was also noted above, the Security Council Resolutions did not bring any substantial development in international law on terrorism whereas it is still questionable whether the STL Decision has indeed cleared the way for the emergence of a customary rule definition of terrorism.

Lastly, the GA negotiations for a draft convention on terrorism have been analysed as a pro-cosmopolitan effort, differing however from the bold judicial activism of the STL. Despite the existence of the system of anti-terrorist treaties, the GA acknowledged the need for a comprehensive convention on terrorism with an agreed universal definition without sidestepping State sovereign interests. Therefore, and without disregarding sound criticism concerning the length of the negotiations, the GA efforts serve so far as the best example of how the required balance between State sovereignty and cosmopolitan theories might be achieved. With these conclusions in mind, the next chapter will try to demonstrate how the 'State sovereignty versus cosmopolitanism' debate is still relevant not only in the process of criminalisation but also in that of definition. Having already argued that aspects of the State sovereignty and cosmopolitan theories were manifest in the Kampala definition of the crime of aggression, the next chapter will suggest how due balance between the two theories could be similarly achieved in the context of defining international terrorism.

References

Akande D (2003) The Jurisdiction of the International Criminal Court over Nationals of Non-Parties: Legal Basis and Limits. JICJ 1: 618–650

Ambos K (2011) Judicial Creativity at the Special Tribunal for Lebanon: Is There a Crime of Terrorism under International Law? Leiden J Int'l L 24: 655–675

Ambos K, Timmermann A (2014) Terrorism and Customary International Law. In: Saul B (ed) Research Handbook on International Law and Terrorism. Edward Elgar, Cheltenham, pp 20–38

Bassiouni MC, Wise EM (1995) Aut Dedere aut Judicare: The Duty to Extradite or Prosecute in International Law. Kluwer, The Hague

BBC (2011) Cuba Anger at US Posada Carriles Verdict. www.bbc.co.uk/news/world-latin-america-13026870. Accessed 21 February 2017

Bianchi A (2004) Enforcing International Law Norms Against Terrorism: Achievements and Prospects. In: Bianchi A (ed) Enforcing International Law Norms Against Terrorism. Hart Publishing, Oregon, pp 492–534

Boister N (1998) The Exclusion of Treaty Crimes from the Jurisdiction of the Proposed International Criminal Court: Law, Pragmatism, Politics. Journal of Armed Conflict Law 3: 27–43

Boister N (2003) Transnational Criminal Law? EJIL 14(5):953–976

Boister N (2009) Treaty Crimes, International Criminal Court? New Crim L Rev 12:341–365

Brichambaut MP de (2001) The Role of the United Nations Security Council in the International Legal System. In: Byers M (ed) The Role of International Law in International Politics. Oxford University Press, Oxford, pp 269–276

Brownlie I (1963) International Law and the Use of Force by States. Clarendon Press, Oxford

Byers M (2002) Terrorism, the Use of Force and International Law after 11 September. ICLQ 51: 401–414

Cassese A (2001) Terrorism is Also Disrupting Some Legal Categories of International Law. 12(5) EJIL 12(5): 993–1001
Cassese A (2004) Terrorism as an International Crime. In: Bianchi A (ed) Enforcing International Law Norms Against Terrorism. Hart Publishing, Oregon, pp 213–225
Cassese A (2006) The Multifaceted Criminal Notion of Terrorism in International Law. JICJ 4: 933–958
Coco A (2013) The Mark of Cain: The Crime of Terrorism in Times of Armed Conflict as Interpreted by the Court of Appeals of England and Wales in *R v Mohammed Gul*. JICJ 11: 425–440
Creegan E (2010–11) A Permanent Hybrid Court for Terrorism. Am U Int'l L Rev 26:237–313
CTC Chair (Ambassador Jeremy Greenstock) (2002) Presentation to Symposium: Combating International Terrorism: The Contribution of the United Nations.
de Londras F (2010) Terrorism as an International Crime. In: Schabas W, Bernaz N (eds) Routledge International Book of Criminal Law. Routledge, London, pp 169–180
di Filippo M (2008) Terrorist Crimes and International Cooperation: Critical Remarks on the Definition and Inclusion of Terrorism in the Category of International Crimes. EJIL 19(3): 533–570
Dugard J (1997) Obstacles in the Way of an International Criminal Court. Camb L J 56(2): 329–342
Fassbender B (2004) The UN Security Council and International Terrorism. In: Bianchi A (ed) Enforcing International Law Norms Against Terrorism. Hart Publishing, Oregon, pp 83–102
Fenelly N (2007) The European Arrest Warrant: Recent Developments. ERA Forum 8: 519–534
Final Document of the XIIth Summit of the Non-aligned Movement (1998) Durban, South Africa. www.nam.gov.za/xiisummit. Accessed 21 February 2017
Fitsanakis J (2013) Turkey refused to extradite bin Laden's son-in-law to US. http://intelnews.org/2013/02/04/01–1189/#more-9905. Accessed 21 February 2017
Fry E (2012) Between Show Trials and Sham Prosecutions: The Rome Statute's Potential Effect on Domestic Due Process Protections. Crim L F 23: 35–62
Gray C (2010) The Use of force and the International Legal Order. In: Evans M (ed) International Law, 3rd edn. Oxford University Press, Oxford, pp 615–647
Heller KJ (2006) The Shadow Side of Complementarity: The Effect of Article 17 of the Rome Statute on National Due Process. Crim L F 17: 255–280
Hinojosa-Martínez LM (2014) A Critical Assessment of United Nations Security Council Resolution 1373. In: Saul B (ed) Research Handbook on International Law and Terrorism. Edward Elgar, Cheltenham, pp 626–650
Hmoud M (2006) Negotiating the Draft Comprehensive Convention on International Terrorism. JICJ 4: 1031–1043
Holmes JD (1999) The Principle of Complementarity. In: Lee RS (ed) The International Criminal Court: The Making of the Rome Statute, Issues Negotiations and Results. Kluwer Law International, The Hague, pp 41–78
ICC Office of the Prosecutor (2003) Paper on some policy issues before the Office of the Prosecutor. ICC Doc. ICC-OTP 2003
ICC Press Release (2015) The President of the Assembly calls on States Parties to fulfill their obligations to execute the Arrest warrants against Mr. Al Bashir. ICC Doc. ICC-ASP-20150613-PR1117
Krisch N (2004) The Rise and Fall of Collective Security: Terrorism, US Hegemony, and the Plight of the Security Council. In: Walter C and ors (eds) Terrorism as a Challenge for National and International Law: Security versus Liberty? Springer, Berlin, pp 879–908
Maogoto J (2009) Early efforts to establish an International Criminal Court. In: Doria J and ors (eds) The Legal Regime of the International Criminal Court. Martinus Nijhoff, Leiden, pp 3–22
Mégret F, Samson MG (2013) Holding the Line on Complementarity in Libya: The Case for Tolerating Flawed Domestic Trials. JICJ 11: 571–589
Morris M (2000) The Jurisdiction of the International Criminal Court of Nationals of Non-Party States. ILSA J Int'l & Comp L 6: 363–369

Morris M (2004) Terrorism and Unilateralism: Criminal Jurisdiction and International Relations. Cornell Int'l L J 36: 473–489
Much C (2006) The International Criminal Court and Terrorism as an International Crime. Michigan State J Int'l L 14: 121–138
Norberg N (2010) Terrorism and International Criminal Justice: Dim Prospects for a Future Together. Santa Clara J Int'l L 8:11–50
Note (2002) Responding to Terrorism: Crime, Punishment and War. Harv L Rev 115: 1217–1238
Nuotio K (2006) Terrorism as a Catalyst for the Emergence, Harmonization and Reform of Criminal Law. JICJ 4(5): 988–1016
Perera AR (2014) The Draft United Nations Comprehensive Convention on International Terrorism. In: Saul B (ed) Research Handbook on International Law and Terrorism. Edward Elgar, Cheltenham, pp 151–162
Reisman M (1999) International Legal Responses to Terrorism. Hous J Int'l L 22: 3–62
Rubin AP (2002) Legal Response to Terror: An International Criminal Court? Harv Int'l L J 43: 65–70
Sailer TM (1999) The International Criminal Court: An Argument to Extend its Jurisdiction to Terrorism and a Dismissal of U.S. Objections. Temp Int'l & Comp L J 13:311–346
Saul B (2005) Definition of "Terrorism" in the UN Security Council: 1985–2004. Chinese JIL 4 (1): 141–166
Saul B (2006) The Legal Response of the League of Nations to Terrorism. JICJ 4: 78–102
Saul B (2008) Defining Terrorism to Protect Human Rights. Sydney Law School Research Paper No 08/125. http://papers.ssrn.com/sol3/papers.cfm?abstract_id=1292059. Accessed 18 January 2017
Saul B (2011) Legislating from a Radical Hague: The United Nations Special Tribunal for Lebanon Invents an International Crime for Transnational Terrorism. Leiden J Int'l L 24: 677–700
Schabas W (2011) An Introduction to the International Criminal Court, 4th edn. Cambridge University Press, Cambridge
Schachter O (1964) The Quasi-Judicial Role of the Security Council and the General Assembly. AJIL 58: 960–965
Schloenhardt A (2004) Conference Paper 'Transnational Organised Crime and the International Criminal Court.' Australian Institute of Criminology International Conference
Schultz G (1986) Low-Intensity Warfare: The Challenge of Ambiguity. International Legal Materials 25: 204–206
Subedi S (2002) The UN Response to International Terrorism in the Aftermath of the Terrorist Attacks in America and the Problem of the Definition of Terrorism in International Law. 4 International law Forum Droit International 4: 159–169
Szasz P (2002) The Security Council Starts Legislating. AJIL 96: 901–904
Talmon S (2005) The Security Council as World Legislature. AJIL 99: 175–193
UNGA (1987) Measures to Eliminate International Terrorism, UN Doc. A/RES/42/159
UNGA (1989) Resolution 44/39 UN Doc. A/RES/44/39
UNGA (1991) Report of the ILC, 43rd Session, UN Doc. Supp No 10 (A/46/10)
UNGA (1993) Report of the ILC, 45th Session. UN Doc. Supp No 10 (A/48/10)
UNGA (1994) Declaration on Measures to Eliminate International Terrorism, UN Doc. A/RES/49/60 Supp No 49 (A/49/49)
UNGA (1995a) Report of the ILC, 47th Session, UN Doc. Supp No 10 (A/50/10)
UNGA (1995b) United States Comments to Ad Hoc Committee Report UN Doc. A/AC.244/1/Add.2
UNGA (1996a) Resolution 51/210 UN Doc. A/RES/51/210
UNGA (1996b) The ILC's Draft Code of Crimes Against the Peace and Security of Mankind, UN Doc. Supp No 10 (A/51/10)
UNGA (2001a) Report of the Ad Hoc Committee Established by UNGA Res 51/210 of 17 December 1996, UN Doc. Supp No 37 (A/56/37)
UNGA (2001b) Resolution 56/1 UN Doc. A/RES/56/1
UNGA Sixth Committee (2000) Report of the Working Group on Measures to Eliminate International Terrorism, UN Doc. A/C.6/55/L.2

UNGA Sixth Committee (2001) Report of the Working Group on Measures to Eliminate International Terrorism, UN Doc. A/C.6/56/L.9

UN Press Release (2004) Security Council Acts Unanimously to Adopt Resolution Strongly Condemning Terrorism as One of Most Serious Threats to Peace, UN Doc. SC/8214. www.un.org/News/Press/docs/2004/sc8214.doc.htm. Accessed 21 February 2017

UNSC (1985) Resolution 573 UN Doc. S/RES/573

UNSC (1990) Resolution 661 UN Doc. S/RES/661

UNSC (1999) Resolution 1267 UN Doc. S/RES/1267

UNSC (2001a) Resolution 1368 UN Doc. S/RES/1368

UNSC (2001b) Resolution 1373 UN Doc. S/RES/1373

UNSC (2004) Resolution 1566, UN Doc. S/RES/1566

UNSC (2006) Report of the Secretary-General on the establishment of a special tribunal for Lebanon, UN Doc. S/2006/893

UNSC (2007) Resolution 1757 UN Doc. S/RES/1757

UN, International Legal Instruments. www.un.org/en/terrorism/instruments.shtml. Accessed 21 February 2017

van Sliedregt E (2007) The European Arrest Warrant: Between Trust, Democracy and the Rule of Law: Introduction. The European Arrest Warrant: Extradition in Transition. EuConst 3(2): 244–252

Ventura MJ (2011) Terrorism according to the STL's Interlocutory Decision on the Applicable Law: a defining moment or a moment of defining? JICJ 9: 1021–1042

Wertheim PJ (2003) Should 'Grave Crimes of International Terrorism' be included in the Jurisdiction of the International Criminal Court? Policy and Society 22(2): 1–21

Wilmshurst E (2006) The Chatham House Principles of International Law on the Use of Force in Self-Defence. ICLQ 55(4): 963–972

Wood M (2014) Terrorism and the international law on the use of force. In: Saul B (ed) Research Handbook on International Law and Terrorism. Edward Elgar, Cheltenham, pp 195–207

Young R (2006) Defining Terrorism: The Evolution of Terrorism as a Legal Concept in International Law and its Influence on Definitions in Domestic Legislation. Boston Coll Int'l & Comp L J Rev 29: 23–106

Chapter 6
A Definition of Terrorism in the Making: Balancing State Interests with Cosmopolitan Ideals

Abstract Having thus shown how State-centric and cosmopolitan concerns have influenced the process of criminalising (or creating a framework for criminalisation of) terrorism, this chapter will focus on the definitional process and principally, on how concerns that relate either to State interests or cosmopolitan purposes should shape the formulation of an international definition for terrorism. The analysis will start with the International Convention for the Suppression of the Financing of Terrorism, as it contains the first example of a treaty law definition that can be tracked down at an international level after the establishment of the UN. Secondly, the UN Draft Comprehensive Convention on Terrorism and the Appeals Interlocutory Decision of the Special Tribunal of Lebanon, as well as some regional instruments and domestic anti-terrorist law, will be compared and contrasted, with the purpose of tracing which definitional elements are the least debated and which ones remain contentious. The comparative analysis of these instruments will reveal some common ground that already exists (and can be used as a safe basis to build upon an international definition) as well as the two major contested elements of defining terrorism: (i) the inclusion of a political/ideological motive requirement and (ii) the exemption of activities carried out by particular groups or individuals from the definition. Subsequently, both these groups of elements will be put under the light of the 'State sovereignty versus cosmopolitanism' debate, highlighting their aspects that pertain to this debate and demonstrating how these aspects should be addressed in the context of finally formulating an international definition for terrorism.

Keywords Financing of Terrorism Convention · International Humanitarian Law (IHL) · Political/Ideological motive requirement · Exemption of particular groups or individuals · UN Draft Comprehensive Convention on International Terrorism · STL Appeals Chamber's Interlocutory decision (STL Decision) · Creation of a state of terror · 'Internationality'

S. Margariti, *Defining International Terrorism*, International Criminal Justice Series 15, DOI 10.1007/978-94-6265-204-0_6

Contents

6.1 Analysing Existing Definitions for Terrorism in International and Regional Instruments: Common Ground and Points of Contention

The crystallisation of some general and common elements of an international definition for terrorism is not an easy task; one could argue that the task would be somewhat facilitated if one tries to unify the main sectoral anti-terrorist conventions[1] listing the several acts they prohibit and then adding some common jurisdictional provisions to reflect the purposes of international criminal justice.[2] This approach would also serve the general argument of this study, namely that definitions of international crimes should be construed in such a manner, so as to reflect both the respect for State sovereignty—the sectoral treaties were drafted by States for States and thus, reflect State interests—and the promotion of international criminal justice purposes, achieved through the international criminalisation of terrorism. However, it seems that using the sectoral conventions as a starting point for criminalising terrorism might be problematic. Firstly and most importantly, the sectoral conventions, where they provide a definition for terrorism, have application only in a specific context. For example, the definition of terrorism in the Financing of Terrorism Convention[3] under Article 2(1a) and (b) is applicable only when someone finances a terrorist activity. It is a functional rather than a general definition and most probably, if it was to be used for attributing individual criminal

[1] Some main anti-terrorist conventions are listed below (n. 7).

[2] Kolb 2004, p. 241.

[3] International Convention for the Suppression of the Financing of Terrorism, opened for signature 9 December 1999, 2178 UNTS 197, (entered into force 10 April 2002) (Financing of Terrorism Convention).

liability, it would not fulfil the requirements of the *nullum crimen sine lege* principle nor capture sufficiently the objective and subjective elements of the criminal act.[4] Moreover, achieving State consensus on the core elements of terrorism and defining the jurisdictional scope of application in order to formulate one general, 'catch-all' definition is anything but simple. In fact, the drafting of several anti-terrorist conventions which oblige for national criminalisation of different sets of terrorist acts, is indicative of the fact that States preferred to circumvent one general definition[5] and avoided dealing with critical questions surrounding the subject. The international instruments under examination in this section, starting with the Financing of Terrorism Convention, will shed some light on the common ground covered so far in the effort to define terrorism but also on the main contentious issues which have led this effort to its current stalemate.

6.1.1 A Comparative Analysis of the Definition of the Financing of Terrorism Convention and Definitions in Regional and Domestic Law Instruments

6.1.1.1 The Definitions Provided by the Financing of Terrorism Convention and Other Anti-Terrorist Instruments

The Financing of Terrorism Convention is one of the most widely ratified anti-terrorist treaties which includes a definition for international terrorism in the particular context of terrorism financing and also one of the few to use the term 'terrorism' as such. Thus, the treaty prohibits the financing of acts of terrorism as defined in its Article 2(1a) and (b). The adopted definition is formulated in a 'two-limb' approach,[6] meaning that the drafters provided both a list of acts that constitute terrorism and then a general definition in which any other act not prohibited by the list could be included. Article 2(1a) prohibits the funding of any act already prohibited by nine anti-terrorist treaties[7] while Article 2(1b) uses an

---

[4] Kolb 2004, p. 234.

[5] Cassese 2004, p. 216.

[6] Kolb 2004, p. 241.

[7] Convention for the Suppression of Unlawful Seizure of Aircraft, 860 UNTS 105 (entered into force 14 October 1971); Convention for the Suppression of Unlawful Acts against the Safety of Civil Aviation, 974 UNTS 177 (entered into force 26 January 1973); Convention on the Prevention and Punishment of Crimes Against Internationally Protected Persons, 1035 UNTS 167 (entered into force 20 February 1977); International Convention Against the Taking of Hostages, 1316 UNTS 205 (entered into force 3 June 1983) (International Convention Against the Taking of Hostages); Convention on the Physical Protection of Nuclear Material, 1456 UNTS 246 (entered into force 8 February 1987); Protocol for the Suppression of Unlawful Acts of Violence at Airports Serving International Civil Aviation, Supplementary to the Convention for the Suppression of

'all-inclusive' general definition, albeit used for the purposes of this Convention only. Apart from the specific acts prohibited by Article 2(1a), a person commits an offence when he or she uses funds for the commission of

> [a]ny other act intended to cause death or serious bodily injury to a civilian, or to any other person not taking an active part in the hostilities in a situation of armed conflict, when the purpose of such act, by its nature or context, is to intimidate a population, or to compel a government or an international organization to do or to abstain from doing any act.[8]

This 'catch-all' formula, which completes the provided list of prohibited acts of Article 2(1a), serves to highlight some core elements of the concept of terrorism which could be useful even outside the context of the particular convention. However, substantial divergence can still be found regarding these elements if one attempts to compare definitions of terrorism provided for in other international anti-terrorist instruments as well as in national legal orders.

To start with, the element of violence against human beings, being 'civilian[s], or…any other person not taking an active part in the hostilities in a situation of armed conflict', would constitute the *actus reus* of the crime of terrorism were the definition to be used for criminal law purposes.[9] What is needed is the commission of a violent act whose victim is a human being. Nevertheless, the requirements of (i) the commission of violence and (ii) the human victim, should not be necessarily considered as a safe starting point in the effort to define terrorism. For instance, the Arab Convention on the Suppression of Terrorism (Arab Convention),[10] although providing a definition very similar to the one in Article 2(1b) of the Financing of Terrorism Convention, requires either an act or a threat of violence under its Article 2. Furthermore, the definition of the Arab Convention is not limited to an act or threat of violence only against humans but also provides that terrorism is 'any act or threat of violence…aiming to cause damage to the environment or to public or private installations or property or to occupy or to seize them, or aiming to jeopardize a national resource'.[11] The more recent UN Draft Comprehensive Convention on International Terrorism also provides in its draft Article 2 that the definition of international terrorism includes 'serious damage to public or private property, including a place of public use, a State or government facility,

(Footnote 7 continued)

Unlawful Acts Against the Safety of Civil Aviation, 1589 UNTS 474 (entered into force 6 August 1989); Convention for the Suppression of Unlawful Acts against the Safety of Maritime Navigation, 1678 UNTS 201 (entered into force 1 March 1992); Protocol for the Suppression of Unlawful Acts against the Safety of Fixed Platforms located on the Continental Shelf, 1678 UNTS 304 (entered into force 1 March 1992); International Convention for the Suppression of Terrorist Bombings, 2149 UNTS 256 (entered into force 23 March 2001).

[8] Financing of Terrorism Convention, above n. 3, Article 2(1b).

[9] Walter 2004, p. 27.

[10] League of Arab States, Arab Convention on the Suppression of Terrorism (entered into force 22 April 1998) (Arab Convention).

[11] Ibid., Article 2.

a transportation system, an infrastructure facility or the environment'.[12] This tendency of including violence against property in a definition for terrorism moves along the same lines with some domestic legal orders. For example, the UK Terrorism Act 2002 extends also to acts or threats of damage to property[13] and the Canadian Bill C-36,[14] the US Immigration and Nationality Act[15] and the Framework Decision of the Council of the European Union of 13 June 2002[16] show a tendency to conceive of terrorism as a violent and non-violent, but definitely destructive, action against public facilities. In this respect, violence in the context of defining terrorism, is not only limited to violence against persons but also tends to include the threat of violence as well as any destructive action against the environment and public or private property.

6.1.1.2 The Issue of Exempting the Activities of Specific Groups or Individuals from the Scope of Terrorism Definitions

The most difficult question to be answered with respect to how to define terrorism is whether one should exempt from the definition acts of national liberation movements carried out in the context of self-determination (the so-called 'freedom fighters') on the one hand, and/or acts of law enforcement agencies on the other. Cassese argues that it was due to disagreements on the freedom fighters' exception that the formulation of a general definition for terrorism was impeded and not because the general concept of terrorism *per se* was in question.[17] However true as that may be, attention should be paid to whether this exception, if adopted, should apply to the scope of application of the convention or to the elements of the definition of terrorism.[18] In other words, it is one thing to leave out of the scope of an anti-terrorist convention acts of freedom fighters because they are covered by another field of international law—for example international humanitarian law (IHL)—and another thing to say that freedom fighters' acts do not fall into the definition of terrorism anyway, regardless of whether they are covered by any other international instrument. Regarding the scope of its application, IHL is applicable in armed conflicts of either an international or non-international character. However, whether an armed conflict indeed exists can be in itself hard to determine, especially in cases of internal violence. Article 1 of the Protocol Additional to the Geneva Conventions, and relating to the Protection of Victims of Non-International Armed

[12] UNGA 2002, Annex II, Article 2(1b).

[13] UK Terrorism Act 2000, c 11, s 1(2b).

[14] Canadian Bill C-36, Part II.1, 83.01(1b).

[15] US Immigration and Nationality Act, 8 USC§1182 a3B.

[16] Council Framework Decision of 13 June 2002 on Combating Terrorism [2002] OJ L164/3 (EU Framework Decision).

[17] Cassese 2004, p. 214.

[18] Walter 2004, p. 41.

Conflicts (Additional Protocol II)[19] defines an armed conflict of a non-international character as an armed conflict

> which take[s] place in the territory of a High Contracting Party between its armed forces and dissident armed forces or other organized armed groups which, under responsible command, exercise such control over a part of its territory as to enable them to carry out sustained and concerted military operations[…]

Article 2 however exempts from the scope of the abovementioned Article, 'situations of internal disturbances and tensions, such as riots, isolated and sporadic acts of violence and other acts of a similar nature'. Nevertheless, for situations that can be found in between what is described by Articles 1 and 2, it is hard to establish whether the appropriate legal framework to be applied is either the rules of IHL or law enforcement. Even though in non-international armed conflicts the combatant status does not exist, as it does in international conflicts, Common Article 3 of the Geneva Conventions, Additional Protocol II to the Geneva Conventions, and customary international humanitarian law all provide safeguards for the rights of the detainees 'in relation to treatment, conditions and due process of law'.[20] It has been argued that, in this respect, the hesitation on the part of the States to recognise that a non-international armed conflict takes place in their territory, is partly due to the political consequences that such recognition brings as well as the obligation to apply rules of IHL.[21]

In terms of substance, there is ambiguity as to what extent the use of force to attain self-determination can be justified.[22] The use of force in the context of exercising the right to self-determination is understood to denote that anti-government force can be legitimately utilised in a 'just cause',[23] namely in a revolutionary context where this right has been denied by the official government of a State. However, it is exactly this point at which struggles against a State's official government can intersect with terrorist offences.[24] While legitimate violence committed in the context of self-determination can be distinguished from terrorism in terms of motivation and means used,[25] it is not uncommon that States would like to stigmatise their opponents as terrorist and would turn to one or other forms of counter-insurgency doctrines usually adopted in anti-terrorist strategies and measures.[26]

---

[19] Protocol Additional to the Geneva Conventions of 12 August 1949, and relating to the Protection of Victims of Non-International Armed Conflicts, opened for signature 8 June 1977, 1125 UNTS 609 (entered into force 7 December 1978) (Additional Protocol II).

[20] For a description of the existing IHL rules that pertain to terrorism see ICRC 2011.

[21] Chadwick 2014, p. 313.

[22] Ibid., p. 300.

[23] Ibid., p. 301.

[24] Ibid.

[25] Ibid., p. 298.

[26] Ibid., p. 314. See also UN Commission on Human Rights 2005, para 56(a).

Closely connected to the debate of the potential overlap between terrorism and self-determination, is also the issue of State-committed terrorism, namely terrorist acts perpetrated by State agents within that State, as a response to political violence committed in self-determination or the fight against oppressive regimes. The question of exempting specific groups or individuals from a definition of terrorism is not limited only to freedom fighters but extends also to State agents that might commit acts of violence as a response to political opposition. Complementary to the issue of State-committed terrorism, is also the concept of State-supported terrorism which generally includes acts committed by third parties in a third State that are funded or prompted by a State's agents. Both of these manifestations of the more general term 'State terrorism' are precisely the second grey area that features in the concept of terrorism, namely the potential overlap between terrorist acts and forms of violence employed by a State which are typically considered as lawful, or violence committed by third parties with direct or indirect State involvement.

Turning now back to the definition of the Financing of Terrorism Convention, there is no reference to any exception for particular perpetrators. In fact, the Preamble of the Convention follows the formulation of the definition given in the 1994 UNGA Declaration on 'Measures to Eliminate International Terrorism', which condemns 'all acts, methods and practices of terrorism as criminal and unjustifiable, wherever and by whomever committed'.[27] In this respect, the formulation leaves no ground for exclusion of either freedom fighters or, at least in principle, terrorist acts committed by State agents. However, the Convention continues by making reference to an 'international element' that has to be fulfilled in order that States apply the provisions therein. Article 3 provides that '[t]his Convention shall not apply where the offence is committed within a single State, the alleged offender is a national of that State and is present in the territory of that State…',[28] meaning that in the classical situations where State agents commit terrorist acts against a part of the population within the State, the 'by whomever committed' clause does not have any application.[29] On the other hand, regarding the question of the freedom fighters' exception, the Arab Convention excludes in its Article 2(a) '[a]ll cases of struggle by whatever means, including armed struggle, against foreign occupation and aggression for liberation and self-determination…', from the definition of terrorism.[30] As mentioned above, both the Financing of Terrorism Convention and the 1994 UNGA Declaration condemn terrorism by whomever committed. Moreover, the UNGA Declaration goes on to condemn

[27] UNGA 1994, Annex I, Article 1.

[28] Financing of Terrorism Convention, above n. 3, Article 3.

[29] Walter 2004, p. 37.

[30] Arab Convention, above n. 10, Article 2a. An almost identical provision is included in the Organisation of the Islamic Conference, Convention of the Organisation of the Islamic Conference on Combating International Terrorism, Annex to Resolution No. 59/26-P (entered into force 1 July 1999) (OIC Convention), Article 2a.

terrorist acts whatever their justification.[31] However, it has been argued that the fact that Additional Protocol I of 1977 to the Geneva Conventions[32] provides for the recognition as lawful combatants of those who 'are fighting against colonial domination and alien occupation and against racist regimes in the exercise of their right of self-determination',[33] might offer an acceptable solution to the problem of labelling 'freedom fighters' as terrorists[34] due to the caveat offered by international humanitarian law to those fighting for their right to self-determination.

6.1.1.3 The Issue of a Political/Ideological Motive Requirement as an Element of Terrorism

Finally, a last major point of divergence between the definitions examined so far, is whether it is necessary to include the element of a political/ideological motivation in a definition for terrorism. The Financing of Terrorism Convention, the Arab Convention and the EU Framework Decision do not make any explicit reference to the requirement of a political/ideological purpose, whereas the 1994 UNGA Declaration explicitly states that 'criminal acts…for political purposes are in any circumstance unjustifiable…'.[35] The UK and the Canadian definitions for terrorism also include a political/ideological element, requiring the 'advancing of political, religious or ideological cause'[36] and an act committed 'in whole or in part for political, religious or ideological purpose, objective or cause'[37] respectively. This divergence can be attributed to the fact that the definitions not requiring such a motivation refer to the minimum requirements present in most national legal systems[38] and did not include elements which may vary from one national definition to another. However, even the definitions of the Financing of Terrorism Convention and the EU Framework Decision, which do not explicitly include a political/ideological motive requirement, do not reject any connection to a political/ideological intent. In the first case, the definition provides that 'the purpose of [the terrorist] act, by its nature or context, is to intimidate a population, or to compel a government or

[31] UNGA 1994, Annex I, Article 3: 'Criminal acts intended or calculated to provoke a state of terror in the general public, a group of persons or particular persons for political purposes are in any circumstance unjustifiable, whatever the considerations of a political, philosophical, ideological, racial, ethnic, religious or any other nature that may be invoked to justify them.'

[32] Protocol Additional to the Geneva Conventions of 12 August 1949, and relating to the Protection of Victims of International Armed Conflicts, opened for signature 8 June 1977, 1125 UNTS 3 (entered into force 7 December 1978) (Additional Protocol I).

[33] Ibid., Article 1(4).

[34] Cassese 2004, p. 217.

[35] UNGA 1994, Annex I, Article 3.

[36] UK Terrorism Act 2000, c 11, s 1(1c).

[37] Canadian Bill C-36, Part II.1, 83.01(1biA).

[38] Walter 2004, p. 35.

an international organization to do or to abstain from doing any act',[39] while the EU Framework Decision definition states that the aims of the committed act should be to

> seriously intimidat[e] a population, or unduly [compel] a Government or international organisation to perform or abstain from performing any act, or seriously destabilis[e] or [destroy] the fundamental political, constitutional, economic or social structures of a country or an international organisation.[40]

It is clear that when the commission of a violent act has as its purpose to compel a government or an organisation to follow or not to follow a particular course of action, or to do serious damage to the fundamental structures of a State, the intention of the perpetrator is driven by political/ideological considerations. On the other hand, it is very rare for a terrorist act to have as its only aim to intimidate the population without any further ideologically-related intention, such as the advancement of a political, religious or any other ideological agenda. Violent acts resulting in the intimidation of a large part of a State's population without the intention to influence politics and/or ideology in a certain way do not reflect the severe impact of terrorism and do not differentiate from non-terrorist but rather violent, ordinary offences.

6.1.2 The Definition of the UN Draft Comprehensive Convention on Terrorism

The second example of a definition for terrorism under examination is the definition provided in Article 2 of the UN Draft Comprehensive Convention as proposed by the Coordinator of the Working Group of the 6th Committee established for this purpose in 2001.[41] The definition is similar to the one of the Financing of Terrorism Convention in that it requires the commission of a violent act against persons with the inclusion however of acts of damage against public or private property, facilities, infrastructure and the environment and providing separately for cases where such damages result in major economic loss.[42] Proposed Article 2(1) provides:

> Any person commits an offence within the meaning of this Convention if that person, by any means, unlawfully and intentionally, causes: (a) Death or serious bodily injury to any person; or (b) Serious damage to public or private property, including a place of public use, a State or government facility, a public transportation system, an infrastructure facility or the environment; or (c) Damage to property, places, facilities, or systems referred to in paragraph 1 (b) of this article, resulting or likely to result in major economic loss, when the

[39] Financing of Terrorism Convention, above n. 3, Article 2(1b).

[40] EU Framework Decision, above n. 16, Article 1(1).

[41] UNGA 2002, Annex II.

[42] Ibid.

purpose of the conduct, by its nature or context, is to intimidate a population, or to compel a Government or an international organization to do or abstain from doing any act.

The formulation of the purpose of such acts is taken verbatim from the Financing of Terrorism Convention, namely that the act's aim is 'to intimidate a population or compel a Government or an international organisation to do or to abstain from doing any act'. The proposed definition as such did not raise any particular issues for controversy.[43] What did and still does raise controversy however, is the scope of application of the UN Draft Convention, which, when delimited, will establish who can qualify as terrorist in a given context.

Despite the fact that the Preamble of the Coordinator's paper repeats the language of the 1994 UNGA Declaration that 'all acts, methods and practices of terrorism' are 'criminal and unjustifiable, wherever and by whomever committed',[44] draft Article 18 provides for two exceptions from the definition: (i) that '[t]he activities of armed forces during an armed conflict, as those terms are understood under international humanitarian law, which are governed by that law, are not governed by this Convention' and (ii) that '[t]he activities undertaken by the military forces of a State in the exercise of their official duties, inasmuch as they are governed by other rules of international law, are not governed by this Convention'.[45] Concerning the first exception, it is suggested that, as it is formulated, it will not cover activities of armed resistance groups or 'unprivileged combatants' against a party to the conflict, groups which do not belong to a State's army and which are otherwise lawful under international humanitarian law.[46] Therefore, there was an alternative suggestion by the Organisation of the Islamic Conference (OIC) to replace the words 'armed forces' with 'parties',[47] so as not to exempt from this provision organisations such as Hamas, Islamic Jihad or Hezbollah which fight against Israeli occupation in Lebanon and Palestine.[48] However, draft Article 18(1), as it stands, already contains a safeguard against the labelling of armed resistance groups as terrorist. Draft Article 18(1), reads as follows: '[n]othing in this Convention shall affect other rights, obligations and responsibilities of States, peoples and individuals under international law, in particular the purposes and principles of the Charter of the United Nations, and international humanitarian law.'[49] Self-determination and the fight against foreign occupation are well-established peoples' rights under the UN Charter and

---

[43] Subedi 2002, p. 163.

[44] UNGA 2002, 4. Similar exceptions can be found in the International Convention Against the Taking of Hostages, above n. 9, Article 12, where it states that, when an act of hostage-taking occurs during an armed conflict and when the Geneva Conventions and their Protocols are applicable, then the said Convention does not apply.

[45] UNGA 2002, Annex IV, draft Articles 18(2) and 18(3).

[46] Hmoud 2006, p. 1037.

[47] UNGA 2002, Annex IV.

[48] Walter 2004, p. 38.

[49] UNGA 2002, Annex IV.

international humanitarian law,[50] and although they need not be violent, success of such pursuits often call for the use of force.[51] While in the past, the scope of the concept of self-determination focused more on fights 'against colonial domination…alien occupation and against racist regimes',[52] today a more comprehensive and broad approach tends to be adopted with the purpose to include also political struggles for greater democracy and human rights.[53] Furthermore, draft Article 18 (3) differentiates the language from Article 18(2), by exempting the activities of the 'military forces of a State'. The difference in language must obviously mean that there is a difference between 'armed forces' and 'military forces of a State', the first term being more comprehensive than the second and thus, including all parties to a conflict.[54]

Regarding the second exception from the scope of the Convention, referring to the activities of the 'military forces of a State, in the exercise of their official duties', draft Article 18(3) does not specify that the acts should be carried out in the context of an armed conflict. Thus, it can be suggested that it refers to acts undertaken only or also in peacetime. However, the provision continues by stating that these activities are exempted 'inasmuch as they are governed by other rules of international law'—'by other rules' obviously referring to rules other than international humanitarian law which applies in cases of armed conflict. If 'inasmuch as' is to be understood as 'to the extent' they are governed by other rules of international law,[55] it is hard to identify the cases where these acts are not governed by any other rule of international law. Activities of military forces in peacetime are covered, *inter alia*, by rules of international human rights law,[56] for example rules that protect civil rights such as the right of free expression, assembly or privacy.[57] Moreover, acts of State-supported terrorism fall into the ambit of the law on State responsibility and, according to the UN Declaration on Friendly Relations,[58] the prohibition of State

[50] Charter of the United Nations, opened for signature 26 June 1945, 1 UNTS XVI (entered into force 24 October 1945) (UN Charter), Articles 1(2) and 55; International Covenant on Civil and Political Rights, opened for signature 16 December 1966, 999 UNTS 171 (entered into force 23 March 1976) and International Covenant on Economic, Social and Cultural Rights, opened for signature 16 December 1966, 993 UNTS 3 (entered into force 23 March 1976) Common Article 1 which unequivocally provides for the right to self-determination to all people; Additional Protocol I, above n. 32, Article 1(4); UNGA 1960, 1970, 2006.

[51] Chadwick 2014, p. 301.

[52] Additional Protocol I, above n. 32, Article 1(4).

[53] Chadwick 2014, p. 301.

[54] Walter 2004, p. 39.

[55] Hmoud 2006, p. 1041.

[56] Walter 2004, p. 41.

[57] Chadwick 2014, p. 311.

[58] UNGA 1970, 1st Principle.

terrorism is an 'instantiation of the general prohibition of the use of force'.[59] Thus, the overall effect of draft Article 18(3) will be to generally exclude acts that would otherwise fall into the definition of the UN Draft Comprehensive Convention, when carried out by the military forces of a State. This effect clearly contradicts the purposes of the Convention as they are formulated in the Preamble, which, among other things, states that acts of international terrorism that have to be suppressed, include also 'those which are committed or supported by States, directly or indirectly'.[60] In an effort to include in the scope of the Convention incidents of terrorist acts committed by military forces, the OIC States made an alternative proposal to the formulation of Article 18(3) suggesting that 'the activities of the military forces of a State, in the exercise of their official duties' be exempted from the scope of the Convention, 'inasmuch as they are *in conformity* with international law'.[61]

All in all, it appears that the most thorny issues about defining terrorism concern more the question of who can qualify as perpetrator rather than what terrorism actually is. It is a fact that there are grey areas that need to be clarified before delimiting the scope of the UN Convention on Terrorism, such as the potential overlap with international humanitarian law or the law on State responsibility. Therefore, it is crucial to see the drafting of the UN Convention on Terrorism as an opportunity to clarify not only its scope but also the scope of other adjacent fields of international law. Although it is not one of the purposes of this book to analyse further the issue of delimitation between the fields of international law that relate to terrorism, it is the author's view that the work of the Working Group mandated with the drafting of the Convention should follow this direction. A clear-cut distinction between the different international law regimes that relate to terrorism could eliminate any gaps in their respective legal frameworks, contribute to the creation of a more uniform perception about the nature of terrorism and establish clearer boundaries on which acts are beyond legitimacy under any circumstances.

6.1.3 The Appeal's Chamber Decision of the UN Special Tribunal for Lebanon

Finally, the most recent example of a definition for international terrorism is found in the STL Appeals Chamber's Interlocutory decision.[62] As was also mentioned in the previous chapter, the STL was established for the purpose of investigating the

---

[59] Hmoud 2006, p. 1034; Trapp 2012, p. 283 where she argues that State obligation to refrain from terrorist conduct is a manifestation of the general prohibition on the use of force under Article 2(4) of the UN Charter.

[60] UNGA 2002, Annex I.

[61] UNGA 2002, Annex IV, Article 18(3) (as proposed by the OIC States).

[62] STL, *Interlocutory Decision on the Applicable Law: Terrorism, Conspiracy, Homicide, Perpetration, Cumulative Charging,* 16 February 2011, Case No. STL-11-01/1 (STL Decision).

2005 assassination of the former Prime Minister Hariri Rafiq and 22 others in a bomb attack and is the first international court with jurisdiction over terrorism.[63] The definition given in the decision addressed the formulation of the subjective and objective elements of the offence and did not elaborate on issues such as the freedom fighters' exception or State-committed terrorism. Besides, the STL, though being a UN-backed tribunal, was bound, according to Article 2 of the STL Statute, to apply Lebanese law,[64] which had already in place a definition for terrorism. However, the judges of the STL held that, due to 'the unique gravity and the transnational dimension of the crime at issue',[65] Lebanese law should be construed in accordance with international law and thus a more extensive definition of terrorism should apply than the one provided in the Lebanese Criminal Code.[66] Thus, after the request of the Pre-Trial Judge that it answer some critical questions which, among other issues, related to terrorism, the Appeals Chamber finally held that there is a customary law definition of terrorism and also determined the objective and subjective elements of the crime of terrorism to be applied by the Tribunal. The controversy surrounding the customary nature of international terrorism was already discussed in the previous chapter. Related to this controversy is also the task of defining the elements of the crime of terrorism based on international law.

The international law applicable on Lebanon is composed by conventional law—in this case, the Arab Convention—and customary international law (which, it held, exists in the case of international terrorism).[67] Thus, according to the Tribunal, the elements to be applied resulting from the abovementioned sources of law are: '(i) the volitional commission of an act or credible threat of an act; (ii) through means that are likely to pose a public danger; and (iii) with the special intent to cause a state of terror'.[68]

Starting from the Lebanese Law, according to Article 314 of the Lebanese Criminal Code,[69] the objective elements of terrorism are (i) an act, whether it is an offence under the Lebanese Criminal Code or not and (ii) the use of means 'liable to create a public danger'.[70] The subjective element, which was retained by the STL Decision in the definition of terrorism, is the intent to cause 'a state of terror'.[71] The Lebanese definition also provides an illustrative list of the means that are considered as 'liable to create a public danger'. Though the list is not exhaustive, it seems that

---

63 Mylonaki 2011.

64 UNSC 2007, Article 2.

65 STL Decision, above n. 62, p. 3.

66 Ibid., paras 43–46.

67 Ibid.

68 Ibid., paras 149–150.

69 Lebanese Criminal Code, Article 314: 'Terrorist acts are all acts intended to cause a state of terror and committed by means liable to create a public danger such as explosive devices, inflammable materials, toxic or corrosive products and infectious or microbial agents.'

70 STL Decision, above n. 62, para 49.

71 Ibid.

some Lebanese courts have preferred a strict interpretation of this objective element of the definition, by limiting the 'means' only to those which, as such, are likely to create a public danger.[72] Thus, it follows that any means not listed therein would only fall into the definition if they create a similar effect to those listed.[73] In this respect, according to the Lebanese case law, non-enumerative implements not envisaged by Article 314 include guns, machine-guns, revolvers, letter bombs or knives.[74]

However, the Arab Convention and customary international law as interpreted by the Tribunal, do not include any constraint regarding the means used for the commission of an act of terrorism[75]; therefore the Appeals Chamber took a broader interpretation of this objective element, extending the domestic definition to include means that are liable to create a public danger 'either by exposing bystanders or onlookers to harm or by instigating further violence in the form of retaliation or political instability'.[76] It held further that this interpretation addresses better the exigencies of modern forms of terrorism and brings Lebanese law closer to the relevant international law which is binding on Lebanon.[77]

Apart from the elements of the crime of terrorism as introduced by the Appeals Chamber, it is also relevant to mention the customary elements of the definition of the crime, as provided for in the STL Decision. In the previous chapter, it was mentioned that this finding of the Tribunal gave rise to controversy surrounding the customary status of terrorism; however, it cannot be overlooked that the STL Decision offered an account of State practice and *opinio juris* that points to the direction of raising terrorism to a crime under customary international law. The Appeals Chamber has used a number of treaties, UN resolutions as well as legislative and judicial practice of States as a basis to conclude that there is a customary crime of terrorism, at least in time of peace.[78] The analysis of these sources of custom led the Appeals Chamber to conclude that the customary rule that has emerged regarding the international crime of terrorism requires:

> i) the perpetration of a criminal act (such as murder, kidnapping, hostage-taking, arson, and so on), or threatening such an act; ii) the intent to spread fear among the population (which would generally entail the creation of public danger) or directly or indirectly coerce a national or international authority to take some action, or to refrain from taking it; iii) when the act involves a transnational element.[79]

[72] Ibid., para 52.

[73] Ibid., paras 51–52.

[74] Ibid., para 52.

[75] Ibid., para 69; para 113.

[76] Ibid., p. 3 and paras 125–128.

[77] Ibid., para 129.

[78] Ibid., para 85. For a detailed analysis of the sources of customary law used by the Appeals Chamber see ibid., paras 86–113. For an opposite view on the interpretation of these sources as a sound basis for the customary status of terrorism see Saul 2011.

[79] STL Decision, above n. 62, para 85.

The articulation of the abovementioned elements as a customary rule is a vital contribution of the Appeals Chamber and can constitute a turning point in international criminal law in the field of terrorism should the STL Decision leave a lasting impact for future cases. The reference to customary law adds legitimacy to the judgment[80] and it has been argued that this ruling can set a precedent for an international definition for terrorism and for the UN to establish in the future special tribunals with jurisdiction over terrorist crimes,[81] offering guidance in terms of how international terrorism should be dealt with. However, if a ruling derives its legitimacy from customary law, it should also take into account a well-rounded interpretation of it, rather than an one-sided one. Generally speaking, customary law can be 'controversial due to its indeterminacy and fluidity'.[82] While one tribunal can use it as a source for its ruling, another might reject it on grounds that it is too vague,[83] and even the Appeals Chamber of the STL acknowledges that customary law is not applicable in all tribunals.[84] Secondly, and with respect to terrorism, customary law has been used in order to show that a customary rule on terrorism has not yet emerged.[85] A decision, ruling on such a controversial issue such as international terrorism, should have reflected all aspects of customary law relevant to it, rather than only those aspects which are in accord with the opinion of the judges.

However, it should be noted that the decision provides a starting point on which discussions about a definition for terrorism for criminal purposes can be triggered. It remains to be seen whether the negotiations for the UN Draft Convention on Terrorism will be influenced by this decision. Furthermore, since this decision articulates for the first time objective and subjective elements for the international crime of terrorism, it constitutes an opportunity to initiate again discussions about the inclusion and definition of the crime of terrorism into the Rome Statute.

The existing efforts of defining terrorism in international law demonstrate some common ground on what is understood as terrorism, but also some points of contention. In summary and as it has been already illustrated, it seems that there is a general consensus that terrorism includes violent acts or threats thereof, that put at risk the physical integrity of human beings, but also destructive actions taken against the environment and public or private property. The purpose of an act of

[80] Puchooa 2011, p. 43.

[81] Mylonaki 2011, p. 338.

[82] Puchooa 2011, p. 43.

[83] Supreme Court of the Netherlands, Chamber of Criminal law, Decision of 18 September 2001, in the case of D D Bouterse, paras 4.4 and 4.7. The Supreme Court overturned an Appeals Chamber conviction for torture as a crime against humanity on the grounds that customary law is too vague as a source of law to base such a conviction.

[84] STL Decision, above n. 62, para 101; paras 114–17.

[85] See generally Saul 2006.

terrorism as has emerged so far, is to intimidate a population or compel a government or organisation to do or to abstain from doing a particular act and the special intent entails the creation of a state of terror. On the other hand, the points of divergence revolve around the questions of (i) whether political or generally ideological motivation should constitute an element of the offence and (ii) whether specific groups should be exempted from the definition, namely national liberation movements or State agents. This latter point however has been an issue only for the drafting of the UN Comprehensive Convention on Terrorism and has not been specifically addressed by the rest of the anti-terrorist instruments examined in this section (with the exception of the Arab Convention), leaving thus room to deduce that terrorism is generally condemned 'by whomever committed'. Finally, the STL Decision raised a point which requires further elaboration: in ruling on the elements of the crime of terrorism, the Appeals Chamber held that terrorism is a customary law crime with its own elements, one of which is the transnational nature of the act. Putting aside the issue of controversy surrounding the customary nature of terrorism, the contribution of the STL Decision to the development of a definition for terrorism in international law cannot be overlooked. Thus, it is essential to examine further the scope and interpretation of the international element of the offence as a potential constituent definitional element of the crime of international terrorism.

However, and regardless of the degree of State consensus on the elements of a definition for terrorism, it is the author's view that a definition of an international crime will not be functional nor serve the purposes of international criminal justice unless it balances properly State sovereignty considerations and cosmopolitan ideals. Thus, in the quest for a definition of terrorism, one should put both the common elements as well as the points of divergence under the spectrum of this approach, namely whether the interpretation and scope of these elements manage to strike the required balance between the need to protect State sovereignty and to promote cosmopolitan considerations. To this end, the second section will first focus on an analysis of the agreed elements of a definition for terrorism in the context of State sovereignty considerations and cosmopolitan purposes. Secondly, it will be suggested that this context can help resolve the most contentious issues surrounding the definition, namely the question of including a political/ideological motive as an element of the offence and that of exempting particular groups from the scope of the definition. Finally, it will be argued that the international element of the crime, introduced by the STL, should be an essential definitional element, as it helps bridge the gap between the protection of State sovereignty and the promotion of cosmopolitan goals. It will be suggested that the threshold of 'internationality' of a terrorist act will place clearer boundaries on the circumstances under which a terrorist act should rise to the level of an international crime without sidestepping national efforts to combat terrorism.

6.2 Reaching the Required Balance: How the Consented, Contested and the 'Internationality' Elements Can Contribute to the Creation of Due Balance Between State-Centric and Cosmopolitan Concerns in Defining Terrorism

The previous section identified three types of constituents of a definition for terrorism: (i) the first type consists of the more common elements, as they are illustrated through international and regional instruments and domestic law, (ii) the second type includes those elements where there is continuous disagreement about how they should be approached, namely the inclusion of a political/ideological motive as an element of the crime and the exemption from the definition of activities carried out by particular groups or individuals, and (iii) a suggestion made by the author and backed up by the STL Decision, to include an international element in the definition of terrorism. This section will try to address the major challenge posed by the drafting of a definition for terrorism, namely how terrorism can be best defined in order to protect both the State interests and the universal values that are threatened by the commission of a terrorist act. For this reason, the abovementioned constituent elements of a definition for terrorism will be placed in the context of the theories of State sovereignty and cosmopolitanism. Thus, it will be demonstrated how the drafting of a definition for terrorism can serve as a means to achieve the desired balance between these potentially antithetical poles and contribute substantially to the development of international criminal law in the field.

6.2.1 'Creation of a State of Terror', the Intention to Influence Politics and the Political/Ideological Motive Requirement

Starting with the least controversial elements of a definition for terrorism, the element of violence against the physical integrity of persons[86] and destructive action against property are the most dominant. The STL Decision ruled that one of the elements of the crime of terrorism, both in the customary definition and the definition to be applied by the Tribunal in the particular case, is the perpetration of a criminal act. Saul argues that the kind of violence entailed in a terrorist act—political or religious violence—cannot be tolerated by States because it both

[86] For the purposes of this analysis, 'persons' or 'individuals' are limited to the civilian population. While Cassese argues that victims of terrorism can be both civilians and military personnel (Cassese 2004, p. 224), this limitation only to civilians relate to the previous acknowledgment made in this chapter that international humanitarian law is the law applicable to armed conflicts where military personnel may be the target of terrorist acts.

jeopardises the safety and human rights of individuals, being their citizens or other persons that happen to be in their territory, and aims at influencing politics or promoting a religious or ideological agenda.[87] In other words, the violence used during the commission of a terrorist act against physical persons or against property is the means used by terrorists to achieve their aim of attacking a State's national security and stability. Therefore, it becomes obvious that even the single element of violence reflects the need to balance carefully the two parallel aims of a terrorist act: the attack on universal values and international community interests through the violation of basic human rights (a cosmopolitan concern) and the attack on national interests (a State-centric concern).

In this respect, it can be said that terrorist violence targets both cosmopolitan and State-centric interests, namely universal values and fundamental freedoms on the one hand and the political stability and national security of States on the other. This dual nature of terrorist violence has to be clearly reflected in a criminal definition for terrorism. Regarding cosmopolitan concerns about the violation of basic human rights, the element of violence should be defined in such a way so as to reflect what Cassese and Delmas-Marty call the 'depersonalisation of the victim'[88] or in other words, indiscriminate violence.[89] Putting aside cases where the victim of a terrorist attack is a political person and whose death would be considered rather 'symbolic' and might not endanger the general public during its commission,[90] random violence against individuals is the most dominant feature of terrorism. The element of random violence is what generates what is considered to be one of the purposes of a terrorist act, namely the aim to spread terror. The deprivation of the sense of security that the citizens of a State, or any other person that happens to be in the territory of a State, should enjoy is the basic cause of terror among individuals and therefore, the *actus reus* of terrorism should entail any act or threat thereof that can cause that effect. To this end, the element of violence should include acts that are already prohibited by the anti-terrorist conventions or by national laws but the list should remain 'open-ended' in order to ensure that any new or unanticipated methods not yet listed would also fall into the category.[91] If, as it has been suggested, there has to be 'an overarching idea of what we understand as terrorism'[92] in order to link disparate acts having a similar effect, then this idea should focus on the creation of a state of terror.

Despite the fact that human beings or private or public property are the direct targets of terrorist violence, the indirect 'victim' is a State's stability and national

---

[87] Saul 2012, p. 91.

[88] Cassese 2004, p. 219; Delmas-Marty 2002, p. 67.

[89] Kolb 2004, p. 235.

[90] This point does not argue that attacks against persons of high political, religious or other status should not be considered as terrorist under any circumstances. However, if the commission of the attack does not endanger the general public, it will probably fall into other categories of crime, e.g. political assassination or murder.

[91] Saul 2012, p. 91.

[92] Golder and Williams 2004, p. 288.

security. Generally, there is consensus that the criminal act that can qualify as terrorist should aim at either the intimidation of the population ('intent to spread fear among the population' as was formulated in the STL Decision)[93] or at compelling a government or an international organisation to do or to abstain from doing a particular act.[94] Having said previously that the element of creating a state of terror should be reflected into the elements of the crime for cosmopolitan-related purposes, it is suggested that the element of compelling a government or organisation to do or refrain from doing a particular act should also be reflected for sovereignty-related considerations. However, the use of 'or' between the two separate subjective elements of a terrorist act seems to signify that either a 'mere' intimidation of a population or a 'mere' compulsion of a government will be enough for an act to qualify as terrorist. This alternative use of either the intention to create a state of terror or the intention to compel a government or organisation to do or refrain from doing a particular act, implies that when one of the two subjective elements is present, the other is not a necessary requirement.[95] If, in this respect, an 'either…or…' approach is followed, then acts with the exclusive aim of spreading terror (without any other political/ideological motivation, such as a crime wave of random violence)[96] will qualify as terrorist. To the contrary, the intention of compelling national or international authorities to do or refrain from doing a particular act, often presupposes a political/ideological motivation,[97] which might be absent from acts intending only to spread terror among the population, such as an attack by a sniper in a public space who does not follow a particular ideology.[98] Therefore, the absence of a political/ideological motivation behind the intention to spread terror among the population or part of it, risks the inclusion into the definition of a much broader category of violent acts, that would deprive of the concept of terrorism its direct link to issues of national security and protection of State interests.

This absence of the element of a political/ideological motive from a definition of terrorism can be seen from a dual perspective in the context of both theories that form the framework of this analysis. From a cosmopolitan perspective, Di Filippo argues that the core context of the fight against terrorism should not be the preservation of a particular State system but rather the protection of individuals and

---

[93] STL Decision, above n. 62, para 85.

[94] Financing of Terrorism Convention, above n. 3, Article 2(1b); EU Framework Decision, above n. 16, Article 1(1); UN Draft Convention on Terrorism, proposed Article 2(1); STL Decision, above n. 62, para 85.

[95] Walter 2004, p. 28.

[96] For example, indiscriminate violence between Shiite and Sunni groups in Iraq based on ethnicity cannot be qualified as terrorist even if the means of violence used resemble to the means commonly used by terrorists (e.g. suicide bombers or car bombs). See Llobet 2012, p. 106.

[97] Arguably, since it is still possible to compel a government or organization for private, non-political reasons (in Saul 2012, p. 89).

[98] Walter 2004, p. 29.

of the human values they embody.[99] Under this perspective, the motivation behind a violent act is made irrelevant, since we cannot exclude that criminal associations which commit particularly violent crimes can have mixed objectives, including, but not limited to, political ones.[100] Therefore, the distinction of terrorism from ordinary crimes by reference to the motive of the offender is unnecessary and can be misleading because the condemnation of terrorism should be absolute irrespective of the context in which it is carried out. Under this approach, terrorism is seen as a method of achieving a particular purpose and whether this purpose is idealistic or materialistic should not determine the qualification of an act as terrorist.[101]

Under a more State-centric perspective, Saul argues that the political motive can serve as a means of distinction between a terrorist and a non-terrorist act, not in the sense that the former is morally worse than the latter, but morally different.[102] He is of the view that political or generally public-oriented violence is morally different than violence carried out for private ends, even if the latter is of equal gravity, and that this differentiation should be reflected into a definition for terrorism.[103] This moral difference between terrorism and other equally violent crimes is based on the view that the former aims 'to disrupt and coerce peaceful political processes through violence' and it is this aim that makes terrorism 'distinctively wrongful'.[104] Therefore, the omission of the political motive from anti-terrorist instruments as a distinguishing element of terrorism results in 'overbroadness', undermining their counter-terrorism character[105] and risking the qualification of other acts of serious violence as terrorist, such as a crime wave or a snipper's attack in a public space. The emphasis should consequently be laid on the aim of terrorism to attack society and democratic institutions,[106] as well as the political system of a particular State.[107]

As was said previously, a political or ideological motive is not specifically included into the requirements of which acts can qualify as terrorist in all international anti-terrorist instruments. However, this is not to say that there needs to be no connection between a violent act and a political/ideological purpose for the act to be categorised as terrorist because a political/ideological motive, even if not explicitly mentioned in a definition for terrorism, is being implied by one of the two aims of a terrorist act. Nonetheless, it is the author's suggestion that a political/ideological motive should be explicitly included in a definition for terrorism, not only in connection to acts carried out with the intention to coerce the

99 Filippo 2008, p. 547.

100 Ibid., pp. 541–42.

101 Ibid., p. 547.

102 Saul 2012, p. 88.

103 Ibid.

104 Ibid.

105 Saul 2012, p. 89.

106 Saul 2012, p. 90.

107 Ibid.

authorities but also to acts carried out with the intention to create a state of terror among the population or part of it. The absence of a political/ideological motive that will connect to both the subjective elements of the crime will result in over-broadness, undermining its character as a crime against non-violent politics and social life.[108] If the motive of the offender is made irrelevant, acts of serious violence whose motive might be economic profit, despair or simply insanity, will be equated with a category of substantially different crimes, whose motive is completely political or ideological in character and definitely requires a different kind of analysis.[109] This overreach would weaken the counter-terrorism character of existing anti-terrorist instruments and measures and will not emphasise the distinctively wrongful character of terrorism which targets individuals and State structures at the same time.

To recapitulate, cosmopolitanism in the context of international criminal justice requires that 'universal standards applicable to humankind should take priority in international affairs'[110] over any national priorities and strategies of the State that has suffered the attack. In other words, the prosecution and punishment of the individual offenders of an act of international terrorism and in this respect, the fight against impunity for these offenders should be given priority despite any national strategies that would opt for a non-judicial response, such as resort to the use of force or political or economic coercion. Therefore, a proposed definition should first of all reflect the need to protect all human beings by preventing grave crimes that 'threaten the peace, security and well-being of the world',[111] and thus have as the *actus reus* of international terrorism the commission of a criminal act with the intent to create a state of terror among a population or part of it. On the other hand, since the intent of a terrorist act is more often than not combined with the intent to attack a State's national stability and security, a definition should equally ensure that violent or non-violent acts aiming at compelling a government or organisation to do or refrain from doing a particular act are clearly included. To this end, it has been proposed that the political/ideological motive requirement will ensure that all acts that will fall into the definition, being acts that either create a state of terror or intimidate the authorities of a State or both, are acts driven by the special intent to promote a certain political/ideological agenda by disrupting peaceful political processes or social life. Additionally, the inclusion of a political/ideological motive requirement will preclude criminal acts driven by non-political/ideological ends, such as economic profit, despair or insanity, from being categorised as terrorist, retaining thus the morally different stigma that a crime of international terrorism should carry.

---

[108] Saul 2012, p. 89.

[109] Habermas 2003, p. 34.

[110] Wilson 2009, p. 6.

[111] Rome Statute of the International Criminal Court, opened for signature 17 July 1998, 2187 UNTS 90 (entered into force 1 July 2002) UN Doc. A/CONF.183/9, Preamble, para 3.

6.2.2 *Exemption of Activities of Particular Groups or Individuals*

So far, it has been argued that, for a definition of terrorism to achieve the fine balance between the protection of both State-centric and cosmopolitan concerns, it has to include: (i) the subjective element of either creating a state of terror among the population through the use of violence or compelling the authorities to do or refrain from doing a particular act and (ii) a political or otherwise ideological motive as a special element required for both of the subjective elements. Turning now to the question of whether activities of particular groups or individuals should be exempted from the definition, such as those carried out by freedom fighters or State agents, it was mentioned previously that, with the exception of the Arab Convention[112] and the OIC Convention to Combat Terrorism,[113] the general tendency does not support the incorporation of any exceptions. Both the Arab and the OIC Conventions provide for an exclusion of activities carried out in the context of self-determination; however the 1994 UNGA Declaration[114] and the Preambles of both the Financing Convention[115] and the UN Draft Convention on Terrorism[116] condemn terrorism 'by whomever committed'. Furthermore, the STL Decision did not address the question of exempting activities carried out in the context of self-determination.

It has been argued previously that the issue of self-determination and activities of national liberation movements in the context of an armed conflict are already covered by international humanitarian law. Activities during war time, in both international and national conflicts, that bear similarities with terrorist offences during peace time are already criminalised as war crimes,[117] including the act of spreading terror among civilians as a separate war crime.[118] Also, the people's right to self-determination is very well established in the UN Charter, IHL and the two UN International Human Rights Covenants[119] and thus, activities carried out in this context cannot fall into the definition of terrorism, regardless of whether a separate exception of this type of activities is finally adopted.[120] The 'by whomever committed' clause that is included in the anti-terrorist instruments mentioned previously

---

[112] Arab Convention, above n. 10, Article 2a.

[113] OIC Convention, above n. 30, Article 2a.

[114] UNGA 1994, Annex I, Article 1.

[115] Financing of Terrorism Convention, above n. 3, Preamble.

[116] UNGA 2002, p. 4.

[117] Saul 2012, p. 95.

[118] ICTY, *Prosecutor v Galić*, Trial Judgment, 5 December 2003, ICTY-98-29-T, paras 65–66; affirmed in ICTY, *Prosecutor v Galić*, Appeals Judgment, 30 November 2006, IT-98-29-A, paras 87–90.

[119] Text to above n. 50.

[120] See Värk 2011, p. 79 arguing that 'the inclusion or exclusion of the activities of armed forces is mostly emotional and symbolic.'

cannot be extended to those who engage in warfare in conformity with international humanitarian law; in case of violations, the perpetrators will be liable for prosecution for war crimes or crimes against humanity.[121] On the other hand, in cases where an internal situation does not amount to an armed conflict for international humanitarian law to apply, then any terrorist-type conduct will be covered by domestic law on terrorist offences.[122] As a result, the reaffirmation of people's right to self-determination and to fight against foreign occupation does not need to be restated in a definition of terrorism to be used in an international criminal law context.

Generally speaking, it is the author's view that the question of exempting or not freedom fighters' activities from a definition for terrorism is somewhat out of place, for the reasons analysed above. However, the same cannot be argued for the exception of the activities of State agents (police, military forces etc.). As was mentioned previously, the UN Draft Convention, despite the reference in its Preamble that, among the acts of international terrorism that have to be suppressed, are also 'those which are committed or supported by States, directly or indirectly',[123] provides for an exception, in its draft Article 18(3) for those 'activities undertaken by the military forces of a State in the exercise of their official duties, inasmuch as they are governed by other rules of international law (…)'.[124] Despite the cosmopolitan aspiration stated in the preambular text of the convention to stand up against international terrorism even when committed by State agents, the caveat offered in its draft Article 18(3) demonstrates its cosmopolitan limitations. The principles that apply to the conduct of military forces in time of peace are those which relate to the law on State responsibility, the use of force and human rights law under general international law[125] and thus, activities of military forces will always be outside the scope of this convention. It has been argued that this interpretation is consistent with the overall direction of the Coordinator's proposal that State-committed or State-supported terrorism will continue to fall into the ambit of other fields of law such as the UN Charter framework, IHL, international criminal law (for acts committed in the context of the crime of aggression or crimes against humanity) and the law on State responsibility, which provide for State obligations in cases where acts of violence are committed by State agents.[126] However, IHL applies only in situations of armed conflicts and thus, any acts committed in the context of 'situations of internal disturbances and tensions, such as riots, isolated and sporadic acts of violence and other acts of a similar nature'[127] are exempted from its scope. Moreover, international human rights law, while being relevant in

[121] Saul 2012, p. 95.

[122] Ibid.

[123] UNGA 2002, Annex I.

[124] Ibid., Annex IV, draft Article 18(3).

[125] UNGA 2010, Annex III, p. 20.

[126] Perera 2014, p. 161.

[127] Additional Protocol II, above n. 19, Article 2.

the context of protecting civil and political rights such as free expression, assembly or privacy, does not include any prohibitions related to State-committed terrorism *per se* and, regarding State-supported terrorism, State responsibility has hardly ever been invoked or established successfully.[128] Concerning the international criminal law framework, the jurisdiction of the ICC over the crime of aggression is not as yet commenced, and consequently, the only branch of international criminal law that is in a position to address acts of State-committed terrorism is the one related to the commission of crimes against humanity. Therefore, if the UN Draft Convention leaves outside its scope the commission of terrorist-type activities by military forces in time of peace, then there will be limited room for any other international legal framework to condemn these activities as terrorist and to directly link criminal responsibility to acts of terrorism committed by State agents.

In sum, for a balance to be achieved regarding the question of exempting activities from the scope of a definition for terrorism, a 'moral symmetry'[129] should be retained: the 'by whomever committed' clause should be understood as covering both activities of non-State actors and State agents if they exhibit the same effect. In fact, the broader a definition is, the more room for exceptions it will have and for this reason, it has to be strictly construed in order to avoid any grey areas that might allow the commission of acts which assume the characteristics of terrorism. Only when the question of a perpetrator is not a qualifier of which acts can be understood as terrorist, will it be possible to further the cosmopolitan aspirations of a definition and push forward the efforts to condemn terrorism in all its forms. The inclusion of activities carried out by non-State actors is obviously imperative to serve the need of protecting State interests pertaining to national security and stability of a State. However, should the definition not cover activities carried out by State agents, then State-centric considerations as to the autonomy of how a State should behave to individuals that live or happen to be in its territory will severely weigh against any cosmopolitan aspirations of fighting impunity for the commission of grave crimes and of applying universal standards that all humankind should equally enjoy.

6.2.3 The International Element of a Terrorist Act

A final suggestion on how a definition for terrorism will best reconcile the somewhat antithetical State sovereignty and cosmopolitan concerns in the fight against terrorism is the inclusion of an 'international element' requirement. As was mentioned previously, the STL Decision ruled that a customary definition for terrorism requires that the terrorist act be transnational. The Tribunal held that this

[128] Trapp 2012, p. 280. Even in the Lockerbie case, Libya accepted civil responsibility only, for the conduct of its officials (ibid) and paid compensation to the victims in order to have Security Council measures lifted (See BBC 2008).

[129] Saul 2012, p. 96.

'transnationality' consists of (i) a connection of perpetrators, victims or means used across two or more States or (ii) a significant impact that a terrorist act in one State has on another, constituting a threat to international peace and security, at least for the neighbouring States.[130] Putting aside the debate whether there is general agreement on the existence of a customary rule concerning the definition for terrorism, this 'transnational element' requirement serves as a distinguishing line between the acts of terrorism that should remain within the national jurisdictional realm and those that can or should justify the intervention of an international tribunal. In sum, the transnational element becomes a threshold beyond which an act of terrorism becomes of international concern and qualifies intervention from an international body due to its international connections or a direct 'spill over' effect to other States. However, if the planning, execution or direct impact of a terrorist act does not have transnational dimensions, then the act is considered of purely domestic nature and only national criminal law is applicable, even when the act has a similar effect to a transnational act of terrorism in terms of the number of victims or social destruction.[131]

Be that as it may, it is the author's view that this requirement should be renamed as an 'international element' rather than a 'transnational element' requirement. While in criminological terms, there is no substantial difference between the two,[132] there is difference in juridical terms, originating from the distinctive nature of transnational and international crimes. Boister argues that transnational crimes, or 'transnational criminal law', form part of international criminal law in general, which is further divided into transnational and international criminal law *stricto sensu*.[133] The former significantly differs from the latter, in that it does not create individual liability but consists of 'an indirect system of interstate obligations, generating national criminal law'.[134] Putting its function in the context of the two theories, one could say that transnational criminal law extends rather than limits the sovereign reach of States in the struggle against transnational crimes.[135] Consequently, this system of interstate cooperation is mostly State-centric and functions on the basis of State sovereignty considerations,[136] contrary to the system of international criminal law *stricto sensu*, which restricts the role of States in the adjudication of international crimes.

With respect to terrorism, terrorist offences were established in international law by the anti-terrorist conventions which fall into the ambit of transnational criminal

[130] STL Decision, above n. 62, para 90.

[131] Ibid.

[132] Mueller 2001, p. 13 as found in Boister 2003, p. 954.

[133] Ibid., p. 955.

[134] Ibid., p. 962.

[135] Norberg 2010, p. 17.

[136] Bassiouni 1974, p. 429 in Boister 2002, p. 200.

law, according to Boister's distinction. Whether the origins of the struggle against these offences have been national or international in character is debated,[137] however, as it stands so far and according to the sectoral regime of the anti-terrorist conventions, the penal proscription against terrorist offences remains national. While the sectoral anti-terrorist conventions could also promote 'a cosmopolitan international morality' in the fight against terrorism,[138] they fail to do so because of this reliance of transnational criminal law to national penal systems. This sectoral regime presupposes the existence of fully developed national criminal systems[139] which pay due regard to cosmopolitan concerns about individuals prosecuted and punished nationally.[140] However, one should be aware that national criminal systems might be poorly developed or heavily influenced by ideals of how criminal law should be, held by the most powerful and influential States.[141] This sectoral anti-terrorist regime demands first and foremost law enforcement expertise in the effort to suppress terrorism and relies for its effectiveness on some influential States which assume the role of an 'international enforcer'.[142] Thus, the outcome is that the ideas of the most powerful States on how criminal law should be, along with their national penal systems, predominate over cosmopolitan values relating to the international legality and the human rights of individuals being prosecuted and punished under this regime.[143] This implicit faith of the sectoral anti-terrorist regime in the national criminal justice systems of its States parties leaves too much room for States to guard zealously their sovereign interests at the expense of international legality and protection of human rights, which constitute cosmopolitan aspirations that international criminal law should embody.

For these reasons, and regarding a definition for terrorism, a formulation which would favour the transnational over the international nature of a terrorist act should be abandoned. The connotations of 'transnationality' of terrorism, contrary to those of its 'internationality', entail ideas of how terrorism should be suppressed, based mostly on State-centric considerations. However, and as the overall argument of this book suggests, the effectiveness of a definition is based on the extent to which State-centric and cosmopolitan considerations are given due regard in order to avoid the effect of cosmopolitan efforts being pushed back by State-centric barriers. Besides, there is no reason in principle why one should preclude the transition of

---

[137] See Norberg 2010, p. 18, arguing that the adjudication of the crimes that are under the ICC's jurisdiction today was initiated at the international level, whereas this 'is not the case with respect to terrorism'. For an opposite view see Boister 2003, p. 955 arguing that '[t]he offences established by the suppression conventions are, in contrast, classed by international lawyers as "crimes of international concern" or "common crimes against internationally protected interests" because although the origin of the norm is international, penal proscription is national.'

[138] Nadelmann 1990, p. 481 in Boister 2003, pp. 957–58.

[139] Ibid., p. 958.

[140] Boister 2002, p. 220.

[141] Boister 2003, p. 958.

[142] Ibid., p. 960.

[143] Ibid.

terrorism from a transnational offence to an international crime with its own definition, should certain requirements be fulfilled, the international element being one of them.

Turning now to the question of the context of this international element, there is substantial convergence among academics and the STL ruling on the 'transnationality' of terrorism, about what this element should entail. Cassese argues that terrorism can amount to an international crime when: (i) it transcends national boundaries, in terms of persons, means and violence involved, (ii) it is promoted or tolerated by a State because State involvement renders a particular terrorist act (iii) 'a phenomenon of concern to the whole international community and a threat to international peace'.[144] Finally, he completes this list by adding that a terrorist act can amount to an international crime when, all the abovementioned requirements being fulfilled, it is (iv) very serious and large-scale.[145] Secondly, Kolb suggests that the internationality of a terrorist act consists of its international consequences, namely whether the rights and duties of more than one State or foreign interests are affected.[146] Thus, for Kolb, internationality is mostly defined by the transnational dimensions of a terrorist act, determined by the persons involved (perpetrators, victims or when the target is a person with an international status) and the number of States that are affected (including cases where the act is committed in a space where no State has exclusive jurisdiction).[147] However, he leaves open the question of whether only a gravity requirement or the element of indiscriminate violence can be sufficient in order for a terrorist act to reach the threshold of internationality.[148] Broadly speaking, even if the persons involved in a very serious or large-scale terrorist act are exclusively from one State, which is also the only affected State, then the terrorist act can still be considered as an attack to universal values and interests of the international community, qualifying intervention from an international tribunal.[149] Besides, it is unrealistic to say that even when a very serious and large-scale terrorist act involves or affects persons exclusively from one State, it does not aim at provoking international concern or attracting the attention of the international community.[150] Therefore, his argument goes, the 'internationality' of a terrorist act should not be strictly determined by its pragmatic transnational dimensions but be extended to include acts of particular gravity that can generally affect international community interests.[151]

However, the question that remains is how the 'internationality' threshold can be defined in such a way so as to respond to the current exigencies of combatting

---

[144] Cassese 2004, p. 223.
[145] Ibid.
[146] Kolb 2004, p. 243.
[147] Ibid.
[148] Ibid., p. 244.
[149] Ibid.
[150] Ibid., p. 246.
[151] Ibid., p. 245.

terrorism without transgressing the boundaries of State sovereignty. The transnational element, as defined by the STL Decision, does not cover acts of terrorism which are of purely domestic nature, even if their impact on a State is similar to the one of a transnational act of terrorism as far as victims and social destruction are concerned.[152] Cassese agrees with this view, arguing that, for an act of terrorism to be an international crime, all the conditions he presents have to be met, together with the requirement that the act be very serious and large-scale.[153] This last condition does not suffice on its own if the act does not present the other characteristics he proposes, namely, the cross-border character, State involvement and the requirement that the act amount to a threat to international peace. This approach of the ambit of 'internationality' precludes the possibility of an act of domestic terrorism amounting to an international crime, based strictly on grounds of gravity and/or indiscriminate violence. This question is left partly unanswered by Kolb who leans, however, towards a more flexible interpretation, according to which an act of domestic terrorism ceases to be purely domestic when being of such gravity so as to affect international community interests. Though in pragmatic terms, one would agree that very serious and large-scale acts of domestic terrorism aim at attracting international attention or attacking international values, their inclusion into a definition for international terrorism, overrides national priorities and strategies in the field. Besides, the sectoral anti-terrorist conventions regulate only transnational acts of terrorism, leaving outside their scope domestic acts,[154] without any reference to their gravity. Therefore, the inclusion of gravity as a sufficient qualifier of which acts can amount to international terrorism even without having a cross-border character, goes far beyond the scope of the existing anti-terrorist conventions and widens the ambit of 'internationality' to an extent that seriously collides with the ambit of national anti-terrorist policies and State sovereignty-based priorities.

Therefore, it seems that the introduction of the element of gravity as a sufficient qualifier for the 'internationality' of an act of terrorism will not bridge but rather widen the gap between the concerns relating to State sovereignty protection and promotion of cosmopolitan aspirations in the fight against terrorism. For this reason, it is the author's suggestion that one should focus on another of the proposed elements, in an effort to eliminate the tension between the two poles of State sovereignty and cosmopolitanism: both the STL Decision and the element of 'internationality' proposed by Cassese support the view that an act of terrorism is 'internationalised' when it constitutes a threat to international peace and security. The STL Decision ruled that an act of terrorism amounts to a threat to international peace and security when it has an impact on more than one State, namely 'when it is foreseeable that a terrorist attack that is planned and executed in one country will threaten international peace and security, at least for neighbouring countries',[155] an interpretation that is consistent

[152] STL Decision, above n. 62, para 90.

[153] Cassese 2004, p. 223.

[154] Saul 2012, p. 93.

[155] STL Decision, above n. 62, para 90.

with the generally accepted cross-border element. Moreover, Cassese interprets the element of 'threat to international peace' by referring to the State involvement in a terrorist act; if a terrorist act is committed with State support or tolerance, then it stops being a criminal activity which can be suppressed within the national realm and becomes a problem of international concern.[156] Finally, Saul also argues that 'if terrorism is thought to threaten international peace and security, an international definition must be limited to acts capable of that result'[157]; what makes them capable of that result can be their cross-border character and/or State involvement,[158] inflicting thus an injury to international community interests and values. In this case, it is highly likely that these acts cannot be suppressed by one State's law enforcement mechanisms and will present a 'spill-over' effect rendering the act a threat to international peace and security. These acts that will present a cross-border element or include State involvement, and also attack, in both cases, international community interests and values, cannot be considered as purely domestic and will fulfil the requirements of 'internationality'.

To recapitulate, it is suggested that the element of 'internationality' will be a necessary threshold in a definition for terrorism, as it will help reconcile the gap between State-centric and cosmopolitan concerns about the suppression of acts of international terrorism. It has been argued that the preferred terminology should refer to the 'internationality' of terrorism, rather than to its 'transantionality', not for reasons relating to criminological differences between the two but to juridical ones. If terrorism is to be suppressed at the international level, an international definition should reflect and put emphasis on the international dimension of terrorism. References to its 'transnationality' relate to the categorisation of terrorism as a transnational offence, which States have an obligation to suppress through State-based mechanisms of cooperation. However, the formulation of a definition for international terrorism should and can constitute a starting point to signify its transition from a transnational offence to an international crime. The establishment of the STL demonstrated that there are particularly grave acts of terrorism that qualify for international intervention. This 'internationalisation' should be further developed by the formulation of a universal definition which will advance the international dimensions of a terrorist act and promote accountability at an international level. Secondly, the inclusion of an international element in the definition will set a clearer distinction between which acts of terrorism can and should be suppressed within the national realm and which acts qualify for international intervention. It is as crucial to protect State sovereignty and national security interests in cases of purely domestic terrorism as it is to protect basic human rights and universal values and international community interests in cases of international terrorism. Lastly, it has been suggested that the 'internationality' of an act of terrorism should be determined not by the gravity of the act as such but by the

---

[156] Cassese 2004, p. 223.

[157] Saul 2012, p. 93.

[158] Ibid.

extent to which it constitutes a threat to international peace and security. Since the Security Council, the only international organ empowered to determine a threat to international peace and security, is not bound to follow any legal rules in order to make such a determination, it is proposed that acts of terrorism that conceptually amount to such a threat should demonstrate either a cross-border element, in terms of perpetrators, victims or means of violence used, or direct or indirect State involvement. The cross-border element of a terrorist act will result in a 'spill-over' effect to other States and State involvement will render the suppression of the terrorist act by the national authorities of that State highly difficult. Therefore, in both cases, international community interests will warrant protection and suppression at an international level will be the only option in order to protect the interests of the affected State(s), the interests of the affected individuals and the interests of the international community as a whole.

References

Bassiouni MC (1974) An Appraisal of the Growth and Developing Trends of International Criminal Law. Revue Internationale de Droit Penal 45: 405–433

BBC (2008) Lockerbie Evidence not disclosed. http://news.bbc.co.uk/1/hi/scotland/south_of_scotland/7573244.stm. Accessed 24 February 2017

Boister N (2002) Human Rights Protections in the Suppression Conventions. H R L Rev 2(2): 199–227

Boister N (2003) Transnational Criminal Law? EJIL 14(5): 953–976

Cassese A (2004) Terrorism as an International Crime. In: Bianchi A (ed) Enforcing International Law Norms Against Terrorism. Hart Publishing, Oregon, pp 213–225

Chadwick E (2014) Terrorism and Self-determination. In: Saul B (ed) Research Handbook on International Law and Terrorism. Edward Elgar, Cheltenham, pp 298–314

Delmas-Marty M (2002) Les crimes internationaux peuvent-ils contribuer au débat entre universalisme et relativisme des valeurs? In: Cassese A, Delmas-Marty M (eds) Crimes Internationaux et Juridictions Internationales. Presse Universitaire de France, Paris, pp 59–67

di Filippo M (2008) Terrorist Crimes and International Cooperation: Critical Remarks on the Definition and Inclusion of Terrorism in the Category of International Crimes. EJIL 19(3): 533–570

Golder B, Williams G (2004) What is "Terrorism"? Problems of Legal Definition. U N S Wales L J 27(2): 270–295

Habermas J (2003) Fundamentalism and Terror: A Dialogue with Jürgen Habermas. In: Borradori G (ed) Philosophy in a Time of Terror: Dialogues with Jürgen Habermas and Jacques Derrida. University of Chicago Press, Chicago, pp 25–44

Hmoud M (2006) Negotiating the Draft Comprehensive Convention on International Terrorism. JICJ 4: 1031–1043

ICRC (2011) The relevance of IHL in the context of terrorism. www.icrc.org/eng/resources/documents/faq/terrorism-ihl-210705.htm. Accessed 24 February 2017

Kolb R (2004) The Exercise of Criminal Jurisdiction over International Terrorists. In: Bianchi A (ed) Enforcing International Law Norms Against Terrorism. Hart Publishing, Oregon, pp 227–273

Llobet M (2012) Terrorism: Limits Between Crimes and War. The Fallacy of the Slogan "War on Terror". In: Masferrer A (ed) Post 9/11 and the State of Permanent Legal Emergency,

Ius Gentium: Comparative Perspectives on Law and Justice 14. DOI: 10.1007/978-94-007-4062-4_5, Springer Science + Business Media B.V., Berlin, pp 101–117
Mueller GOW (2001) Transnational crime: Definitions and Concepts. In: Williams P, Vlassis D (eds) Combating Transnational Crime, Concepts, Activities and Responses. Frank Cass, London, pp 13–21
Mylonaki E (2011) Defining Terrorism. Criminal Law and Justice Weekly 175. http://www.criminallawandjustice.co.uk/features/Defining-Terrorism. Accessed 3 July 2015
Nadelmann EA (1990) Global Prohibition Regimes: The Evolution of Norms in International Society. International Organisation 44: 479–526
Norberg N (2010) Terrorism and International Criminal Justice: Dim Prospects for a Future Together. Santa Clara J Int'l L 8:11–50
Perera AR (2014) The Draft United Nations Comprehensive Convention on International Terrorism. In: Saul B (ed) Research Handbook on International Law and Terrorism. Edward Elgar, Cheltenham, pp 151–162
Puchooa P (2011) Defining Terrorism at the Special Tribunal for Lebanon. Journal of Terrorism Research 2(3): 34–48
Saul B (2006) Defining Terrorism in International Law. Oxford University Press, Oxford.
Saul B (2011) Legislating from a Radical Hague: The United Nations Special Tribunal for Lebanon Invents an International Crime for Transnational Terrorism. Leiden J Int'l L 24: 677–700
Saul B (2012) Civilising the Exception: Universally Defining Terrorism. In: Masferrer A (ed) Post 9/11 and the State of Permanent Legal Emergency, Ius Gentium: Comparative Perspectives on Law and Justice 14. DOI 10.1007/978-94-007-4062-4_4, Springer Science + Business Media B.V., Berlin, pp 79–100
Subedi S (2002) The UN Response to International Terrorism in the Aftermath of the Terrorist Attacks in America and the Problem of the Definition of Terrorism in International Law. 4 International Law Forum Droit International 4: 159–169
Trapp KN (2012) Holding States Responsible for Terrorism Before the International Court of Justice. JIDS 3(2): 279–298
UN Commission on Human Rights (2005) Report of the Special Rapporteur on the Promotion and Protection of Human Rights and Fundamental Freedoms While Countering Terrorism, 62nd Session, UN doc. E/CN.4/2006/98
UNGA (1960) Resolution 1541 (XV) UN Doc. A/RES/1541
UNGA (1970) Declaration on Principles of International Law concerning Friendly Relations and Cooperation among States in accordance with the Charter of the United Nations, UN Doc. A/Res/2625 (XXV)
UNGA (1994) Declaration on Measures to Eliminate International Terrorism, UN Doc. A/RES/49/60 Supp No 49 (A/49/49)
UNGA (2002) Report of the Ad Hoc Committee established by UNGA Res 51/210 of 17 December 1996, 6th Session, UN Doc. Supp No 37 (A/57/37)
UNGA (2006) Resolution 60/145, UN Doc. A/RES/60/145
UNGA Sixth Committee (2010) Report of the Working Group on Measures to Eliminate International Terrorism, UN Doc. A/C.6/65/L.10, Annex III
UNSC (2007) Statute of the Special Tribunal for Lebanon, Resolution 1757, UN Doc. S/ RES/ 1757
Värk R (2011) Terrorism, State Responsibility and the Use of Armed Force. Estonian National Defence College Proceedings 14: 74–111
Walter C (2004) Defining Terrorism in National and International Law. In: Walter C and ors (eds) Terrorism as a Challenge for National and International Law: Security versus Liberty? Springer, Berlin, pp 23–43
Wilson P (2009) Aggression, Crime and International Security: Moral, Political and Legal Dimensions of International Relations. Routledge, London

[illegible] Goodman [illegible] (2006), [illegible]
[illegible] Burlington (Gower).
[illegible] 2011.
[illegible]
[illegible] Whistleblowing [illegible]
[illegible] Law [illegible]
[illegible] (eds.) [illegible]
[illegible] (2011) [illegible] The Code [illegible]
[illegible]
[illegible] (2011) [illegible] Germany [illegible]
[illegible] (2010) [illegible]
[illegible] Pub[illegible]
[illegible]
[illegible] Whistleblowing [illegible]
[illegible]
[illegible]
[illegible]
[illegible]
[illegible]

Chapter 7
Conclusion

Abstract As the overarching argument of this book goes, State sovereignty considerations and cosmopolitan ideals are the two principal driving forces in the development of international law in general and international criminal law in particular. However, these two dynamics ofter appear to conflict, with the former, typically based on political interests and exigencies, trying to push back any developments aspired to by the latter. For this reason, more often than not, international criminal law developments have been slow and often confronted by States which tend to have a rather conservative view of how international law should work in practice. This book has been an attempt to demonstrate how these two dynamics can be potentially reconciled in an effort to define and criminalise terrorism for international criminal justice purposes. It is the author's view that not only is there an imperative need to finally agree upon a universal definition for terrorism but also that this definition should be more than a compromise between those who aspire to cosmopolitan ideas and those who prioritise State concerns over those ideas. The formulation of an international definition for terrorism, if ever achieved, should be seen as an example of how States and international criminal justice can work together towards the achievement of a common end which will eventually benefit all sides involved, States, individual victims and the international community, contributing meaningfully to the effectiveness of the international criminal justice system as it stands today.

Keywords Security Council · ICC · State sovereignty · Cosmopolitanism · International Criminal Justice · International Terrorism

Contents

S. Margariti, *Defining International Terrorism*, International Criminal Justice Series 15, DOI 10.1007/978-94-6265-204-0_7

7.1 Putting the Pieces Together

This book has been an attempt to show that the effectiveness of definitions of international crimes relies heavily on the extent to which concerns of State sovereignty and aspirations of cosmopolitanism are balanced properly. The paradigm of aggression served to highlight how these dynamics shaped its definition and criminalisation throughout history, starting from the League of Nations period and until the Review Conference in Kampala. On a similar basis, the paradigm of terrorism was examined, demonstrating that State sovereignty and cosmopolitanism constitute the same driving forces towards this direction, and their antithesis is most of the time the main reason why the most contentious issues surrounding the matter cannot be adequately addressed. In this 'State sovereignty versus cosmopolitanism' scheme, the Security Council was sketched as an organ with primarily State-centred priorities and the ICC as an institution whose priorities have a cosmopolitan basis, though in practice, their priorities might well be mixed. Finally, a suggestion was made on how an international definition for terrorism should be approached taking into account sovereignty- and cosmopolitanism-related parameters, as this is, according to the author's view, the most workable way of achieving a meaningful development in this direction.

After analysing the concepts of State sovereignty and cosmopolitanism and their interplay with international law, emphasis was given early in this study on the complementary mandate of the ICC. One could argue that this emphasis might seem somewhat out of place since there is still a long way before terrorism is actually defined for the purposes of international criminal justice, let alone from being included into the jurisdiction of the ICC. Apart from its contribution to our understanding of the modalities of ICC prosecutions under its complementarity regime, this analysis reveals once again in the history of international law the 'tug of war' relation between politics and law, a relation that all members of the international community, States and international organisations, have to deal with. In the ICC context, this relation is primarily manifested in two ways: firstly, in the implementation of the Rome Statute provisions by its States Parties and secondly in the prosecutorial policy in the selection of cases. Despite the fact that many States Parties have already harmonised in some respects their national laws concerning international crimes with the Rome Statute provisions as was shown in Chap. 2, it is hard to speculate to what extent States Parties (or which of them) will conduct themselves in a similar way to the ICC regarding the implementation of the Rome Statute definitions, the prosecutorial policies, sentencing, immunities etc. While, obviously, differentiation between the Rome Statute and national legislations is not a ground for admissibility *per se* and the spirit of the complementarity regime does not support such a view, examples of the ICC's prosecutorial policy have shown that there might be instances where this differentiation might be extended to a degree that covers the grounds for admissibility, provided by Article 17 of the Rome Statute. This tendency to intervene in cases not strictly envisioned by the Rome Statute can be said to constitute the pro-cosmopolitan facet of the ICC, in the sense that international prosecutions predominate over the conduct of national proceedings.

This need for balance between State sovereignty and international criminal justice purposes did not come to the surface with the establishment of the ICC. The paradigm of aggression showed that the two World Wars drew the attention of the international community to the need for outlawing, criminalising and finally defining the crime of aggression. This process has been undoubtedly slow, not the least because of the implications it bore on the sovereign interests of the most powerful States. This long process, marked by the establishment of the first security system of the League of Nations, the cosmopolitan legacy of the Nuremberg trials, the creation of the Security Council as the ultimate authority in international peace and security matters and finally, the criminalisation and definition of aggression for the purposes of the Rome Statute, made it clear that no substantial development can be made in the field unless sovereign priorities and cosmopolitan ideals are properly balanced. The Kampala definition for the crime of aggression seems to have provided a way forward, by introducing an adequate legal framework at the international level for the prosecution and punishment of political and military leaders found to be implicated in acts of aggression.

It remains to be seen in practice however, to what extent this newly-adopted definition will accomplish the hopes of those who aspire to an international justice system free of politics. Much is left to the ICC's discretion in the interpretation of the definition but it is equally true that much is left to the relation that the ICC will form with the Security Council if and when a case of aggression comes before the former. It was highlighted in Chap. 4 that the pragmatic limitations that permeate any future aggression prosecutions, posed by the role preserved for the Security Council by Articles 15*bis*(6) and (8) of the Kampala Resolution[1] cannot be overlooked and therefore it would be better for the ICC to try to minimise them than to pretend that they do not exist.[2] The Security Council, having a primary and key role in international peace and security matters, might ultimately exercise control over which aggression prosecutions will or will not take place and therefore, the ICC should make the most of its autonomy as provided by the Rome Statute provisions.

The issue of defining and criminalising international terrorism has similarly at its centre this 'State sovereignty versus cosmopolitanism' antithesis. Especially after the 9/11 attacks, where terrorism drew international attention in the most tragic way, counterterrorism responses by individual States focused mostly on the

[1] Resolution RC/Res.6, Annex I, Amendments to the Rome Statute of the International Criminal Court on the Crime of Aggression (11 June 2010) (Kampala Resolution) Article 15*bis*(6) (providing that the Prosecutor 'shall first ascertain whether the Security Council has made a determination of an act of aggression committed by the State concerned') and Article 15*bis*(8) providing that 'the Prosecutor may proceed with the investigation in respect of a crime of aggression, provided that the Pre-Trial Division has authorized the commencement of [this] investigation…and the Security Council has not decided otherwise in accordance with Article 16').

[2] Schabas 2012, p. 259 referring to the political factors that might influence the ICC Prosecutor in the selection of situations to be brought before the ICC.

protection of their own sovereign interests without due regard to cosmopolitan aspirations relating to the administration of international criminal justice. For the Security Council and the most powerful individual States, it suffices that terrorism be addressed nationally, despite the differentiation of each State's understanding of what constitutes terrorism and the lack of a commonly accepted definition. The ambiguous drafting of some post-9/11 Security Council Resolutions which provided the US with the latitude to respond with the 'war on terror' and the substantial discretion they also provided to individual States to fight terrorism unilaterally, widened further the gap in States' understanding and response to terrorism and encouraged an abusing use of the term in order to include a wide range of other ordinary offences. On the other hand, the Decision of the Special Tribunal for Lebanon surpassed State sovereignty considerations and held that a customary law definition for terrorism in times of peace actually exists. While this is a very welcome conclusion for those who support the criminalisation and definition of terrorism for the purposes of international criminal justice, this cosmopolitan judicial activism to apply to the Lebanese case a widened definition for terrorism, different from the national one, raised concerns about whether such a customary definition exists and whether overlooking a national definition to apply a customary one was justified under the circumstances of a national case. Finally, the United Nations General Assembly negotiations on a draft Comprehensive Convention on Terrorism were examined as another pro-cosmopolitan effort to this direction, which however tries to accommodate the different State views in the issue of a terrorism definition. Though the process has been slow and no agreement has as yet been reached, the outcome of these negotiations, despite any flaws it might have, is bound to achieve a better balance between State concerns and cosmopolitan aspirations without being heavily influenced by the most powerful States' understanding of the concept of terrorism nor raising any legitimacy issues.

Chapter 6 exclusively focused on the question of defining international terrorism. This question was approached by a two-tier analysis: firstly, an effort was made to trace the common ground as well as the main points of contention among the elements of terrorism in definitions as provided by several international anti-terrorist instruments and national law. Secondly, both the consented and the contested elements were put under the light of the State sovereignty and cosmopolitan theories in an effort to argue in favour of balance between these two theories. As such, it was finally concluded that a definition for international terrorism should reflect: (i) the element of indiscriminate violence that (ii) will have as its aim to spread fear to the population or part thereof or to compel a government or organisation to do or abstain from doing a particular act, (iii) with a special intent of promoting a political or otherwise ideological purpose, (iv) without any exception as to the category/class of perpetrator (v) provided that the conduct meets the proposed threshold of 'internationality'. This proposed threshold, included in the STL Decision as an element of the customary definition of terrorism, should be determined not by the gravity of the act *per se* but by the extent to which it constitutes a threat to international peace and security. This extent, in its turn, is determined by a cross-border element, in terms of perpetrators, victims or means of violence used, or direct or indirect State involvement.[3]

The purpose of this book was not limited only to the suggestion of a potential definition for international terrorism to be used in the context of international criminal justice, but extended also to the affirmation that defining international crimes effectively presupposes a degree of balance between State sovereignty interests and cosmopolitan ideas. To this end, the crime of aggression as defined in the Kampala Resolution was used as a paradigm of how these concepts of State sovereignty and cosmopolitanism have or have not been balanced in the case of aggression, and whether this paradigm can give some insights with respect to how terrorism should or should not be defined. Chapter 4 proposed three lessons to be learnt from the Kampala definition of aggression, which according to the author's view, are relevant in the context of defining international terrorism: (i) the 'leadership requirement' clause in the definition is a manifestation of the acknowledgment that individuals found in a position to threaten States can and possibly should be prosecuted and punished at the international level, (ii) the 'manifest threshold' demonstrates that the Kampala definition appears to provide little guidance to the ICC as to which aggression cases can eventually fall under its jurisdiction and finally (iii) the provisions regulating the role of the Security Council in the adjudication of aggression cases show that cosmopolitan aspirations in the adjudication of international crimes can only be partially addressed without the explicit support of the Security Council.

Combining these lessons with the abovementioned proposed definitional elements, some particularly useful conclusions can be drawn: firstly, the proposed element in the definition for terrorism that no exception on the category/class of the perpetrators should be included can be paralleled with the 'leadership clause' requirement in the definition of aggression. On the one hand, under a textual approach, these clauses significantly differ in the sense that the proposed 'no exception' clause means that anyone, being a high-ranking official or a common individual, can constitute a potential perpetrator of an act of international terrorism while the 'leadership requirement' clause substantially limits the number of potential perpetrators of the crime of aggression only to political or military leaders. However, what the 'leadership requirement' clause has to contribute in this respect is not that it allows for a limited number of individuals to be found accountable for aggression but for the acknowledgment that individuals can be indeed found accountable for a crime directed against a State. While the rest of the Article 5 crimes refer to crimes committed by individuals against individuals, the crime of aggression is first and foremost a crime committed by individuals against a State. The proposed definition of international terrorism has as subjective elements either the intention to create a state of terror among the population or part of it or to coerce the authorities of a State, or international authorities, to do or abstain from doing a

[3] STL, *Interlocutory Decision on the Applicable Law: Terrorism, Conspiracy, Homicide, Perpetration, Cumulative Charging,* 16 February 2011, Case No. STL-11-01/1, para 90.

particular act. It was also proposed that for both of these subjective elements, there should be a special intent on the part of the perpetrator to promote a certain political or otherwise ideological agenda aiming at disrupting peaceful political processes and social life. Thus, any acts committed with the mere purpose to create a state of terror or the mere purpose to coerce the authorities will not automatically fall into the definition if this special intent to target a State's national security and stability is lacking. It follows therefore that a crime of international terrorism, as defined in this book, targets States (as well as individuals). The Kampala definition demonstrated that the ICC can be an appropriate forum for the prosecution of individuals that target States and this is a model to be adopted with respect to how the individual aspects of a crime of international terrorism should be also addressed.

With respect to the second lesson, it was also shown in Chap. 4 that the 'manifest threshold' does not help in reaching some degree of balance between State sovereignty and cosmopolitan ideals as it ultimately allows for a wide discretion on the part of the ICC to determine which cases will or will not fall under its jurisdiction, and finally to lean towards either a pro-cosmopolitan or a pro-State sovereignty approach. Instead, the proposed definition of terrorism includes another threshold which is not based on the gravity of the act but on the extent to which it constitutes a threat to international peace and security. Again, the link to the text of the UN Charter is unavoidable not the least because the characterisation of terrorist acts as threats to international peace and security is common in Security Council's practice, which is also the only organ empowered to make such a determination. However, just as the Security Council is empowered to determine acts of aggression without being obliged to follow any legal rules or criteria, the same is equally true for any potential determination of an act of terrorism as a threat to international peace and security. In this respect, should the Kampala Amendments acquire the desired number of ratifications, it is doubtful that the Security Council will change its practice in light of the fact that any determination on the existence of an act of aggression will have legal consequences for the political or military leaders of the involved State(s). Therefore, similar complications will also be present if prosecutions of international terrorism take place only after a Security Council's determination that a specific act constitutes a threat to international peace and security. For this reason, it was finally suggested that an act of terrorism can conceptually constitute a threat to international peace and security if it demonstrates either a cross-border element, in terms of perpetrators, victims or means of violence used, or direct or indirect State involvement. Thus the proposed threshold for an act of international terrorism to fall under the ICC's jurisdiction differs from aggression's 'manifest threshold', in that it does not introduce new and ambiguous language, such as the 'manifest violation' or the criterion of character[4] and is also in accord with the STL's ruling on the transnational element of a terrorist act as a part of the customary definition for terrorism.

[4] Kampala Resolution, above n. 1, Article 8*bis*.

This unavoidable interplay between Security Council's powers and ICC competence brings us to the third lesson derived of the Kampala definition. While Article 15*bis* of the Kampala Resolution appears to achieve a reasonable compromise between the primary role of the Security Council in international peace and security matters and the judicial autonomy of the ICC to initiate an aggression investigation, Chap. 4 has concluded that the overall impact of the provisions relating to this balancing of powers will finally favour Security Council's priorities rather than international criminal justice purposes with respect to which (if any) aggression situations will warrant ICC's intervention. The cosmopolitan theory reaches its maximum with Article 15*bis*(8) which provides for the Prosecutor's competence to initiate an aggression investigation after the authorisation of the Pre-Trial Division, in case of Security Council's inaction. However, this provision does not clear the way for the promotion of international criminal justice despite Security Council's inaction or opposing view in a particular case; without Security Council support, the ICC will appear unable to make the most of its autonomy and its mandate to fight impunity will be severely undermined if this mandate collides with any differing view of the Security Council (or any of its permanent members) in a particular case.

It was also discussed in Chap. 4 that this state of affairs will not be manifest exclusively in cases of aggression but it has already been manifest with respect to other cases before the ICC and will be manifest in case international terrorism becomes criminalised under the Rome Statute. While this study did not elaborate on the modalities of how Security Council's powers and ICC competences should be balanced in case of prosecutions of international terrorism, it follows that, at best, these modalities cannot significantly differ from the modalities regulated by the Kampala Resolution with respect to aggression. The Security Council's primary role with respect to international peace and security matters cannot be overlooked or rejected by the international criminal justice system. However, it is equally crucial for the current international criminal justice system to make full use of its competences and fulfil its mandate to the maximum extent possible.

It is already known and very well understood that the competing relation between politics and law permeates all international developments, political and legal alike. The concepts of State sovereignty and cosmopolitanism were used as the most representative continuations of politics and law respectively in the context of international criminal justice. However, this 'State sovereignty versus cosmopolitanism' debate that was framed for the purposes of this book is actually one aspect of the much wider debate between politics and law. As such, according to the author's understanding, any developments that have been, are, or will be advanced in the field of international law are the middle, minimum ground of agreement between these two opposing dynamics. These developments can be viewed in a dual perspective, both as the maximum concessions that politics can make to law and as the maximum control that law can exert on politics. Regardless of which perspective one chooses, the result is the same: all developments in international law are a mixture of political considerations and legal aspirations, which most of the time are improperly balanced. This book was written with the hope that, at least in the context of defining and prosecuting international terrorism, this balance can be achieved, not as a compromise between the two opposing dynamics, but as the outcome of a common effort to achieve a common end.

Reference

Schabas W (2012) The International Criminal Court: Struggling to Find its Way. In: Cassese A (ed) Realizing Utopia: The Future of International Law. Oxford University Press, Oxford, pp 250–260

Index

S. Margariti, *Defining International Terrorism*, International Criminal Justice Series 15, DOI 10.1007/978-94-6265-204-0

MIX
Papier aus verantwortungsvollen Quellen
Paper from responsible sources
FSC® C105338

If you have any concerns about our products,
you can contact us on
ProductSafety@springernature.com

In case Publisher is established outside the EU,
the EU authorized representative is:
Springer Nature Customer Service Center GmbH
Europaplatz 3, 69115 Heidelberg, Germany

Printed by Libri Plureos GmbH
in Hamburg, Germany